"In her newest book, Janet Edgette encourage late some of the most hoary and archaic rules us that therapy is rooted in our capacity to thin and that it's not just about what to *do* with our a how to *be* with them."

**Brad E. Sachs, PhD**, *psychologist and*
Teen, The Good Enough Therapist, *and* ...on No One Understands

"Janet Sasson Edgette has yet again proved to us that she has her fingers on the pulse of what it's like to be an adolescent today. This book illustrates the range of issues that kids face from the inside out and the range of responses that therapists can utilize to engage this population. I couldn't put this book down! Janet's insight, perception and authenticity are so refreshing!"

**Amy Fantalis, MS, MSW, LCSW**, *psychotherapist*

"*Therapeutic Conversations with Adolescents* is an unprecedented and extraordinary guide for therapists treating teens and families. It's an elite handbook that demonstrates what to DO in session. Therapists will learn how to respond in real time and sequence interventions, to name a few of the tools taught throughout the book. This is an invaluable resource."

**Joseph Dowling, MS, LPC**, *author of ZONEfulness: The Ultimate Guide for Student-Athletes*

"Edgette's honesty and her professional experiences will keep you reading more and then more. She's not lecturing. She's sharing. She's reminding us that we can engage with teens without the pings, rings, dings and all things tech and instead choose face-to-face conversations with truths and vulnerabilities."

**Kat Rowan, MA, NCC**, *CEO and creative director of TiffinTalk and owner of Rowan Therapy*

# Therapeutic Conversations with Adolescents

*Therapeutic Conversations with Adolescents* takes readers into the office of a seasoned therapist, where they can be a fly on the wall of live therapy sessions. Full of actual dialogue and the processing behind the choice of responses and interventions, this book stands in contrast to the dozens of books about adolescent therapy that discuss mainly theory, conjecture, and generic strategies.

Teenagers today need therapists who can offer robust and unpretentious therapeutic relationships, as well as conversations that matter enough to hold their clients' attention and make them want to come back for more.

Readers will come away from this book understanding how to tread the delicate balance between the support and confrontation, the forthrightness and discretion, and the humor and tenacity that therapists need to make a real and lasting impact with teenagers.

**Janet Sasson Edgette, PsyD**, therapist, author, and speaker, has worked with teenagers and their parents for over thirty years in her Philadelphia-based private practice.

# Therapeutic Conversations with Adolescents

## Helping Teens in Therapy Thrive in an Ultra-Competitive, Screen-Saturated World

Janet Sasson Edgette

Routledge
Taylor & Francis Group

NEW YORK AND LONDON

Designed cover image: © Getty Images

First published 2024
by Routledge
605 Third Avenue, New York, NY 10158

and by Routledge
4 Park Square, Milton Park, Abingdon, Oxon, OX14 4RN

*Routledge is an imprint of the Taylor & Francis Group, an informa business*

*Library of Congress Cataloging-in-Publication Data*
Names: Edgette, Janet Sasson, author.
Title: Therapeutic conversations with adolescents : helping teens in therapy
thrive in an ultra-competitive, screen-saturated world / by Janet Sasson
Edgette, PsyD.
Description: New York, NY : Routledge, 2024. | Includes bibliographical
references and index.
Identifiers: LCCN 2023018158 (print) | LCCN 2023018159 (ebook) |
ISBN 9781032189369 (hardback) | ISBN 9781032189376 (paperback) |
ISBN 9781003257080 (ebook)
Subjects: LCSH: Adolescent psychotherapy.
Classification: LCC RJ503 .E343 2024  (print) | LCC RJ503  (ebook) |
DDC 616.89/140835—dc23/eng/20230630
LC record available at https://lccn.loc.gov/2023018158
LC ebook record available at https://lccn.loc.gov/2023018159

ISBN: 978-1-032-18936-9 (hbk)
ISBN: 978-1-032-18937-6 (pbk)
ISBN: 978-1-003-25708-0 (ebk)

DOI: 10.4324/9781003257080

Typeset in Helvetica Neue and Optima
by codeMantra

*To my three boys — Casey, Jake, and Austin –*
*in whose company I will always rejoice.*

# Contents

# About This Book

Twenty years ago I wrote my first book about doing therapy with teenagers. Entitled, *Adolescent Therapy That Works: Helping Kids Who Never Asked for Help in the First Place*,[1] this book was my first effort at presenting the ideas and practices I'd developed over the decade prior working with adolescents in both residential placement and my private practice.

The book had been prompted in part by the countless case reports I'd heard and read about of teenagers sitting listlessly in front of their therapists, denying the problems for which they had been referred, and frequently mocking the well-intentioned efforts of clinicians and the mental health profession at large. "Resistance" became the universal descriptor for these teens, often obscuring the earnest intentions of many of them to get help.

Believing we could do better, I set about to discover how I could have more constructive and rewarding experiences with my own teen clients. As a result, I developed a different approach to working with adolescents in therapy, one that averted the power struggles and going-nowhere dialogues that derailed so many of the relationships between therapists and teenagers and their respective therapies and led to better outcomes and better experiences for both parties.

Ten years later, I wrote an article in *Psychotherapy Networker* magazine entitled "Why Teens Hate Therapy: Mistakes Therapists Should Avoid."[2] Out of the dozens of articles I've written, this one has been my most popular one to date. It tells us something about our collective desire to better understand what goes wrong when we try to help adolescents through our craft.

---

1 W.W. Norton & Company. NY, 2002.
2 Sept/Oct 2012.

A lot has changed since the publication of *Adolescent Therapy That Works* and "Why Teens Hate Therapy," including my own self. It was time for an update.

*Therapeutic Conversations with Adolescents* stands on the same principles upon which my earlier works were shaped – therapist credibility, an enduring respect for clients' autonomy, and the role of accountability in successful clinical work – and uses them to advance a more comprehensive, intricate and nuanced approach that is more attractive, applicable, and useful to the historically underserved population of adolescents and their parents.

Teenagers who are brought into treatment usually have enough people telling them what they should be doing differently. What they don't have are opportunities to reveal the things they really think and worry about where it's understood that talking about problems doesn't mean you're necessarily ready to take action on them. You can't resolve problems without being able to talk about them broadly, and teens need places where they trust us to hold a space where they can do that without us jumping in immediately to solve for x. That's how you get the kind of animated dialogue that engages them and brings their full selves into the room.

In conversational spaces that are prescription-free – that is, where we're not telling teen clients to stop it, change it, apologize for it, or analyze it, they are freer to think about what they genuinely want to stand by and how they want to show up in their lives. In that kind of holding space, they're much better able to hear us, and don't need to push back so hard when we begin to share our candid thoughts, impressions, and even our frank suggestions. It's in this way that teenagers who balk at all the "good advice" they get from well-meaning parents, teachers, mentors, and counselors start taking ownership of their choices and making the changes necessary for their mental health and quality of life.

Some of the best work I did as a therapist took place at a summer camp where I worked for six years as a psychologist/consultant. I love this camp, and have for half a century, having grown up there almost every summer from the time I was three years old until my mid-teens. On board decades later to help kids and staff with their transition to a seven-week overnight camp and adjustment to living in cabins with six or so other kids or your co-counselor, I had to learn how to transpose the craft of therapy from a 45-minute session in a suburban office to the intimate but casual and open-aired setting of a summer camp. For me, this distilled down into two things: credibility and practicality. Relying on only my own person and no outer trappings, I needed to establish myself as credible, as somebody in whom one's attention and faith were well-placed. And whatever I offered needed to be unobtrusive, graspable, fast-acting, and able to fit seamlessly within the rhythms of camp life.

Every year, and just like the campers, in that climate of leisure, whimsy, vigorous activity, and boundless affection I too became a bigger human being – more generous, more patient, more present. I came to recognize the value and sheer power of connecting with kids in a thoroughly unadorned, uncontrived way and want to believe that I brought a lot of that back home with me. What was helpful for those kids and counselors were the multiple small moments of grace, of connecting, of sharing or responding, of becoming comfortable letting oneself be known by another person. It was therapy on the go, and it was beautiful.

It's easy for me to romanticize my experience at camp, but there are real takeaways too. I think the biggest one was seeing that we've let some of the principles and processes of therapy become too sacrosanct. Inviolable, hallowed tenets keep us wedded to older models of therapy and older ways of relating to our young clients and their parents that don't really suit today's kids, today's larger communal needs, or even today's therapists, many of whom are looking for more effective, more authentic ways to work with children and teenagers. Those ways do exist, and I hope you'll find some of them in this book and add to them others you discover elsewhere. I'll never believe that it's from our prescriptions or directives that people find what they need in order to live their better lives. I think our strongest influence is sourced from a far more organic and compelling offering: our person, our perspective and wisdom, our advice and warmth, and our patience and respect, among many other things, including, and perhaps especially, our demonstrations of our own human fallibility.

With deep respect for, and appreciation of, your kind attention.

JSE
January 29, 2023
Exton, PA

# Acknowledgements

My clients, younger and older, and everyone in between, and the people who are doing their best to care for them – their parents and guardians and grandparents and godparents and aunts and uncles and other caregivers. I thank you for opening your hearts and minds in my presence and allowing me the opportunity to be part of your healing. And to those for whom that didn't happen, I do hope that you have found the solace and strength you needed elsewhere, with others better equipped than me to bring your best forward.

My own beautiful family: my three sons, my best fans, always gracious and kind, funny and considerate, who every day reaffirm my deeply held belief that for parents and their children, the generation gap is more apparent than real.

And Bill K. of course. The driving. The grilling. More important, your devotion and affection and unbounded love. Your generous words of support and your warm, infectious humor. Lucky girl am I.

My wonderful friends, who've been traveling a long time with me, and whom I adore. Thank you, each and every one – the ones I see often, the ones I see too infrequently. I love you all very much.

Oh, my darling pit bull, Libby, as brilliant and lovely and gracious a cotherapist as one could ever want. Rest in peace, my sweet girl. You should know that you were a huge part of why clients kept returning, of why they got better.

Anna Moore, my publisher at Routledge, for your confidence in this book when it was still embryonic.

My professors and clinical supervisors at Hahnemann (now Widener) University in Philadelphia. Never had I loved learning as much as I did for those five years. You were wonderful teachers of both the art and science of psychotherapy. And such a wealth of knowledge you shared, rich and nuanced, a profound gift. Thank you all.

Rich Simon, may he rest peacefully, who for years would invite me to write something for his magazine, only to ask me a seemingly never-ending stream of questions while I wrote and re-wrote and re-wrote some more. We all joke about having been "Simon-ized," but I'll be the first to say that it made me a better writer, a better therapist, and a better human being. Thank you, Rich.

Jane Friedman, who assured me I'd publish again.

Brad Sachs, Kat Rowan, and Sheri Gardner, who so kindly took the time to review the original proposal and offer their insights on what would become this book – thank you.

And finally, with profound respect and love, my sister, Carol Sasson, my best friend, without whom … well, I don't even know. I just love you, C. And of course, her blue-eyed Connemara, Ronan, as well – kind and hardy and patient, for decades waiting his turn to have his picture in a *real* book. Alas, the timing was off for this one; with it going to press in January, Ronan worried he was just too woolly for his long-awaited glamour shot. But I got you, Ronan. After all, you deserve a book of your own for what you've given those little kids you carry around on your strong back, leaving them with a confidence and jubilation they didn't know they had in them. Here you go, my man.

All names and identifying details in this book have been changed to protect the privacy of clients. The majority of therapy conversations included were re-created verbatim from notes written right after a session, while others are re-created from memory but true to the spirit of the encounter. A few conversations are hypothetical, in other words, they are conversations or exchanges that I would try to have under the circumstances discussed. Those are identifiable by comments such as, *Here you could say ...* or *I could imagine saying ....*

Please know that everything is so disguised that any client's resemblance to a real, living person is pure coincidence.

# CHAPTER ONE

# Growing Up in a Culture of Social Media, Disconnection, and Unrelenting Pressure

## Adolescent Mental Health in the 2020s

Never has the adage, "I was a teenager once too, you know," been more tone deaf to the experience of being a teenager today. So much has changed in the past decade plus, and it's changed in ways that have altered the DNA of how kids communicate with one another, stay connected or don't, relate with family members, acquire information about the world, and plan for their futures, among many other things.

Many of the changes are welcomed, long past due. The embracing of mental health care among youth, and the national dialogue about it that they have brought forward is unprecedented and noteworthy. Kids have both the language and the courage now to talk about how they feel, and to reach out for help when they are overwhelmed or frightened for their own safety. Also welcomed is the uptick in the availability of mental health services, even if it's still not enough.

But some changes are not so welcomed. The explosive growth of social media and its ubiquitous presence in our kids' lives is devastatingly consequential. It's robbed our children and teenagers of so much of their curiosity and creativity and imagination. Boredom has become unendurable, as has the silence that fills bedrooms at night when not bombarded by the cacophony of YouTube and TikTok. The pervasiveness and popularity of social media has also provided fertile soil for a peer culture in which harsh criticism and judgment reign. Kids' appetites for off-the-grid hobbies or interests wilt in the anxiety that engaging in such would mark them as losers, middle school girls especially. Boys who grow up on a near constant diet of video gaming leave home at eighteen

DOI: 10.4324/9781003257080-1

without having ever developed the social and emotional skills to successfully, let alone confidently, navigate the tasks of independent living, the temptations of the all-you-can-eat buffet of alcohol and drugs they'll find at college, or the challenges of creating relationships with others that they crave but have no idea how to sustain.

What troubles me the most though is probably what troubles teens and their families themselves the most – the lonely sense of disconnectedness that too many family members feel while in close physical proximity of one another. It's just like what Mary Pipher said in her book, **The Shelter of Each Other: Rebuilding Our Families** – "Being thirsty in the rain."[1]

And then there's the weed. So much of it, all the time. Kids getting high before school, during school, after school, when they're with friends, when they're alone. Some are self-medicating for anxiety or depression, or both. Some are bored and don't know how to create a more stimulating world around them. Some are just wanting to escape the stress in their lives for a few hours. But it's everywhere at once and insidiously takes the mental edge from our teenagers. They lose their motivation for activities that involve any kind of emotional or physical effort, even ones they have enjoyed. They become complacent about their lives; they aren't particularly happy but don't care to do anything about it at the moment. They let themselves become spacey and dull in their thinking, in their discernment, in their ability to extract important information from their surroundings and make good meaning of it. Parents know all about this but can't stop it.

The Covid-19 pandemic during 2020 and 2021 made everything worse. Kids now had (seemingly) *only* their phones for connection and entertainment. We learned what months of isolation will lead to in teenagers: increased rates of depression, anxiety, lethargy, apathy, and suicide risk. Education was another casualty; so was a sense of security about our world and the people who run it. Teenagers looked into their future and saw an adulthood that became less and less appealing over time, a morass of unwelcome responsibilities, unrelenting stress, and unremitting conflict. How did that happen? Here's how: they looked at *us* — a generation of parents who argue too much, drink too much, work too much, complain too much and play too little. *Thanks, but no*, they rejoin. *Plus, the climate?* they ask to anyone willing to listen. *Will there be a viable planet left when I'm a parent? Will I even want to have children of my own?*

Meanwhile, in another display of the vast disconnect between adults and the generation they are trying to raise, parents, educators, guidance counselors, and family relatives are ceaselessly (and prematurely) exhorting teenagers to load up on all the things believed to afford them the advantages they'll need to be sure to "get into a good college." C'mon, are there really any bad ones?

Omg. No wonder our kids are struggling.

## What Does This Mean for How we Practice
## Therapy with Our Teenage Clients?

Years ago, I was asked to comment on a case study[2] in which the counselor/author, Howard Honigsfeld, a school social worker in the South Bronx, talked about the value of what he described as the "homelier" values of therapy – things like compassion, patience, and common sense – in other words, those values or skills that are often overshadowed by high tech interventions or complicated methodologies. I loved that, and appreciated the gentle push back on trainings that highlighted acronyms and prescribed techniques and manualized protocols at the expense of warmth and clinical sensibility. Mary Pipher also spoke to the merits of "applying earthy solutions" to our modern dilemmas, adding that mental health needs to transcend technique[3]. Hallelujah.

So maybe that's the place to start, not with manuals or itemized treatment plans or psycho-educational worksheets. Not with interviews about problems or protocols based on diagnoses. Maybe the place to start is with a relationship and a conversation that matters enough to hold a young person's attention and makes them want to come back for more. I tell trepidatious new clients, "Come in and let's start a conversation. If it helps, we'll have another. If not, I'll help you figure out something else you can do." I love the challenge.

We can offer these kids opportunities to join us in robust and unpretentious therapeutic relationships that are characterized, at least from our end, by an emotional intimacy, a candor, a respect for the person of the other, and a cultivation of hope and play and thoughtfulness. Through such relationships we can teach our clients the value of relationship repair and of empathic accountability regarding the impact of their choices and behaviors on those around them. We can demonstrate how apologizing can feel good, explain that being right is a victory in name only, and encourage both the expression and comfortable acceptance of small gestures of care. We can model prudence and patience, as well as a passion for that which moves us. We can push back against all the messaging telling adolescents they need to know what they're going to do for the rest of their lives by the time they graduate high school, robbing them of opportunities to see a bigger and more differentiated world and *self*, and turning post-secondary education (college) into nothing more than dressed up trade schools.[4]

That's how we can offer our young clients antidotes to their loneliness, disillusionment, complacency, and untethering. That's how we can try to instill hope in them that they can have worthwhile and fulfilling adulthoods, and spark the curiosity and resilience they will need to build lives like that, with breadth and color and an appreciation for that which brings us awe. Getting their eyes on that prize can be instrumental in the collateral resolution of so many of the personal problems and issues that compromise the quality of their lives.

Fred Rogers, the beloved creator, show runner, and host of the preschool television series Mister Rogers' Neighborhood, remains a hero of mine for many reasons, one of which was his commitment to talking about those experiences that make us bigger human beings – moments of connection and wonder, an openness to that which we may not yet know or understand. His model of empathy and acceptance and kindness is the perfect antidote to the cynicism and guardedness that's infected large swaths of our citizenry.

Turns out his program wasn't just for children after all.

## Notes

1  Mary Pipher, *The Shelter of Each Other: Rebuilding Our Families*, Putnam Adult, 1996.
2  Supporting the overwhelmed child, sometimes it just takes time, Howard Honigsfeld & Janet Sasson Edgette, *Psychotherapy Networker*, March/April 2016.
3  Pipher, Mary. [Keynote address]. Psychotherapy Networker Symposium. Washington, DC.
4  J.S. Edgette, Let's stop stressing out our kids with career choice pressure, Opinion. *Philadelphia Inquirer*, March 11, 2019.

CHAPTER TWO

# A Crisis in Confidence and Credibility Among American Parents

The changes over the past couple of decades have not made it any easier for parents to raise their kids than it has for their kids to grow up. The face of modern adolescence has brought a markedly new set of challenges to parents, one of which is the endeavor to maintain an authority and credibility in what are felt to be the critical and judgmental eyes of their teenagers. Social phenomena such as the broadening informalities between the generations, the idealization and subsequent empowering of youth culture, and teenagers' appropriation of electronics serve to chip away at the self-possession and conviction parents need in order to follow through on their choices regarding the best interests of their adolescent children and make what they know will be unpopular but healthy decisions.

In the wake of all these sociocultural changes and what's been described as a mental health crisis among youth, parents are, as they should be, very worried about their kids. Many have lost their inner compass and are left with a gnawing sense of doubt regarding their judgment and decision-making. *What's normal these days?* they wonder. *What are the new red flags? Will bearing down on getting chores done around the house really make my daughter's depression worse, like she says?* Parents find themselves second guessing decisions about everything from curfews to screen time to how disrespectful is *too* disrespectful, and feeling intimidated by the emotional reactivity of teens. Collectively, and over time, these different challenges to parents have effectively neutralized much of the parental authority in the home, something Jerome Price was already writing about in 1996.[1]

And then there's this, too: Adults who romanticize the adolescent life-style sometimes begin to idealize the *presumed adolescent knowledge base*. So, when teenagers start acting as if they know better than the adults about

DOI: 10.4324/9781003257080-2

what's hot and what's sexy and what the new rules are, these adults believe them. They want to raise kids who are confident and independent but fall prey to their teenager's demands to be in control. It's easy to think, "Well, maybe she's right."

## Teenage Angst: Fact or Fiction?

Fifteen-year-old Lauren arrives home after school and isn't even through her front door before her mom, Paula, asks her how her day went.

> "It was pretty good," Lauren replies, looking into the refrigerator, to both find something to eat and avoid her mother's focused gaze.
>
> "Just *pretty* good?"
>
> "No, it was good," Lauren backtracks, trying to settle on just the right combination of words so that her mother will stop with her questions.
>
> "What was good about it?" Paula inquires, restlessly.
>
> Lauren sighs, and closes the refrigerator door.
>
> "Why do you have to sigh like that?" whines Paula. "I can't ask you a question about your day?"

Lauren looks over at her mother, and tries to feel sorry for her. After all, she figures, she's been home alone all day, and is probably eager for some company and conversation. But Lauren, to the contrary, has been around people all day, and just wants to go up to her room. She can't summon up the empathy she knows she should be feeling. Instead, she thinks, *Why can't you just ask me how my day was and leave it at that? And what's the matter with "pretty good" anyway? I just got home, I don't feel like talking, and whenever I do you start asking a million questions and trying to solve problems I didn't even know I had!* What she says to her mom is very different, though. "Actually mom, no, you can't. Not right now." And with that, she grabs her backpack, slings it across her shoulder, and walks upstairs. The door to Lauren's room closes a few moments later.

This is a story that Paula will recount later to Lauren's father, when he comes home from work.

> "I don't understand why it's such a big deal to talk to us," she says, with an edge. "And after all we do for her? I'd think the least she could do is be more open."
>
> "Don't worry about it, Paula. C'mon, she's fifteen. What fifteen-year-old talks to their parents anyway?" Lauren's father offers.
>
> "She talks to you," says Paula, sounding plaintive.
>
> "Yeah, well, I don't know. Maybe it's a father–daughter thing."

But maybe it's not a father–daughter thing. Maybe it's because when Lauren's father asks Lauren a question, he listens and thinks about her response and doesn't immediately jump to the next question. Maybe it's because he doesn't only ask questions, but also volunteers interesting stories or experiences from *his* day, so that it feels to Lauren like a real conversation, not an interrogation. Maybe it's because he doesn't grow alarmed when Lauren says she's fighting with her best friend, and doesn't try to find out exactly what happened, figuring that if his daughter wanted to tell him more about it, she would. Talking with her dad is pleasant for Lauren, and she welcomes it. Not so with her mom, whose urgency and radar-lock attention feel oppressive, and seem to be much more about Paula, than about Paula and Lauren.

How much of this is adolescence, per se, and how much of it is a function of the relationship between Lauren and her mother, and the way they try to communicate with each other?

Unfortunately, because Lauren's parents aren't thinking about the differences in their communication styles, or other things that might account for the contrasting ways in which their daughter relates to each of them, they simply attribute the paucity of communication between Lauren and her mom to Lauren's *being a teenager.* It's an awfully convenient excuse, but a regrettable one as well. It's also a perfect example of how the current American narrative surrounding adolescence has played and continues to play a role in compromising the quality of relationships that parents and teenagers establish with one another.

---

"This is exactly how adolescence gets its undeserved reputation for 'sturm und drang,' a self-fulfilling prophesy disguised as developmental theory that lulls parents into complacency with their adolescent's moodiness or defiance. Adolescents really don't have to be all that moody or defiant, and they certainly do not have to be rude. *They're just wired that way,* we've been led to believe, unfortunately. No – they go there because we let them."

Janet Sasson Edgette

from, *The Last Boys Picked: Helping Boys Who Don't Play Sports Survive Bullying and Boyhood*[2]

---

## Adolescent Brain Development and Behavior

"He couldn't help it because his brain is still maturing…."

Uh, no. By failing to see the difference between teenagers, and teenagers who behave badly, we leave room for things like disrespect and indolence to be understood as a natural part of being a teenager, rather than as a red flag.

Recent advances in brain research support the idea that the adolescent brain is qualitatively different from that of a child or an adult. Dan Siegel's[3] work in particular highlights the significant structural and physiological changes taking place within the brain during adolescence that impact the way teenagers remember, think, reason, focus attention, make decisions, and relate. These changes then drive the emergence of new qualities in teens, such as a search for novelty and the company of peers, emotional intensity, and creative exploration. It's not hard to see how some of these qualities might be expressed impulsively, recklessly, audaciously. But how much do they really account for some of the more aggressive or disrespectful behaviors we see in teenagers?

Saying that your teenager can't control his frankly aggressive temper or his mouth because his brain is still maturing (or his hormones are raging) is a very different conversation than the one Dan Siegel is having about teenagers experiencing an increase in emotional intensity and engaging in riskier behaviors. A teenager who is impulsive or dysregulated, or who plans poorly – for example, maybe we see a kid who's freaking out over a canceled concert or who's doing something stupid, maybe even dangerous – is displaying very different behaviors from one who walks over to his younger brother rummaging through the refrigerator and shoves him out of his way in order to assert his dominance, or a sixteen-year-old who tells her mother to F*@k off! when told to hand over her phone.

Instead of, *Teenagers behave differently because their brains are different,* how about, *Teenagers behave differently AND their brains are different.*

Puberty, hormones, immature brains — these things have been blindly adopted as reasons why teenagers do things that annoy, worry, or enrage their parents. Of the many problems associated with this cultural narrative about adolescence run amok, one of the worst is that parents have come to expect their kids to become defiant, irresponsible, or even rude upon entering adolescence, as if hard-wired for it and predetermined. When their kids oblige, the parents react not with correction but with resigned accommodation. Soon, everything their pre-teens and newly minted teens do is examined through the lens of "typical teen behavior," with so much of it having become normalized.

As soon as we start dismissing bad behavior with excuses such as *They will grow out of it,* or *It's just a phase,* or *It's their hormones,* or *They can't help it because their brains are still developing,* we cloud our own judgment in terms of being able to discern what's really a function of adolescence, and what's really a function of low expectations. And believing those things to be true diminishes everyone involved – teenagers, who are thought to be at the mercy of their physiology and neurobiology, and parents, who are discouraged from expecting more from their teen than the stereotypes about them suggest. By not differentiating between *unchecked* behavior and *undeveloped* behavior, we leave room for unacceptable behavior to be seen as just another part of adolescence.

**Brain changes during adolescence are not the reasons why some teenagers display disrespectful or bullying behavior.**

One of the more disturbing things about all this is that it's not only American parents who fall into this trap – it's educators and psychologists too, guidance counselors and pediatricians, child psychiatrists and so many others, weaving into the fabric of family life, education, and mental health this idea that adolescence is this mystifying phase of life during which children become insufferable tyrants. Instead of facilitating understanding and compassion between parents and their children, this ugly, inaccurate narrative creates unnecessary conflict, misunderstanding, isolation, and despair. Here's how that happens:

- *by promoting divisiveness between the generations*
  An "us" versus "them" mentality grows splendidly in a culture where parents are repeatedly warned that once adolescence hits, their son or daughter isn't going to want to talk to them, be seen with them, feel close to them, or listen to them. It proposes a template for parent–teen relations that entrenches families in conflict for years. If you're convinced your teenagers have no interest in speaking with you or listening to you, then you're probably not going to spend a lot of time trying to make that happen. *Why would you bother?* However, the truth of the matter is that most teenagers *do* want to talk with their parents and crave real engagement with them. I sit with teenagers all day long and will say this unequivocally: That despite all the talk about teens wanting to individuate or break free from their parents, what they really want is *connection*, not separation. Becoming independent doesn't mean disconnecting from those who have previously overseen your life. But our steadfast belief in the idea that teenagers are always trying to get as far away from their parents as possible leaves the door open for parents to see their teenager's withdrawal from the family or refusal to communicate as a just another mark of "healthy" adolescence.

I think a more accurate understanding of why adolescents don't *appear* to want to engage or talk with their parents is this: *It's not enjoyable.*

As mentioned earlier, too many parents try to jump start conversations with their kids by asking questions, one after another after another. "I don't even answer the first one," said one of my teen clients, "because if I do, there are twenty more behind it." Never was there a less appealing or less effective way to get one's kid to open up. Moreover, a lot of what start as conversations between parents and their teens morph quickly into old familiar lectures, boring monologues, or annoying reprimands. *That's* why kids leave the conversation, the room, the relationship—not because they're teenagers.

- **by discouraging parents from addressing real problems their kids are having**

A mother came into my office with her thirteen-year-old son who had finally convinced her to set up an appointment for him with a therapist. "He's been saying he feels depressed," the mother explained, "but I just thought he was going through a tough time, you know? I mean teenagers have days like that, don't they? I didn't think he was really *depressed*."

Thankfully, parents have become more sensitive to their kids' mental health over the past several years as mental health awareness and advocacy has spread exponentially, and especially during and post Covid-19. But we may need to keep reminding them that teenagers resist their directives or advice for reasons other than "defiance." There are still too many parents who are unable to see past the stereotype of the defiant adolescent to explore the reasons behind their teenager's puzzling behavior in a supportive and constructive manner. They continue to dismiss it as adolescence and wait for it to go away.

- **by encouraging parents and other adults to set the bar low for teenagers and expect less responsible and less respectful behavior than these kids can demonstrate.**

When parents think of their teenagers as irresponsible or lazy, they're probably not going to expect as much from them as they could. "I don't even bother trying to get him to do chores around the house," parents will say. "It's much easier to just do it myself." Of course it is. Your teenager is making sure it's more frustrating for you to get him to unload the dishwasher than it is to simply grumble under your breath and unload it yourself.

I always tell parents that in order to get their kids to change some of their behaviors, they themselves need to be willing to be grossly inconvenienced. That means putting some kind of system in place through which they can hold their teens accountable for completing tasks and following up with consequences if they skip out on the job. But that's easier said than done, and besides, what's a good system anyway, and who has time to follow up on all these things?

It's more than just chores though. It's our expectations about how our kids treat their twin sister or their friends, or how they respond to a grieving relative or their own parents when visibly distressed. Parents accept behavior they don't like or find disappointing because they believe it's the best their teen can do. "If my daughter ever came home from school and asked me how my day was, I'd drop to the floor!" said one mom to me when I asked if her kids ever reciprocated her efforts to see how their day had gone.

This mother's kids had already struck me as very self-absorbed, showing little interest in anyone else but themselves and maybe their friends. I wanted this mom to know that she could expect more from her kids, that their self-centeredness had much less to do with being a teenager than it did their awareness that their mother thought teens could only care about themselves.

"What if you were to tell your daughter that, every once in a while, you'd like her to ask about your day?" I asked her. "I don't know," the mom said, seemingly bewildered by my question. "I think she'd just look at me and say, like, *'Why would I want to do that?'*" "Yeah, she might," I replied, "which would be a perfect invitation for you to talk with her about how sometimes you just do things you don't necessarily feel like doing, and you do them because someone you care about wants you to do them. You're not talking to her to lecture her; you want to have a conversation. You could tell her what you told me the other day – that you often feel alone when you're with her, as if you were invisible, as if your presence didn't matter. *Talk to her not because you want to get her to change her behavior, but because you want her to know* you, *and what it's like for you when you're with her*. Without the directive in there for your daughter to change, she'll be freer to actually think about what you said."

Some young people save their best and most generous selves for their friends and people outside the home. Some of that is only because their parents never thought their teenage son or daughter could really show up that well at home. Because of that, they accepted a level of treatment and regard that is thoroughly inappropriate and a blight on family relationships.

- **... and, perhaps in one of the most important ways, by absolving parents of their own responsibility for the conflicts taking place between them and their teenagers, or the remote quality of the relationship**

When a mother can look at her teenage daughter and pass off her reluctance to share information about her day as "typical teen behavior," there's no reason for her to reflect on her own contribution to this disconnect.

When a father can look at his teenage son being mopey or snappy around the house and, again, think he's just being a typical teenager, there's no reason for him to consider other reasons why his son behaves this way in his presence. Maybe the son doesn't like the dismissive tone he hears from his father when he shares an opinion or an idea about his future. Maybe he resents all the sarcasm. No one will ever find out, as long as such behavior gets dismissed as something "all teenagers do."

Brain changes during adolescence may account for a lot of the misplaced focus, poor time management, impulsiveness, and circuitous reasoning that we see in teenagers, among other things, but they aren't the main reason why teens become rude, act defiantly, or communicate sarcastically. Those behaviors take place within the context of their *relationships* with others – the ones with their parents being the most significant. Importantly, these relationships are *bidirectional*, meaning that each person in the relationship affects, influences, and reacts to the other person. Considering these things, I believe we ought to be looking more closely at factors *within the relationship* as the primary forces behind our teenagers' angry or inappropriate responses to adults rather than dismissing them as functions of brain changes or "adolescent angst."

When we do look more closely at parent-teen relationships, however, we can see that the lens is pointed inordinately toward the teen. People always focus on what teens are saying to their parents and how they are acting toward them. We pay much less attention to what parents are saying to their teens (or *not* saying to them) or how they are responding to them. And to be fair to our kids, I think we have to acknowledge that some of the ways in which adults show up to teens in their relationships with them are as unbecoming or disrespectful as what they observe in teenagers. But here's the thing: What parents say to their teens, even when they're angry, is generally far less brazen and bombastic than what teens are willing to say to their parents; they therefore escape the scrutiny that our teens' more colorful comments and snap backs draw. Moreover, if angry enough, they have something to exploit that the teen doesn't – their teenager's dependence on them. You don't need to be loud or flashy to shut a kid down with that; you just have to be mean.

All this is very unfortunate, because it too reinforces the narrative that teen defiance and disrespect are biologically determined and allows the research on adolescent brain development to be hijacked in order to corroborate the running stereotype of teenagers. And the overall result? The outright vindication of parents (and some teachers and therapists) who need to believe that the trials they experience with teenagers – the ones that leave them feeling powerless, baffled, and sometimes afraid – are developmentally pre-determined, universal in nature, and inherently unavoidable. Meaning, it's not their fault.

It will be no easy task to replace the current narrative about teenagers with a new one in which adults and teenagers are each accountable for their respective roles in the quality of their relationships with one another, and teenagers seen through a more flattering lens. Parents like being told their teenagers are crazy. It keeps the spotlight off of them, and serves to bond them together as one big troop of weary soldiers charged with raising their teenagers as best they can. Telling a parent that her daughter's moodiness may have less to do with "puberty" or "hormones" and more to do with what's happening at home may be a tough sell. **After all, when you have a fixed and widely accepted explanation for the behavior of others, you really don't have to reflect on your own.**

## Notes

1 Jerome Price. *Power and compassion: Working with difficult adolescents and abused parents.* The Guilford Press, 1999.
2 Penguin/Berkley, 2012.
3 *Brainstorm: The power and purpose of the teenage brain.* TarcherPerigee, 2015.

# CHAPTER THREE

# Playing the Long Game
## Leading Teens Out of the Rabbit Hole

### Teens and Disillusionment

In the pressure-cooker of American society, parents prime their children to compete and succeed in a world that has become less and less desirable to adolescents and young adults. Consider this exchange I had with a client, an eighteen-year-old high school senior named Scout, lamenting a future which held little appeal for her or her peers:

SCOUT:   People say these are the best years before everything gets serious and if that's the case, sorry, but we're all fucked.

ME:   What do you mean you're all fucked? How so?

SCOUT:   All my friends are depressed, they're not particularly excited about going away to college next year –

ME:   Why not?

SCOUT:   Well because if we're already sick of high school then what's there to be excited about for college? More of the same?

ME:   For what it's worth, it's not really the same. I mean the scene is different of course and you're living away from home, but I mean the education part is different, too.

SCOUT:   Whatever. I don't know. I just want to get through college, get a job, and be done with it.

ME:   Done with what?

SCOUT:   With school! But even then, there's nothing to look forward to.

ME:   Oh my god.

SCOUT:   What.

ME:   That's just the saddest thing I've heard all day.

 DOI: 10.4324/9781003257080-3

SCOUT:      What, that there's nothing to look forward to?
ME:         Uh yeah, doesn't that sound sad to you?
SCOUT:      Yeah, but that's the way I figure things are, so it's not sad, it's realistic.
ME:         Oh god now you're talking really sad stuff.
SCOUT:      What? (Starting to laugh)
ME:         That you believe your own sad-ass vision of the future!
SCOUT:      (Really laughing now) Well, what's yours?

How do you help a kid like Scout retreat from such a fixed forecast and consider another, brighter perspective? If you try to bump her out of her disillusionment and cynicism too quickly, you'll lose her; you will have become one more in a succession of adults who have told her or will tell her that she's crazy wrong and that she has such an exciting future ahead and that life is just getting started and yada yada. All of that may be true, but she can't hear it yet. I think the best thing that came out of my conversation with Scout was her question at the end: *Well, what's yours?* (vision of the future).

That's the opening I want. I didn't plan it, but it's a good example of what I mean when I say that some of the better moments in therapy are serendipitous but not unintentional. With that one question, I can open a new path of conversation having to do with one's future, Scout's future. Not all at once – in fact, I might have responded with only a sentence or two: *Well, let's just say I'm looking through a different lens than you are when I look forward. I just don't know how to get you to come over and peek through mine without sounding like I'm pitching a sale.*

A cynical kid like Scout will always engage the attention of people who will try to pull her out of her cynicism in order to see things in a more promising light.

In therapy, it would look like this:

THERAPIST:  Claudia, there are so many things for you to look forward to! I can't believe you have such a negative attitude about being an adult.
C:          I'm not negative, I'm realistic.
THERAPIST:  What's so realistic about thinking you'll never find a job or career that you'd really want to do, or that you won't even be able to afford your own car, let alone an apartment?
C:          Have you been listening to the news lately? It's all bad. People hate their life, hate their jobs – that's if they can find one.
THERAPIST:  (trying to be clever) Maybe you shouldn't follow the news ...
            Claudia gives the therapist a sideways look, as in, *Right, so that's the answer ...*

Changing someone's perspective is never an overnight job. With someone who's become cynical, you have to sidle up to them first and find out how they got there in the first place (personal experience, hearsay, the zeitgeist?). Then you want to take the time to find out what keeps them there. Only then, much like the racetrack outrider who, at the end of the race, catches up to the race-horse in order to slow him down and "pony" him back to the stable, might you have sparked enough curiosity for the cynic to look at things afresh.

You have to play the long game.

Here's another kid, thirteen, freshly suspended from school for refusing to take off his hoodie. I've seen Denny a few times already, sometimes in tandem with his twin brother, Miles.

ME:    Denny, what's your end game?

D:    I don't know. I don't care.

ME:    Okay, so this is different.

D:    What's different?

ME:    You. You're different. I've never seen you this negative.

D:    Yeah, well, whatever.

ME:    Tell me what the deal is with the hoodie.

D:    No one tells me what to do. I don't have to follow anybody's rules.

ME:    I don't know, buddy, it's not much of a mountain to die on.

D:    I don't care. I'm done with school. It's stupid. I don't need to go.

ME:    What will you do instead?

D:    I don't care. I'll work at Dairy Queen.

ME:    I feel like you're trying to get me to say, *Oh my God, Denny! What are you talking about! You can't quit school!* All that tommyrot ….

D:    All that what?

ME:    Tommyrot. New word, just learned it. Means nonsense. Was looking for some place to use it. Yeah, I feel like you're waiting for me to like bug out and get all lecture-y, telling you you're crazy to talk about quitting school.

D:    Not really.

ME:    Okay good, cause I don't really want to say that stuff.

D:    I don't need school. I'm just gonna work at a stupid job like Dairy Queen and live my life and that'll be all.

ME:    Well, I'm not going to sit here and try to talk you out of it. I just don't know how you look at the picture you just painted and say, *Yeah I'll go with that one.* Besides, you think you're bored at school? Wait til you been swirling soft serves for a few months …

D:    There's nothing else for me to do. I'm bad at sports. I'm not unique.

ME:    (quiet for a few moments) I'm sorry you feel that in order to matter you have to be good at sports or special in some recognizable way.

D:      It doesn't matter.

ME:    Denny, the way you've been talking today sounds like you're saying *you* don't matter.

D:      I don't know, whatever, maybe …

The *maybe* here is priceless. It's the opening you need to return to a sensitive topic without coming off as pushing your own agenda; he's given you permission to go there. I say return, because I wouldn't jump on it at that moment; I'd worry about making Denny too careful about what he says. I'd come back to it later in the session, or on another day. And it's easy enough to get back to. For example …

- *Remember that day we were talking about working at Dairy Queen and I said it sounded like you didn't think you mattered, and you said, I don't know, maybe …?*
- *Your argument with your dad reminds me of when you said you were bad at sports and not unique, as if that meant you didn't really matter … remember that?*
- *Your words are different today but I'm getting the same message that I got the day you came in here after getting suspended over your hoodie — that you don't feel you matter….*

From there you take the conversation further, only little by little though with a quick-to-shut-down kind of kid like Denny who has, at the moment, less interest in self-reflection than in wearing his depression, disaffection, and hopelessness on his sleeve for everyone to see.

Kids like Denny have been showing up in therapists' offices since therapy became a thing. It's just that there are so many of them now, and they're younger.

I'm all about finding ways to make therapy with kids and teens more incisive and brief so that they can get back on the road more quickly. But some things take time, and these kinds of problems – disillusionment with one's future, disaffection with authority, kids disheartened from a lack of confidence in themselves to do adulthood "right" – especially so. Moreover, these problems of malaise and depression and paralyzing anxiety among our youth are bigger than psychotherapy; they're sociocultural problems, deeply rooted in the ideas that parents and educators and counselors have about what's important, and about what will stack the deck in favor of living a satisfying, happy life.

The pressure and disillusionment felt by many adolescents today may have started anywhere, but the Covid-19 pandemic and quarantine certainly didn't help. In the new world of ambiguity, parents and teenagers both want to latch on to something certain or permanent. America's culture has shaped in us an appreciation of all things abbreviated and finite, and sometimes we take it too far.

Unfortunately (I say), when it comes to standard measures of success among American youth, educators and parents have opted for the quantifiable and binary kinds – grades, class rankings, RBIs, how many extracurriculars, uses drugs or doesn't, in National Honor Society or not. What's left out are, arguably, the better determinants of healthy adjustment, things like communication skills, interpersonal sensitivity, empathy, perspective-taking, insightfulness, an ability to manage one's strong emotions, resilience, flexibility, and a tolerance for the unknown or yet unanswered.

That first set of measures yields numbers, nice and neat, like a quick-read meat thermometer. And a lot of adults and most institutions like numbers; they make it easier to brag, to compare, to evaluate, to choose. But numbers don't tell stories. And without our stories, we can all look alike, at least on paper. Even something like "having good leadership skills" leaves a lot to the imagination. Alexander the Great, Rosa Parks, the Dalai Lama, and Cleopatra were all considered great leaders, but none of them is anything like the others. I think teenagers need us to look at them and see not numbers, and not even "teenagers," but *them as individuals*, and teach them to measure themselves by that second set of unquantifiable but truly indispensable qualities that contribute to good character and a meaningful life.

## Teens and an Absence of Self

Denny felt like a failure because he was bad at sports and wasn't unique. Others feel like failures because they don't know what to do with themselves when they aren't doing homework or scrolling social media on their phone. Like Louie.

Louie is eighteen years old and a graduating senior. An outstanding student with a high GPA and a transcript filled with AP courses and extracurriculars, he is riddled with anxiety – the reason he asked his mother to see a therapist.

When he came for his first appointment, I reminded Louie that I'd spoken briefly with his mother the week before and understood that he often felt overwhelmed.

"How are you hoping I might help?" I asked Louie.
"I really don't know."
"Okay," I said. I thought about what an easier question might be to start off with. "Tell me something about you then, Louie. What you like to do, what's important to you, who's important to you. Stuff like that."
But it wasn't any easier. Louie sat for a moment, uncomfortable and self-conscious. "I don't know. I'm not really good at talking about myself. Not really much of a talker …"

"No problem," I said, wanting to take any pressure off Louie to "do therapy right." "Your mom said you're a strong student, play soccer, have a job, take a lot of AP courses …. Sounds like a lot on your plate to me."

"Totally," he replied, and with that little assist, Louie began to talk with me about what the last two years had been like for him. They weren't good, despite his academic and athletic success and supportive family ("I have the best parents").

"What do you do when there's nothing you *have* to do?" I asked Louie.

"I don't know," he said. "Now that soccer's over, I just go home and go on my phone, I guess. I don't have homework anymore, so there's nothing really to do."

*Nothing to do.* It breaks my heart when I hear this. In a world so rich with offerings, that anyone would find there to be nothing to do is, to me, just so sad. But try explaining that to someone who isn't aware of what he's missing. Louie doesn't know how different he might feel were he to avail himself of what his community, other communities, nature, or people from other walks of life, had to offer. He doesn't miss wonder or awe because he doesn't know what it's like to walk around in the world experiencing them. He avoids making any decisions on his own and, other than soccer, enjoys no extracurricular activities.

Later in his session, Louie talked about feeling low at times. "It's usually when I'm in my room, on my phone or gaming, and I'm not sure what I'm supposed to be doing. I think I should be doing something else, but I don't know what. I'd *like* to be doing something else but have no way of figuring out what that would be. Saying it out loud like this, it makes me sound pathetic."

Louie is one of countless teenagers who don't know what to do when they're left on their own to fill their time. It's part everything: social media for sure, where kids learn to be passive consumers of other people's lives and lose their desire to explore the world around them; all the weed being smoked or vaped that can wipe out one's motivation to try new things and learn new things; school districts that prioritize state rankings over the quality of education they offer students; parents who join the bandwagon of encouraging their teens to pursue activities that will look good on a college application rather than ones that might inspire their kids; the inescapable judgment among peers that inhibits the less secure from owning publicly who they are and what they like to do. Therapy can help a lot of these kids, but we need something bigger to help out with the larger picture; we need a social course correction.

## Teens and Social Media

I'm talking with fourteen-year-old Levi about his social media use.

ME:    Best guess. How many hours a day?
L:       I don't know exactly.

ME:     Just letting you know that whatever you tell me I'm gonna double it.

L:      (laughing) Then why am I gonna bother counting?

ME:     You don't have to count. You can look it up on your phone. I'm still gonna double it.

L:      (Looks at his phone.) Okay so yesterday it was seven and a half hours.

ME:     On your phone.

L:      Yeah.

ME:     Scrolling.

L:      Mostly. Maybe Netflix, some texting. Mostly Instagram and TikTok.

ME:     Your brains are all melting and nobody knows.

L:      It's fine.

ME:     God I hope you're right.

This is one of several conversations about screen time that Levi and I have had over the course of months. They are breezy and casual, and I try to inject some humor into them. I understand it's the only way he and I are ever going to have conversations about this stuff and that's fine; I'll take it. Every other conversation he has with adults about being on his phone – although they're more like lectures – is anything but breezy and casual and they certainly aren't fun. I want my conversations with Levi to be everything those others are not, in the hope that we can take them further, past the point of *Oh this is probably something you should limit before someone else limits it for you* to somewhere that he might begin entertaining the thought that maybe all that scrolling isn't everything it's thought to be.

## Teens and Weed

It can be tricky working with teenagers who are smoking a boatload of marijuana or thoroughly lost in the rabbit holes of social media. You want to talk about it with them, but you can't go on a lecture or psycho-educational rant. How do you approach these issues or respond to them when they come up in session? How can you tell when a teen is looking for some help with their habit but not coming right out and asking for it?

Taytum has been smoking more and more lately, and already has one school suspension under her belt for vaping in the bathroom. She tells me, one day, for no apparent reason, "Oh, and I get high every day now."

"All right …. you okay with that? The way you said it, I can't tell."

"Yeah, I'm *fine*. I'm totally fine."

"Okay." Pause. "If you weren't, though, what would be different about you?"

"Nothing."

You might be tempted to respond with, *If there would be nothing different about you, then how will you know if you're no longer fine?* This, however, is an invitation to your client to arm wrestle over this whole issue of how much weed is too much weed. It backs the teen into a corner, forcing her hand. Now she has to either reiterate her standing response ("I'll be fine") or change the subject.

I'd go with, "Okay, I was just curious."

"No, I'm doing great."

"Is there someone telling you you're not?"

"No. Why?"

"Oh, no, just the way you keep saying that made me wonder."

"No. No one's said that. Why, what are you thinking?"

Here's an invitation to share some of your thoughts, but you don't want to lay it on. I'd use it as an opportunity to obliquely share a sliver of my concern while seeing if I could get Taytum curious about how *anyone* knows when they're okay with how much they're smoking or vaping versus when they're really in trouble.

"Yeah, there are some things I'm thinking," I'd start out, "but not a lot of things for me to say. I mean I'm not going to tell you that you're not what you say you are – fine – and how would I know anyway? I just think about if you weren't, how would you know? How does anyone know? That's what I was thinking." And then I'd want to let the conversation rest with that as the closing note so that it might resonate for a while in Taytum's mind before she pushed it away.

This is an example of one of several conversations I might have with clients about their smoking, each one encouraging them to become increasingly mindful about the impact of their smoking on their overall mood, energy level, social functioning, and interest in activities, including school. I wouldn't be concerned about the kid who occasionally gets high with friends on weekends, but my ears do perk up when I hear from kids that they are vaping several times a week, including on school days, not to mention the increasing number of kids who are getting high every day, all day.

The next time Taytum and I talk about weed might be two or three weeks later, when she's talking with me about being bored all the time.

"Ugh my life is so boring, I can't stand it. I go to school, come home, watch Netflix, go to bed."

"What would you like to be doing?"

"Nothing. I don't feel like doing anything. I'm just bored."

So I laugh at this, and Taytum says, "What?"

"I don't know, it's just I'm trying to imagine how once conquers boredom while keeping everything the same …." Taytum changes the subject.

No problem.

A week later, the boredom thing comes up again. "I think that's part of why I feel depressed sometimes," Taytum says. "Can being bored make a person depressed?"

"Sure. And being depressed can make someone feel bored, if they're not doing anything interesting anymore."

"Hmm," is the response.

It's two weeks later and Taytum opens her session with, "Do you think my getting high has anything to do with why I sometimes feel depressed?"

"Yeah, I do," I replied. "I've been wondering about that. It can have an impact on how your brain functions and often makes people not feel like doing things they used to like doing. Their world shrinks, they get bored, depressed." Pause. "What makes you wonder about that today?"

"I don't know, I heard something on TikTok and started thinking …."

This is a conversation I'll want to keep revisiting with Taytum. Either she'll bring it up, or I can, since we have enough of a foundation laid down on the topic that she won't feel blindsided by my introducing it in a session. I like the direction of Taytum's thinking here and therefore it's highly unlikely that I would feel any need to take the issue outside of the therapy in service of her safety. The question gets thornier when a young client is smoking/vaping (or drinking) so much that they are endangering their immediate health or safety (for example, driving while high or inebriated) or – thornier still – sacrificing what have been longstanding aspirations for their future (for example, a historically strong student with designs on a particular post-secondary course of study or an exceptionally talented musician or athlete getting offers to attend colleges of their choice).

All these scenarios call into question the role of depression and/or anxiety in the teen's behavior, as well as the question of which came first. There is no one right answer here; it's one of those professional conundrums that requires us to balance a whole host of factors in order to come up with what we hope is the best course of action in service of our client(s). Do we say that we don't feel comfortable keeping their story to ourselves any longer? Do we ask them to talk with their parents about it? Do we refer them out for a medication eval? Do we talk with them about a need for rehab or a partial program or a more intensive outpatient program? Can we locate any reputable AA or NA groups for teens, or a group therapy or another therapist in a practice that caters to adolescents who are running up against that line of recreational versus habitual/problematic use? What if the client says no? What if they say they'll leave therapy? What if they say their parent won't let them go to college if they find out they've been using at all? Yikes.

People think that if you've been in the mental health business long enough, you have all the answers to these questions. Sometimes I think that I *should* have the answers. But I don't, and still look to colleagues, professional associations, and the literature to guide my thinking when the "right" decision isn't apparent. Often enough, you can't tell if it will be the right decision until *after* you make it, and sometimes there are multiple right ones, just as much as there are multiple wrong ones. And it's not like with the next kid you can now just press repeat. All the factors, all the contingencies, all the resources, and all the personalities are different, and you have to start with somewhat of a fresh slate. This won't be the last time you hear me say in this book that doing therapy with teenagers is not for the faint of heart.

The cases in this book span a wide range of problems, diagnoses, and presentations. Many are "evergreen" cases, meaning, they are about the kinds of problems that teenagers and families have always had. Others, like the ones in this chapter, are problems related in large measure to sociocultural conditions that have evolved over the past two decades. That's part of what makes them so challenging to treat. Because of the infiltration of social media into every crevice of teenagers' lives, they are inculcated 24/7 by a heady pop culture with values about family, relationships, recreation, education, and personal responsibility that are often at odds with what we know to be important for sound mental health.

These social and cultural forces are pervasive among youth, and they are robust. There's another challenge worth noting, too: People don't miss what they never had or never felt. We can't expect teenagers to appreciate what it would be like, what *they* would be like, if they were more familiar with and invested in their capacities for imagination and inventiveness, and the reverence that being in the natural world can bring forth. No wonder their eyes glaze over when we start yakking about the good old days, before electronics took over.

But I think there are changes on the horizon. And they're coming from those who are in the best position to influence kids and teens – the kids and teens themselves. I see some of them turning away from social media, others experimenting with flip phones. My teen clients tell me they're deleting social apps, putting down the vape pen, wanting to read. "I'd like to start reading more," a handful of teens have told me recently. I've not ever heard that before. They haven't quite gotten there yet, they add, but it's on their radar. They're thinking about it, and that's great. It's a terrific start.

# CHAPTER FOUR

# Therapy's Blemished Reputation Among Teenagers

Despite so many advances in the field of psychotherapy, some challenges have remained pretty much the same – engaging teenagers in a therapy they might not have ever asked for; generating conversations where their thoughts and feelings are brought forward in ways that intrigue them; expressing compassion for their plights while being able to hold them accountable for their actions, and; constructively navigating simultaneous therapeutic relationships with them as well as with their parents/caregivers, among many others. Like I said just a few short paragraphs before, therapy with teenagers is not for the faint of heart.

Most industries – electronics, say, or communications or fashion – innovate quickly in order to continue meeting the needs of consumers. Mental health, not so much – especially regarding doing therapy with adolescents. Clinical innovations in mental health tend to be in other areas – brain science, mindfulness, trauma, and attachment theory, for example.

But if any single population struggles with mental health, it's our nation's teenagers (and pre-teens). Rates of depression, anxiety, and self-harm, among other problems, are soaring among kids, with hospitals, mental health facilities, and school counselors overwhelmed and unable to provide adequate services. And forced to witness their kids in distress without access to sufficient resources, the parents and caregivers of teens suffer as well. The long-term impact of the pandemic quarantine, the omnipresence of social media and its liquidation of our youth's capacities for curiosity and wonder, the families whose members are all but emotionally detached from one another, and the pressures exerted on teens to excel in all domains of life have given rise to a daunting milieu that has many young people throwing up their hands in defeat or disillusionment before they've even graduated high school.

DOI: 10.4324/9781003257080-4

One summer while I was in graduate school I worked as the director of horseback riding at a day camp. Since it wasn't a camp that specialized in riding, the kids didn't have their own riding equipment or attire. That meant that all 100 kids in the riding program shared the same collection of riding helmets, which they would pull out of a big brown box inside the barn.

A week or so into the season, I was preparing for the first group of morning riders to arrive. Suddenly I saw the camp director running across the field toward the barn from his office. As he got closer, I could see that in his hand was a gigantic can of Lysol Disinfectant spray. Rushing over to me and out of breath, the director quickly explained that he'd been fielding phone calls from parents all morning; apparently, there had been an outbreak of head lice among the campers. I immediately thought of all those shared helmets and assumed our response would be to shut down the program until the problem was under control. But the director had a different idea, specifically, spraying all the helmets with Lysol, and then carrying on as usual. "David," I said, "Lysol doesn't exterminate head lice. Applying it to their heads will more likely exterminate our campers." "I know," said David, plaintively, "but, at least we'll be doing *something* ...."

This idea – of *at least doing something*, even if you have little reason to believe it will work – reminds me of the somewhat agonizing situation many mental health professionals end up facing when working with teenagers with whom it's not clear what to do. They've tried everything they learned and maybe even made up a few things on their own – but it's just not working. They have parents and perhaps a supervisor getting restless on the sidelines wondering when some positive change will show. They feel accountable for the work they're doing and want a better outcome as much as anyone else, but they're out of ideas.

I think that if these therapists knew of something different to try, they'd try it. However, for decades we have just been putting teens in the same chute as all our other therapy clients and pushing until they come out the other end, many of them in the same condition in which they came to us. Historically, there hasn't been too much attention paid to the difference between doing therapy with adolescents, and doing therapy with everyone else. Graduate courses especially focused on child and adolescent *development* more than therapy per se, supposing, I assume, that students would be able to extract from the course material what they needed once they were in their offices – an unfortunate oversight.

## Why teenagers have (historically) "hated" therapy[1]

Teenagers balk at therapy (often but not always) because ...

**It feels awkward**. They're sent into a room with an unfamiliar adult to answer questions about problems they don't believe they have or aren't ready to admit they have. Many encounters are tense and awkward, and don't invite return visits.

**It feels unnatural.** Teenagers generally don't go about solving problems by talking about them in depth, so they're not real sure how therapy is supposed to work. In addition, everything about therapy – from meeting a new therapist to being asked dozens of questions – operates under an unnatural set of principles. It's just not how people ordinarily meet and get to know one another in real life. It feels weird and makes teenagers feel self-conscious.

**It appears irrelevant**. Wanting to avoid going too deep too soon, many therapists spend early sessions asking about school, hobbies, friends, etc. Putting aside for a moment the problem of trying to start conversations by asking questions, the issue here is that unless the therapist is able to talk about these things in a meaningful way, it's all just fluff, and the teen's suspicion that therapy is a waste of time is reinforced.

**It's often ineffective.** So many attempts at therapy fail, some epically. We don't get many chances before kids decide therapy isn't for them, and then good luck getting them back. Many young clients don't find the conversations, exercises, or experiences very helpful. The sooner we can make the conversation interesting and relevant to the things our clients are thinking about – but without pushing an agenda on them – the better are the chances at getting them to give therapy a shot.

**It can feel controlling.** Too often, conversations between therapists and adolescents deteriorate into some kind of power battle – solicitous appeals or quasi-lectures on the therapist's part, a gamey withholding or anxiety-driven silence on the teen's, resulting in protracted tugs-of-war. Therapists get frustrated, feel ineffective, and get impatient. Clients feel misunderstood, disillusioned, and lose confidence in therapy. Innumerable fractures in the relationship derail the process before it can even get started.

**It's often too reliant on questions.** Teenagers walk into a new therapist's office and are often hit with dozens of questions – either because there's an intake form to be filled out, or because the therapist finds it hard to start a conversation without asking questions. What I find funny about this thing with questions is that nowhere else in our lives – not with family members, colleagues, our adult friends – do we ever try to start conversations by asking a lot of questions. Usually, we just start talking – about ourselves, our day, our worries, the things we thought were funny – and then the other person starts talking and then we're having a conversation. Only with teenagers do adults (therapists, parents, teachers) try to jump start conversations with kids by firing off questions in the hope that one of them might spark a real conversation.

## Why is adolescent therapy so challenging?

- Many of the teenagers we see have not asked to be in therapy. They were brought by parents or other caregivers or sent there by their school or the courts, making the therapy, at least in the beginning, non-consensual. This changes almost everything about it, drawing into play issues of power, respect, and implicit communication that profoundly affect the relationship between therapist and teen, as well as the course and outcome of therapy. Yet there's been very little attention paid to this in training programs. In addition, as mentioned earlier, there has been **insufficient attention paid to the differences between therapy with adults and therapy with teenagers.** Graduate and other training programs will have separate courses for treating adults and treating kids and teenagers, but much of that content is related to developmental theory and not the nuances of therapy and the micro skills needed to be successful with the latter.

- Moreover, there is **not enough training in family therapy,** where therapists learn how to be an organizing influence on a family and present themselves as on everyone's side, working harmoniously with their teen clients and their parents. I will hear from some of the therapists I supervise that they have difficulty being taken seriously by their teen clients' parents. They lack the credibility to be strongly influential, or have difficulty controlling sessions or discerning salient points. Unfortunately, many family therapy sessions simply end up being family meetings, where participants say their piece but nothing changes.

- There are entrenched executive policies reflecting **ideological clashes between administrative and clinical staff**, for example, paperwork requiring therapists to discuss treatment goals in the first session – a big ask, and a big turn off, for most teens. We need greater congruence between administrative/agency protocols and the service needs of adolescents. We will always lose kids when we start out talking about "treatment," with all its medical and patient connotations. How attractive will that be to a fifteen-year-old girl who's wondering why she's not as happy as her friends seem to be, or who wonders why she's afraid to speak up in class or at her lunch table, or who simply wants a place where she can think out loud with a trusted adult? Therapists forced to fit human change processes into administrative protocols or the needs of the institutions are compromised from the start by offering services that are often unappealing to young people.

- **Not everyone is well suited by personality to work with an adolescent population.** This has nothing to do with age, gender, background, values, preferences, or choice of clothing. It has to do with feeling comfortable around adolescents, with being able to balance a spontaneous interpersonal style with a mindfulness regarding the impact of one's reactions and words on young clients. Therapists who work with teenagers need flexible perspectives on all things, an ability to handle provocations deftly and non-defensively, and a willingness to be taught by their teen clients and remain comfortable when things don't make sense. They need also to be able to relinquish control over the conversation, their client's feelings, and their client's ultimate choices. Can you help a teenager to see that what's inside him is interesting? Are you credible? Can you play? this latter question because there is always an *element of sport* when doing therapy with teenagers.

- Therapists need to **maintain an even perspective** in the face of extraordinary stories, affects, and dynamics. This requires therapists to be able to respond authentically and emotionally while also demonstrating thoughtfulness and self-restraint.

- **The relationship dynamic is different with teenagers than it is with adults.** Anyone who has sat with a teenager reluctant to engage in therapy will be familiar with that miserable feeling of not having a clue what to say or do next. Teens are experts at discerning adults' vulnerabilities and anxieties and, if they choose, will exploit them like no one's business. All those things we hope to be in session – helpful, trustworthy, competent, credible – are exactly what we might feel stripped of. For example, those therapists to whom it's important to appear in control of the session will find themselves struggling to keep any semblance of that. Those who try to hide their anxiety about not knowing what to say are rendered speechless in no time flat. And those who try to meet all the wishes of the teenager in an attempt to establish a rapport find that the conditions they've agreed to simply wind up compromising the integrity of the therapy to begin with.

- It's also important that therapists **recognize the importance of helping kids to save face**. Teenagers appreciate adults who understand that saving face in some circumstances can be more important than doing the "smart" thing. For example, some kids can work in therapy as long as you don't make a big deal about their "participation" or "cooperation." Some need you to downplay the working relationship or refrain from putting too fine a point on any collaboration you have established. Some kids can join you in therapy as long as it's never acknowledged aloud between the two of you that they have "consented to treatment" (one of the reasons why I object to the idea of having kids sign agreements about therapy goals or objectives). Some kids are very comfortable with the idea of being in therapy and will tell anyone who asks (and many who don't), while others can get better only if they're scaring the bejesus out of everyone around them. Doing therapy successfully with teenagers calls for an alertness to the kind of approach that will best suit each individual.

## In addition, doing therapy successfully with teenagers also calls for a unique set of communication skills

### A fluency in nonverbal communication

Some of the richest information about adolescents will be communicated nonverbally. This requires therapists to read in between the lines of what kids say – or don't say – as well as to be able to express themselves through their own body language, voice tone or absence of response. The subtlety, artistry, and nuance involved in communicating successfully, compellingly, and credibly is challenging to convey in a textbook, but ever so important to highlight. At times, it can even seem at odds with the frank, unvarnished and urgent expression of distress we see in our teen clients, but it plays a terrifically important role in keeping the conversation moving forward. For instance, being able to recognize when a client's muted response is nonetheless an affirmative one may be one of the differences between therapists whose clients stay with them, and those whose clients leave prematurely.

> Looking down toward his lap and sighing heavily, a teenager remains silent after his therapist quietly asks him whether he is ready to try returning to school after a two weeklong truancy stint. His answer, *Yeah*, is implied in his body language and muted response. For this kid, questions from adults have always been opportunities to push back, and the absence of any push back in this moment should have been answer enough; it should be understood that he'll go. But his therapist doesn't understand that and so, after a few moments, repeats, "So, you're not answering …. Are you ready to go back?", which annoys the kid, who is thinking, *I already told you … I already said I was going and if you make me say it out loud I'm going to give you a different answer ….*

### A personal comfort with mosaic, rather than linear, communication patterns

Organic conversations with teenage clients that are not a part of a programmed treatment plan tend to have patterns that are mosaic, that is, they combine a broad range of seemingly non-related references into a single conversation. Therapists who prefer a more linear style of communication and a more methodical approach to therapy with specific goals and plans may get anxious during a conversation that doesn't stay close to specified treatment objectives or that bears little resemblance to the one the therapist anticipated. Similarly, a teenager accustomed to having conversations that bounce around may get anxious during one in which the therapist tries to keep everything very focused and task oriented. My best conversations with teenagers are often a mix of banter, encouragement, challenge, stories, questions, reactions, and self-disclosure, as well as brief periods of silence in order to punctuate a point, allow for reflection, or rest the conversation.

## Ideas That Don't Downscale Well from Adult to Adolescent Therapy

In addition to important stylistic differences between conducting therapy with adults and with teenagers, there are also **fundamental tenets about therapy that are less relevant for teens** than they are for adult therapy clients. For example,

### "Insight is important for change"

Not only is insight unnecessary for effecting change, the tasks associated with acquiring insight distract from the more immediate task of therapy, that is, getting kids to feel better or do things differently, or to think about things or themselves or others differently. The language of traditional, insight-oriented therapy is foreign to kids and, despite an openness to getting help, they just may not know how to carry on that type of dialogue. Martha B. Straus[2] talks about this in her book, *No-Talk Therapy for Children and Adolescents,* describing how many kids, especially younger ones, don't know how to respond to questions about their inner emotional life or how to respond to questions asking them to "clarify" what they meant in something they just said.

### "Rapport is king"

In the spirit of establishing rapport with adolescent clients, therapists sometimes set the scale too heavily in favor of empathy and support over issues of accountability. In doing so, they end up avoiding thorny but key situations or topics. Kids pick up on this right away, surmising correctly that their therapist is walking on eggshells around them. Some find the behavior ingratiating and lose faith in the therapist who they see as someone willing to sacrifice their authenticity in order to keep a false peace. More on this later.

### "Talking about feelings is important"

The great effort that many therapists make to get teenagers to talk about their feelings is one of the bigger reasons why their therapies derail. We all are so much more than a compilation of our feelings, and the partisan emphasis on expressing one's feelings minimizes the colorful, complex tapestry of our identity, psyche, and soul. At the very least, if you're going to ask about feelings try doing it in a more oblique manner that doesn't isolate them from a larger and more meaningful or interesting context, for example:

- What do you hear on the news that makes you want to jump out of your seat and do something?
- What do you hear about these days that makes you cry? Want to run and hide? Want to hug someone?
- Oh my god, I can't even imagine how crazy excited I'd have been to have the opportunity to meet the band backstage. What was it like?

Besides, what kid doesn't roll her eyes when hearing that tired phrase, *"How did that make you feel?"* We need to bury that one.

## "Therapy should be experienced primarily as a 'safe' place"

What exactly are we promising our clients when we describe therapy as safe? Safe from unwarranted judgment and breaches of trust? Of course, that goes without saying. However, it's come to mean something more than just that, something that doesn't always support the work we're trying to do with them. If some part of therapy is engaging kids in relationships that are authentic, then that part has to also include the dimensions of a relationship that make it real – accountability, transparency, vulnerability.

Therapy should be safe in all the right ways: no judgment, no snark or sarcasm, no "making a point" in order to feel you're "doing something," no provocation or criticism because you're feeling frustrated or annoyed with the client. But it shouldn't mean that clients won't be challenged, or that they shouldn't have to account for their choices when they choose to be mean or manipulative or disrespectful or irresponsible. Accountability makes some clients feel defensive, disillusioned, or vulnerable – unsafe. But done sensitively and artfully, your endeavor to hold clients accountable for some of their indecorous decisions becomes an indispensable part of the therapy: *Wow, you said that to her as casually as if you were telling her what you just had for breakfast. What is so very easy for you to say would be hard for most. How were you hoping she'd respond?*

The role of accountability in adolescent therapy is never a matter of getting a teenager to "own up" to problems or agree to work on them. The therapist is simply *ascribing intention* behind the client's actions or choice. Accountability is valuable for its ability to *dis-illusion* the teen, that is, to reinforce the idea (without confrontation) that one cannot necessarily control the (public) narrative surrounding one's actions. It's a way for therapists to not have to go along with something objectionable, while also not feeling any pressure to directly criticize their client at that time.

One needs to always be kind in their work with clients – no matter the age. But therapies that are all about being "safe" wind up being therapies that are all about being "nice," in which case we're not even talking about therapy anymore.

## "Avoid too much self-disclosure and try to remain neutral in your interactions with clients"

Huh? Few things foretell the demise of therapy with teenagers more than the reluctance of the therapist to "show up." By that I mean being truly present in the room with the client – attentive, emotionally resonant, an active contributor to the conversation underway. I don't know how anyone does that without their person and values naturally being expressed – which is different from being imposed. How can we put ourselves out there as facilitators of healthy, reciprocated relationships if we sit there withholding the very ideas, experiences, and stories that make each of us unique?

It's so easy to blame teenagers for the failures in our therapeutic work with them, especially with all that the concept of adolescence conveys culturally, historically, and sociologically. After all, teenagers are irascible, defiant, coy, pseudo-independent, imprudent, puckish, and argumentative – *aren't they?* Not really. Teenagers are not alien, hostile or exotic creatures and they are not crazy, despite what some of the popular works on adolescence expound. They can be generous and passionate and witty and amenable and uncommonly empathic. They also happen to be disarmingly astute about the operative dynamics in human relationships which, I suspect, is why so many adults feel intimidated or defensive when engaging with them. Teenagers see right through adults' attempts to placate, trivialize, camouflage, patronize or otherwise relate with them in efforts to reinforce their tenuous sense of control.

Unfortunately, these same teenagers have few ways of pushing back on that without it being seen by most adults as oppositional or difficult or argumentative or as simply "typical teen behavior." No wonder so many adolescents depend as much as they do on their "second families," [3] those powerful friend groups that threaten to overwhelm the first family of adults at home. Theirs is a collective understanding and easy camaraderie.

We don't have to offer the same things to adolescents that their peers offer them in order to become valued members of one or another of their social families. We can't, and those who try wind up looking foolish. As therapists, we offer something very distinct – a relationship and an experience that's different from ones they have with other people, and especially with other adults. With us they can reinvent themselves if they so wish, or stay the same as they are, or do something in between. We support them no matter what.

## Notes

1  I say "historically" because that statement is truer for the past that present. Advances in the provision of mental health services for adolescents and changes in the way clinicians approach them has made therapy more appealing to teens. Moreover, the mental health social movement of the past several years, boosted by the Covid-19 pandemic, has made teenagers better informed and more engaged consumers of therapy, which inevitably raises the quality of services available.

2  W. W. Norton & Company, 1999.

3  Ron Taffel, *The second family: Dealing with peer power, pop culture, the wall of silence – and other challenges of raising today's teens*, St. Martin's Griffin, 2002.

CHAPTER FIVE

# What Teenagers Need from Our Therapeutic Relationships

When we first learned about therapy and the importance of a good therapeutic alliance, our attention was directed toward a small but unwavering group of principles that were understood to be critical in fostering this connection. We were taught to demonstrate to clients our capacities for empathy, keeping confidentiality, and unconditional support so that they could tell we were compassionate and safe to talk with. Basically, we chased them.

We were also taught to avoid challenging clients before we had a strong alliance with them, and that the alliance building itself would take weeks of listening, reflecting, mirroring, and supporting. The problem of course is that by then any teenagers were long gone, put off by the obliging demeanor of their therapists and protracted onboarding.

Some therapists will need to be convinced in order to abandon the time-worn idea that good therapy with teenagers is principally about providing "safe places" and a lot of empathy, or should at least start off that way. This may feel good (temporarily) to the teenager in trouble, but it usually does very little to change anything. Even the good feeling wears off. Countless teenagers have said to me some version of the following: "My other therapist was nice, but she didn't do anything to help me. All she did was feel sorry for me and try to act understanding." We can do better.

Here's what we weren't taught in graduate school. In spite of all the hours spent discussing how to connect with clients, we really weren't taught *how to be so they'd want to connect with us*. These two undertakings are very different from each other and shape the ensuing therapy in distinct ways. When we understand how to use our best selves to be *compelling* rather than banking on our empathy or benevolence to draw young clients in, we will show up more fully to our clients, and find we no longer need to chase them. I think we pose

DOI: 10.4324/9781003257080-5

the wrong question when asking, "How do I get this teenager to talk with me?" I believe a better one is, "How can I become an inviting and relevant enough figure to teenagers so that they actually *want* to talk with me?" It's better because it reflects the importance of the teen being drawn into the field of the therapist rather than the other way around and serves to mitigate the dynamic wherein therapists work harder than clients at making therapy work.

Adolescents, being especially keen on the dynamics surrounding interpersonal influence, pick up quickly on adults who play to their favor. Solicitous appeals on the parts of parents, teachers, or therapists to engage them are met not with cooperation but with suspicion (someone wants something from them) or boredom (here come more questions about school) or resistance (*Sorry, just not interested.*). That's why therapists who try too hard to gain the attention or engagement of their teen clients often struggle to do so; despite the apparent benevolence on a therapist's part, many teenagers don't find that type of invitation to talk or relate very appealing. In order to be effective in our role, it can never become more important to us than to our clients that we connect, or that "something therapeutic happen" during sessions. We may *want* it to happen more than they do, we may *apply more thought* about how to engender it than they do, but when we try too hard to *make* it happen, that's when things hit the skids.

## Critical Dynamics in Therapist~Teen Relationships

Teenagers enjoy a privileged position of having something that their parents and therapists want but cannot extract: their words and, to some extent, their approval. So, when we allow the act of speaking in therapy to matter more to us as therapists than it will to our clients, we inadvertently play up the value of words as currency. As a result, many therapists end up working very hard for the words they get from their adolescent clients.

These two cards that kids hold – talk and approval – are empowered only by their therapist's complicity. For certain teens, volunteering information about themselves and accepting the process of therapy can feel like a big concession of power. As a result, words and approval are dispensed sparingly. Therefore, if a therapist's interaction style or behavior allows her teen clients to believe that either their chattiness or their endorsement of therapy (or of the therapist) is important for the therapy to move forward, then all any teenager has to do to stop the process or stump the therapist is to withhold one of the two.

Even the teenagers who come to us of their own accord, who seek us out themselves or prompt their parents or other caregiver to make the call, can get a little spooked when their new therapist comes on strong with messages about how helpful they want to be. We don't need to lead with that; kids already figure, correctly, that we are there to help simply because we are showing up in our respective roles. It's the nature of who we are because of what we've chosen to do.

What follows are some twists on conventional ideas and practices in adolescent therapy that have enhanced my ability to establish strong working relationships with teenage clients:

## Empathy is great – until it's too much

Adolescents are very attuned to what's real and what's not real in the relationships that adults try to establish with them, and strong expressions of empathy from therapists who barely know them come off as unnervingly disingenuous. Compassion is great, but when presented too early in a relationship (any relationship, not just in therapy) and especially when too forceful, it can be off-putting.

The reason why banking on empathy as a pathway to rapport can be misguided is that the compassion a therapist had hoped to demonstrate is registered by the teen as something else – more along the lines of, *Here's another adult (like my parents, like my teachers) who is willing to work much harder than I am to "connect," or help me with my problems.* When we try to connect with adolescents with only (or primarily) our empathy and concern, it's difficult for the therapeutic relationship to gain any traction. Renowned family therapist Carl Whitaker spoke about this decades ago, saying that such relationships are compromised because only half of the relationship is present – the "nice" half – and it feels out of order; the contract is all wrong. Teenagers recognize this and can feel unnerved.

It's this inauthenticity in the relationship that causes so many teens to go ballistic when adults try to get them to calm down. What happens is that when trying to get an agitated teen to settle, many adults take a step back from the relationship. They speak to the teenager from a cool and distant place of logic and rationality that is incongruent with the distress and urgency *they are actually feeling* in the face of that teenager's rage. And that lack of congruence between what the adult feels and what the adult says breaks or interferes with any connection they might have had with the teen they are trying to help. The adult won't know that they are no longer connecting. But the teenager feels it acutely and, in the absence of the genuine contact and authenticity he seeks, responds in the only way he can – that is, *dramatically*.

Here's how such a dynamic could show up in therapy with a teen client. Let's say a sixteen-year-old boy starts to get agitated during a session. One therapist might try to intervene by saying, *"Let's take a minute to calm down so we can talk about what happened …,"* but this is the sort of thing that Whitaker advised us against. I think a better response in that situation might be to say,

THERAPIST:    Zane, hang on! I can't understand what you're saying. Tell me again.

TEEN:    Well, fuck that. I said what I wanted to say.

THERAPIST:    Yeah, but I didn't catch all of it. I don't know, maybe I could be mad along *with* you. At the very least, I could be in that *conversation* with you.

TEEN:    (Sighs) I was just saying that ....

The clinical task here is balancing one's empathy and discretion with other dimensions of our role as therapist – in this case, maintaining connection during disharmony – in a way that holds the teenager in because what is being offered is a very real and unfeigned relationship that happens to also be a therapeutic one.

## The idea that rapport leads to engagement is backwards

As taught in graduate school, therapeutic rapport is thought of as something built over time, meaning, it is the *time together* that leads to its emergence. Many therapists are surprised, however, when suddenly, after weeks of pleasant-ish conversation, the kid drops out of therapy. There's not a lot of traction in *pleasant*. And to grow, rapport needs not time but traction, and that comes from engagement and from respect.

That's why rapport-building "techniques" don't make sense to me. My understanding of true rapport between therapists and clients is that it develops after clients decide that there is something of value for them in relating with their particular therapist. The value can be anything that matters enough to clients that they continue engaging – it could be anything from finding their therapist easy to talk with, to finding their therapist knowledgeable about their predicament, to finding their therapist entertaining; it doesn't matter. What matters is that they keep coming back for more.

That's why I consider the idea that rapport leads to engagement as backward. Specifically, a therapist engages a teenager in active conversation and, if the teen likes what she sees, then she engages for real. And more deeply. *Now* you have rapport. It kicks in *after* there's been a connection.

Is this just semantics? I don't know. I wanted to introduce this conversation about rapport because I worry it's become a hackneyed phrase – dog-eared and threadbare, its meaning lost from indiscriminate use. We all know what it means, but we also might have become so overly familiar with the term that we stopped thinking that we had to continue unpacking it in our practices and in our understanding of how we and our clients connect. We just spoke of "building rapport" and left it at that, overlooking the value of understanding what it was exactly that we were doing in our pursuit of this Holy Grail.

### Showing up as authentic is far more influential and inspiring than showing up too eager to help

Authenticity in relationships is one of those things that's hard to define. It shares a DNA with other personal qualities such as being nice or kind. After all, most people think of themselves as a decent person, fairly nice and, for the most part, kind. Same with authenticity. Everyone believes they are authentic.

But ask people to define authentic, and most stumble. It's one of those terms where the harder you try to prove that you know what it means, the less authentic you sound. I think the closest description of authenticity comes from how the secretary to Mahatma Gandhi, Mahadev Desai, replied when asked how Gandhi, attending a round table conference in 1931 in order to influence the British public over the plight of India under British rule, spoke so eloquently and for so long without any notes, mesmerizing his audience. Desai replied as follows: "You see what (Gandhi) thinks is what he feels. What he feels is what he says and what he says is what he does. What Gandhi thinks, what he feels, what he says and what he does are all the same."[1] I guess we can say that when we are able to recognize that *through line of consistent character*, that integrity, we have found authenticity.

### Until teenagers see their therapists as willing to recognize their behaviors and expressed attitudes as "choices" (not things they can't help doing), there will be little traction in the therapy

Few things cut into a therapist's credibility with young clients faster than the reluctance of that therapist to stand behind what both parties know to be true – that this particular teenager could have helped it, that he did know better, that he understands all too well that if he does A, then the world around him will always and can only respond with B. And, in contrast to the common assumption that in asking the teen to be accountable the therapist risks fracturing their connection, I believe it's more likely to be the very thing that cements it.

People young and old respect those who own and will say what they believe, especially when tempered by graciousness and free from directives or prescriptions. When directed toward therapists on the part of teenage clients, this unsolicited respect becomes an important vehicle through which they will allow themselves to be influenced, guided, coached, known. These kids have a lot of adults in their lives who get in their faces and try to muscle their points across the divide. They also have a lot of adults in their lives who over-accommodate their poor behavior. What these kids don't have enough of are adults who have their back and at the same time can help them see through their own b.s., who can talk with them about their problems without raising their defenses or having them bolt prematurely from conversations.

**The Paradox of Trying to Avoid Conflict When Doing Therapy with Teenagers**

Unless a therapist communicates an easy and forgiving, but unapologetic, willingness to call the adolescent out on his behavior, choices, and the beliefs governing those choices, there won't be any real connection.

Therapists lose credibility (and thus the ability to influence) when they sideline the truth in order to appear supportive (lending the idea that the two are incompatible). However, a therapist's quiet, understated refusal to go along with what no one had ever really believed in the first place yet had been left unchallenged (she can't help it, he didn't mean it, it was just a joke), is a very powerful intervention.

This is the role of accountability in adolescent therapy and in an adolescent's emotional maturation – its ability to dis-illusion the teen without directly confronting him. It should never be a matter of "getting" the teen to own up to problems or agree to work on them. Rather, the teen is drawn in by the authenticity of the therapist, as evidenced by a) an honesty about their encounter and unwillingness to sacrifice it in order to "keep the peace," and b) the absence of any effort to "get" the teen to change, reflecting the therapist's respect for the client's autonomy. That is the condition under which many teenagers who had previously kept themselves impervious to outside opinion will begin to open themselves up to being helped.

## A quick word about treatment goals

I can't think of any good reason to ask a new teenage client – who may not even be sure how therapy works – a question about treatment goals that suggests a big, up-front buy in and sounds about as welcoming as a sales contract.

The question itself being unappealing is one problem. Another is that the therapy can easily get bogged down by the therapist and teenager trying to broker some kind of agreement. This is especially true when the teen wasn't the one to initiate the therapy. When we ask teenagers what their goals are for a therapy they never asked for, we are saying that we're more attached to our vision of what therapy is supposed than we are open to a vision of what it might become with each different client. Meanwhile, the kid's thinking, *Is there anything on my face that says I have a freakin' treatment goal??*

Sometimes therapists like treatment plans because it gives them what feels like a road map. But as I hope to illustrate in subsequent chapters, some of the best therapy you can do with teenagers will happen as a natural part of the conversations you're having with them and not through the targeted pursuit of a treatment goal, which can put too fine a point on symptoms, resulting in wooden, labored exchanges over what steps a kid took (or didn't take) toward progress.

The funny thing is that if the therapist and teen are in sync, they both know why they're meeting and where they're trying to go anyway. They may have different words for it, or maybe the teen doesn't have an articulated purpose for meeting but knows that he doesn't want to feel so depressed anymore or doesn't want to keep starting fights with his parents all the time or needs a better way to react when his friends piss him off or is tired of wanting to be high all the time or doesn't want to keep flirting with self-harming behavior or needs to figure out whether he wants to keep playing basketball or instead go after his real interests, the act of which will incur the wrath of his dad/coach, and so on. And, as far as a roadmap, there are many ways to get there from here.

## Teenagers in Therapy: No Place for Neutrality

Having gone through a psychology graduate school program in which all but two of my professors were psychoanalysts (!), I am well versed in all the reasons why therapists shouldn't disclose much about themselves when conducting therapy and should try to maintain a stance of neutrality.

But apart from the fact that this therapeutic approach didn't really suit my personality, it became clear once I graduated and started seeing clients, especially young ones, that this was no way for me to work; it felt, and I felt, colorless, measured, and restrained.

Kids don't want neutrality in their therapy. They want to know who you are and what you think, what you like and what you're willing to go to the mat for. Just like we want to know about them.

You can't be present if you're trying hard to be neutral. At best, it's experienced by the teenager as stingy and aloof. At worst, it's unkind, and just plain weird.

There are many ways in which we disclose parts of ourselves to our clients, both intentionally and otherwise. Our office decor, the photographs and playlists we choose to share, our stories and dress, our reactions to what our clients share with us, the issues we choose to attend to and the ones we take a pass on – these are the points of self-expression we're aware of. Some clinicians prefer to keep a lower profile, muting their personal preferences for music, favored activities or vacation spots, ideologies. Fair enough; most teenagers will find what they need as long as there's *something* real for them to latch onto.

I like bringing my full self into my work with all my clients – teens, children, their parents, college-age kids, and the other adults I see. I am also very mindful – or so I like to believe – of being discreet and discerning when it comes to what I share and what is on display in my office. But I do self-disclose frequently, showing up the same whether my client and I are meeting in a therapy session, bumping into each other at the grocery store, sitting next to each other in a classroom on Back-To-School night, or competing against each other at a horse show. It works for me and it works for my clients but I understand it's not for everyone.

What follows are several ways in which I have used self-disclosure specifically and *intentionally* as a therapeutic tool.

## Self-Disclosure with Teenage Clients

### Self-disclosure to expand a teenager's emotional landscape

I'm talking with sixteen-year-old Annika, who is a music aficionado. She watches a lot of music videos, loves a cappella, and is a fan of the a cappella group Pentatonix.

"Have you seen their video of Hallelujah?" I ask.
"Yeah, but I deleted it because it made me cry."
"Oh my god – I keep it in my play list *because* it makes me cry …"
Annika looks up at me, quizzically. I imagine she's thinking, *Why would anyone keep something around that makes them cry?*
I take a chance. "There's *sad* sad," I say, "where you feel worse, and then there's *beautiful* sad, where you feel like your heart just grew three times its size, even though it's sad. That's the kind of sad I feel when I watch their video of Hallelujah. It's kind of cool…

I think my response to Annika does a couple of things:

- It seeds the idea that having *that* strong an emotional reaction is something some people might seek out instead of trying to avoid.
- It suggests that some people feel a sense of comfort rather than discomfort when affected by something emotionally, and that allowing oneself to be moved like that can be a desirable experience.
- It suggests there are times when feeling sad about something can expand your love or appreciation or generosity.

41

- It suggests that some people find beauty in a certain kind of sadness.
- It lays down the scaffolding for a later, larger conversation that moves from the avoidance of emotions when listening to music to their avoidance in everyday life and in relationships. Here you are playing at the edges and gradually moving toward the center.

These are all new concepts for Annika and her exposure to them matter more here than they would in some kind of lecture, mainly because of the emotional tenor of our conversation which rivets our attention on each other and to what we're saying. There is gravitas, which gives the messages weight, but there is levity too, which allows them to be assimilated without any need for Annika to become defensive.

## Self-disclosure as an expression of communion

I once sat with a reticent boy of thirteen whose name I'll say was Declan. Just about the only thing I knew about Declan is that he had pet rats and loved them. So, I said to him that I was really happy to hear about rats getting good homes, with all you hear about them in labs or used as food for snakes. I went on to tell Declan about how I'd kept water turtles as pets several years back but, after finding out that they'd need a diet of live fish in order to remain healthy, I made the decision to find them other homes. "One time," I said to this sad looking, withdrawn boy, "I bought fish at the pet store for my turtles. Driving home with them, I felt like an executioner and apologized to each one during the entire ride. I hated putting the fish in the tank with my turtles, knowing they'd have no escape. I never did it again, but here I am thirty years later, still haunted by its memory."

And the face of this closed off and largely mute kid opened up as he peeled his eyes off the floor and brought them up to meet mine, softly, accompanied by a small, warm smile. It lasted only a few moments, but it was enough; we had found a scratch of common ground and built a relationship up from there.

Maybe some people wouldn't share their playlist with a client or tell this story about their turtles and that's fine. What's important is that you define for yourself the parameters within which you are comfortable disclosing personal stories, and always make a point to understand why you are choosing to tell them. How will your disclosure mesh with the needs of your client? What is it you intend? To reveal a little of your personality? To let clients know you're not going to expect them to do all the talking? To show your individuality or human-ity or benevolence? Or to look cool or well versed in pop culture? Or maybe to coax clients into telling you something about themselves? There's a huge dif-ference between disclosure as a gesture of reciprocity and contribution to the conversation and process of therapy, and disclosure that proposes a deal along the lines of, *I'll tell you things about me as a person that most other therapists wouldn't share with you, as long as you agree to open up and tell me about yourself.* Scrap anything that hints of the latter.

## Self-disclosure to normalize and seed a conversation for later

Eleven-year-old Gabby – very social, but also very bossy – talks in session about the rules she made for her neighborhood friends about who could play with who on which days. She's getting a little sheepish as she realizes how it sounds. I had reasons to suspect there were times when she outright bullied some of the kids. I also understood that Gabby cared what I thought of her, so I figured I'd try to capitalize on it in service of her therapy, the presenting problem of which was Gabby's anxiety and difficulties with social adjustment.

"You wanna know something, Gabby?"
"What?"
"I made rules for everyone in the neighborhood too when I was a kid."
"You did?"
"Yup. I was a tomboy back then and didn't like that a lot of the girls wanted to play with dolls, so I made a rule that no one on the block could play with Barbies except on Friday. Still not sure how I pulled that off...."
"You were top dog," she says, without missing a beat.
"Maybe so," I replied, taken aback by her swift, correct assessment. "Actually, I was kind of bossy. I don't like saying it, but it's true," I add.
"Yeah, I'm kind of top dog too, but I don't get bossy."
"That's cool. You're better at being top dog than I am .... I thought I had to be bossy to get anyone to listen to me."

And then I moved onto something else, gently leaving this conversation behind. The temptation might have been to stay with it in an effort to "get to" Gabby's feelings about being top dog and making the rules for everybody. But it would have been too much, an unnecessarily protracted conversation about a sensitive topic, and she'd have scooted away.

By leaving the conversation at that juncture, before Gabby had become uncomfortable, I was making it easy for me to return to it at a later date and invite her to join me again in talking about being top dog. This would be an easy one to circle back to, any of the following conversations serving as a bridge:

- Gabby mentions something about a friend who's bossy.
- Gabby again talks about her neighborhood friends who she makes rules for.
- Gabby mentions any situation (at home, at school, at a sleepover, etc.) where she calls the shots and exercises control over her friends'

decisions (what snacks to get, which video game to play, who to FaceTime, etc.)

A week or two later, in a meandering conversation in which Gabby and I were discussing other kids among her neighborhood homies who also liked to make rules, I said, "Hey, Gabby, remember the other day when we were talking about each of us being a top dog and I said that I thought being bossy was the only way I could get anyone to listen to me?"

"Yeah," Gabby says, largely disinterested.
"Well I think it was pretty cool you were able to be top dog without having to be bossy."
"Yeah." I know this conversation isn't grabbing her, but I'm just trying to fast track a reference to the topic of being bossy.
"Yeah, it's one of those things …" I say easily, before pivoting to, "Do you ever wonder if some of the kids don't love all your rules but follow them anyway because they don't want you to be mad at them?" which brings the conversation around to something more interesting for Gabby. She looks up now and scrunches up her nose.
"Not really," she replies.

I could have just as easily pivoted to …

*… Hey, Gabby, has anyone ever said to you, 'Hey I don't think I like that rule,'*
OR
*… Hey, I'm curious, Gabby, was anyone the boss before you?*
OR
*… Hey, Gabby, so how did you become the boss of the neighborhood without getting bossy?*
OR
*… Do you ever feel like you don't want to be top dog anymore but you still have to be?*

Notice though that I'm saying "or" and not "and"! You'd ask one or two of these, tops. You can always come back another time, especially if you keep each conversion short, and exit before Gabby gets defensive or bored. But in that sequence of conversations, you are able to touch upon a number of issues related to Gabby's problems making and keeping friends, especially her need to be in control of the action or of the people involved. This is not only a function of her anxiety, but a consequence of the very behavior her anxiety is fueling.

It's easy to segue from those conversations about the neighborhood social dynamics to ones about her anxiety:

*… Gabby, does it ever bother you when your friends don't let you be the top dog, or don't follow your rules?* – a sentence which morphs imperceptibly into *Does it bother you when your friends don't do what you want them to?* which can be followed with, *Is that one of the times when you start to feel a little anxious, like we were talking about when your mom was with us the other day?* And boom, we're there, right where we need to be.

## Self-disclosure to share a favorable impression of your client with her

I'd known nineteen-year-old Eleni since she first came for therapy at age fourteen, with her hair dyed and spiked and her attitude even sassier. We connected right away and have been working together ever since.

But for a variety of reasons, none of them good ones, Eleni over the years had abandoned her remarkable vocal and musical talents. This kid, who had regaled community audiences had parked her gifts in favor of deliberate recalcitrance at home and at school, anywhere she could get the attention she desperately sought.

And so when, a couple of years later, Eleni one day said to me, "Hey I'm getting my muse back with the cello, and even with singing …. I feel creative again …," I responded genuinely by saying, "Oh Eleni, I never stopped thinking of you in that way …." At this point, Eleni slowly looked up at me, tears in her eyes. I think she was surprised that anyone at all still held a space for those softer, more generous, and colorful parts of her that, in her depression and anger, she had spitefully abandoned.

## Self-disclosure to draw out themes

I remember fourteen-year-old Gina telling me that she wasn't having any kind of birthday party because she was "over all that," her depression having robbed her of an ability to appreciate such things. Besides, all the popular girls were having birthday parties and she wanted nothing to do with anything they fancied.

"Over all *what*?" I asked.
*"Birthdays,"* she scoffed, as if I were the biggest idiot in the world. "I'll probably just go over to a friend's house."

That's when I leaned forward and told Gina this story:

"When my mom was turning 82 years old, she said the one thing she really wanted was a birthday party with Elmo. Not any old birthday party. One with Elmo."

After several moments, Gina asked, "So what did you do?" seemingly embarrassed to have been interested enough to ask.

"We gave her a party and we got her Elmo, too." I replied, opening my phone to show her my mom, all smiles, standing next to the Elmo (impersonator) my dad had found. "Gina," I whispered, putting my phone away, "please don't ever let yourself get too old to play."

## Self-disclosure to both model and employ an emotional expressiveness in the service of re-orienting clients lost in battle

A mother and father are arguing in a family session because their sixteen-year-old son doesn't want to go out Christmas tree shopping with them this year. The argument is going nowhere so I decide to join in.

"Do you know that every year I feel sorry for the trees that don't get bought, all lonely, sitting in those lots?" I said. All three of them turn to look at me. "I think of them like the animals at the S.P.C.A., waiting for their forever homes." The two parents and their son are wondering whether I'm serious.

"Totally serious," I say, and they start to smile and look at one another. I see that they can appreciate, if not experience for themselves, someone else's whimsical emotionality, and they relax a little. In the wake of their softening, I say to them, with a sense of gravitas now, "Family rituals need the flexibility to change as kids get older. You guys can do Christmas differently and it can still be good."

This model of working with teenagers in therapy puts the greatest amount of attention on factors that I've come to believe have the strongest chance of influencing our young clients – content that matters, a commitment, our presence and attention, our discernment, frank advice that's useful and informed, our wisdom, and genuine emotional affection. It's important to me that the model be understood as being much more disciplined than it might appear at first glance. I can see where it would be easy for it to be misinterpreted as a "fly by the seat of your pants" approach, where you talk chummy and say whatever comes to mind, but nothing could be further from the truth. My approach requires an immense amount of self-discipline and self-restraint, so that even in a context of easy and spontaneous conversation, therapists are mindful of and intentional about every single word they say. Interventions are thoughtfully worded and made judiciously, and must always and only come from a place of benevolence.

These kids – whether voluntarily or not – are, in many ways, at our mercy. We know their history a great deal more than they will ever know ours. We know about where they hurt and maybe why as well; we know about the failing grade they received in phys ed; the psychological evaluation that revealed multiple learning disabilities or an autism spectrum diagnosis; maybe the "real" reason their parents divorced – something to which they were not privy; terrible decisions they've made that a caregiver chose to share with us without the teen's consent; the fact that they were bullied for years; the fact that they tried once to fight back and got the crap beat out of them, becoming the laughingstock of their grade … the list is endless. Some of these things matter more to some teenagers than to others, and some are ashamed by this one thing but not that one, and some will wear on their sleeve behaviors that would make others cringe in utter shame. In our presence, in order to remain whole or become whole again, to remain curious, and to heal, our teenage clients are forced to rely on our humanity, our emotional clarity, our decency and good will. This is something of which we must never lose sight.

## Note

1  Steve Pauley, Be First Class blog, www.be-first-class.com/gandhi-story-he-needs-no-notes/?doing_wp_cron=1671850780.6361908912658691406250

# CHAPTER SIX

# Better Engagement with Teens Through Credibility, Respect, and Accountability

My first job out of graduate school was being a staff psychologist at a residential treatment center for socially and emotionally challenged teenagers. I had just completed a five-year full-time clinical psychology program the orientation of which was psychoanalytic. Not just psychodynamic. Psycho*analytic*. Almost every single one of my professors was a psychoanalyst.

The teenagers at that treatment center had little interest in or respect for therapy in general and even less so for an approach that would have required them to free associate and self-reflect. It's kind of funny to think about it now – such a mismatch. In fairness to my schooling and my professors, though, I will say that I loved my training and still do. It informs my clinical work every single day, when I think about character development and structure, interpersonal dynamics, conflict, ego defenses and strengths and the like. For the most part, however, it stays inside my head and rarely shows up directly in that space between my clients and myself.

It didn't take long at my new job for me to find out that grad school was just the beginning of my education about doing therapy, especially with teenagers, and especially involuntary ones. Sure, there were many who craved the attention and support of their therapists, but there were just as many who didn't, and they made no bones about it.

Since the feedback from the teens there was immediate – say something of interest and they'd stay in the room with you, say something that was boring or missed the mark and they'd leave – I learned quickly how to gauge relevant content. As I looked around at the other therapists, though, what struck me was the adversarial nature of the relationships they had with their clients. They frequently challenged them on issues where their only goal was to prove a point

DOI: 10.4324/9781003257080-6

or exert some measure of control. They often assumed the worst about their clients – that they were manipulative and unmotivated for treatment. Both of those things were probably true, but they were more a function of how these kids were being regarded rather than a reflection of who they were or what they could accomplish. Seeing that many of the kids at that center were shown little respect for their person or their anguish, I wound up thinking a lot about the function of and need for respect in therapeutic relationships. This concept became the cornerstone of my psychotherapy practice, as well as of my parenting of my own three sons.

Of all the characteristics I would ascribe to my model of therapy, respect for clients comes to mind first. A close second is a regard for the natural order of things between humans, for example, the ways in which they naturally connect, learn to trust, become more transparent – or don't. Another characteristic is restraint, coupled with active engagement. Sound paradoxical? It is, actually, reflecting the counter-intuitive responding to clients that is very much a part of this therapy model, in that you often need to wait or hold back just when you feel like moving in, or have to move in and act just when you might have been tempted to wait or hold back. And a final one I'll mention is this: That the less *direct* pressure we put on teens to change, the more the conversation expands, as teens learn to trust that the space we are holding for them in the room is one without coercion or injunctions, one in which they are free to think out loud and try on different ideas for size.

## The Three Pillar Foundation

What I talk about in this chapter are three pillars of a triadic foundation upon which my approach to adolescent therapy is based – credibility, respect, and accountability. Embracing them in clinical work allows us a good shot at bringing forward therapeutic conversations that have the power to hearten, animate, awaken, prompt, embolden, revitalize, enrich, or champion our young clients. I find it a profoundly robust and adaptable platform from which to work.

Embracing these three pillars means:

1) becoming credible figures to our clients,
2) expressing a strong measure of respect toward them, and
3) unapologetically but compassionately holding them accountable for the choices they make and the impact of those choices on the people affected by them.

Let's look at them one by one.

## Credibility

My idea of being credible as a therapist corresponds to exhibiting the qualities of trustworthiness and expertise and self-command. It also includes the attributes of being convincing and, especially important for us as therapists, inspiring belief.

I think of credibility as *our most powerful conduit of influence*, one of the more reliable ways through which we can gain kids' attention as well as help them open up to new perspectives, opinions, ideas, or behaviors. It is as non-threatening and unalloyed a human force as anything could possibly be, while still being able to hold sway. In therapy, it's the unforced leverage you will need in order to effect the difficult changes you invite your clients to make, or to actively support the ones they choose to make for themselves.

In therapy one's credibility is evident, or not, very quickly. It's most immediately expressed in a therapist's countenance – everything from posture to facial expression to composure, and it shows up in how confidently (without swagger or righteousness) and graciously (versus unmindfully or inattentively) you greet your clients. It is expressed in how you position yourself vis a vis your young clients' parents (deferentially versus respectfully authoritative), in how active and effective you are in shaping the conversation, and in how deftly and tactfully you handle challenging moments or exchanges in session. It shows up in how you normalize certain behaviors in order to put a client at ease, and in how you isolate points you believe are important without putting anyone on the spot.

For a superb and very moving example of how a human being's credibility can be forceful enough to change the mind of a seemingly immovable man, you need look no further than the video recording of Fred Rogers in his 1969 appearance before the United States Senate Subcommittee on Communications, where he spoke in support of continued funding for PBS and the Corporation for Public Broadcasting. In his six minutes of testimony, Rogers' earnestness, conviction, and grace stood up stunningly to the gruff impatience of subcommittee chairman Senator John O. Pastore, transforming him from cynic to unabashed supporter. "Looks like you just earned the $20 million," Senator Pastore tells Rogers when he was done making his case, to the cheering applause of the hundreds in attendance.[1] It's really a beautiful thing to watch.

Examples of enhancing one's credibility during therapy sessions include:

### *Shrewd discernment coupled with a droll sense of humor*

You're in a family session with a school avoidant teen whose return to the classroom is obstructed by his need to save face with parents who are always making a big deal about "knowing better" and "being right." Rather than going into a long-winded explanation of the family dynamic, you say, smiling ever so slightly, "I actually think your son would return to school if he knew the two of you wouldn't do a victory dance across the kitchen floor." Not only do you get the kid's immediate attention, but you get his respect too, for discerning the operative dynamic in the family that he would never be able to articulate, but can recognize in a snap.

## Deft handling of awkward situations or potential conflicts

To a kid who likes to dangle his high-risk behavior in front of your face … instead of getting into a tug-of-war over how dangerous is too dangerous, you can say, "I don't want to get into a never-ending game where you say, *Look at these dangerous things I do!* and then I say, *Don't you see how dangerous that is?* and then you say, *Gee, no.*"

And continuing, you can say, "I look at the things you do and get queasy. You look at them and go, *Lemme at it.* I'm not interested in trying to convince you of something. I'm more interested in finding out how it is that you and I can look at the exact same things and view them so differently."

In these kinds of situations, I find the question, *Are we connecting?* to be much more useful than *Are we agreeing?* It liquefies the battle for control, and productively redirects the conversation.

## Sharing an illuminating point about adolescent psychology

Your client is a fourteen-year-old girl with little self-esteem and even less confidence. She might be the most self-conscious person on the planet. Lyla comes into her session one day with a new haircut and she's rocking it. She knows it, too, but doesn't say anything about it. Her mother joins us, and proceeds to applaud Lyla's new look, telling her how great she looks and how she should plan to show it off the next day at school. Lyla scowls at her mother and pulls the hood of her hoodie over her head. "Lyla, why are you being like this?" asks the mom, genuinely baffled. "Don't you agree about the haircut? You said you liked it in the car!"

To the mother you say, kindly, "Louise, this kid, your daughter, spends all day every day trying to stay under the radar of other kids, and you want her to waltz into school tomorrow and show off her haircut? No. She may love it. She may rock it. But what you had in mind – it's not gonna happen." Helping the mother understand that Lyla will still want to avoid any extra attention *even though she likes her haircut* is a gift to both of them; the mom begins to see that being self-conscious is about so much more than how you look, and Lyla learns that she can count on you to have her back.

## *Being congruent*

Credibility also comes from being congruent – meaning that what you think and feel and say are all in alignment. It's the best way I know of describing what it means to be authentic. One of the ways therapists lose credibility with their teen clients is when they speak out of both sides of their mouth, for example, conspicuously supporting a parent's efforts to engender more cooperation around the home but downplaying that support when talking with the teenager.

TEEN: Why did you tell my parents that I should be helping more around the house?

ME: Because you should be helping more around the house.

TEEN: Why? I help out plenty.

ME: I know you do, but it's only when you feel like it, and when you like what it is you have to do.

TEEN: I don't see why you care so much about it.

ME: I care about it because I care about you growing up to be a good citizen of this earth.

TEEN: What? That sounds stupid.

ME: I knew you'd say that. That's why I told your parents that they should be asking more of you. They've asked less of you as you've struggled in high school. They see you feeling depressed and anxious and feel bad for you, and it makes them think they should ease up on the stressors they can control.

TEEN: Well, they should.

ME: (I'd be smiling here in response to her remark.) Oh my god, Marissa, they've been doing it for too long already. None of it helps you to feel better, or cope better with the avalanche of stressors you were hit with this year. What you're learning instead is that if you feel shitty, you get a pass. I'd rather you learn that you can do stuff that helps other people, like your parents, out even though you feel kind of shitty.

TEEN: Oh, cause *that's* gonna make me feel a whole lot better, *yeah*....

ME: (Smiling again at her shrewd push back) No, it'll probably just piss you off for now, but ... the other way is pissing everyone else off at home, and I think that's worse.

TEEN: Why should I care?

ME: Tell me you did not just say that.

TEEN: Why?

ME: Oh my god.

TEEN: Seriously, did you really tell them that they should take my phone if I don't do the dishes or clean my bathroom??

ME:       Of course! What else are they going to do? Put you in time out on
          the stairs? (This cracks my client up and we both laugh and move
          on to something else.)

## *Dodging traps and engendering curiosity in the process*

In addition to presenting as credible to your teen clients, you'll want to show
up as credible to their parents or caregivers as well. I was consulting to parents in Israel over Skype. Their thirteen-year-old daughter was exhibiting severe behavior problems including threats of suicide, verbal abuse toward her
mother, and a refusal to do any schoolwork. Like most young depressed, unhappy teens who appeal to the sympathy of helping adults, Tamar had been
able to distract her school counselor and a consulting psychiatrist with her
complaints and draw them unsuspectingly into a power battle. After talking
with her parents twice, I introduced myself to Tamar and excused her parents from the room. Dismissive and aloof, Tamar sat in front of her computer
screen waiting for me to do what therapists have always done with her – try
hard to get her interested in talking with them. They might have asked things
like, *So, how are you doing?* (Okay) or *What's going on at home*? (I don't
know, nothing really) or *Tell me about yourself*? (What's there to tell?) or *What
would you like to talk about?* (Nothing, my parents told me to come over to
their computer).

Instead, I ask Tamar,
"Hey, what do you think about the conversation I was just having with your
          parents?"
"I don't know. I wasn't part of it."
"Are you kidding? Every time they opened the door to see if you were listening,
          you almost fell into the room. Of course you were part of it. You just weren't
          talking, that's all."
Tamar smiles despite herself.
There's a pause. Tamar is waiting for me to pursue her. I sit in front of my
          screen and just smile gently at her, as if I'm thinking about stuff, and not
          waiting.
After a few moments I asked, "What did they tell you the reason for contacting
          me was?"
"They just said you were going to try to help them be better parents," Tamar
          says.
"Do they need to be better parents?"
"I don't know. I guess."
"If they were better parents, what would be different for you?"

"Nothing probably. I'm just a miserable teenager. It's okay – all teenagers feel
   like this. I'm just going to have to wait until my adult life to start living."
"Seriously? What will you do in the meantime?"

Afterward, in consultation with Tamar's parents, I said that I felt as if their daughter were just waiting for me to step into her trap by trying to convince her that
things weren't really that bad. *Oh, no, Tamar, not every teenager is unhappy*,
or *Don't you want to start feeling better now, instead of waiting until you grow
up?* Apparently, no one had ever caught onto that dynamic in their daughter or,
if they did, they hadn't known how to respond. By not falling into Tamar's trap
I was able to establish good working relationships with all three parties that
endured the challenges of a cross Atlantic therapy, and allowed me to a) share
perspectives with Tamar about her fractious social relationships, b) support
Tamar's parents in their efforts to repair the relationship with their daughter as
well as to set up some boundaries for behavior within the home, and c) consult
with the family about what kind of school environment would be best for Tamar
as she entered high school.

## Respecting clients' autonomy about their choices and their therapy

Of all the things that my clients could feel when they share a space with me,
I want most for them to know and to feel that they are respected. What that
means to me is that not only their *person* is respected but their autonomy, too,
as well as any proprietary leanings they have toward their symptoms/problems
and their degree of interest, or lack thereof, in doing anything about them.

   In this model of therapy, it's important that clients recognize they're not
obligated to respond to interventions, or remain committed to something they
committed to earlier, or return to earlier topics of conversation with the same
degree of interest they showed before. They don't owe us an interest in getting
better that they may never have expressed in the first place. And even if they
had, they're allowed to change their mind.

   I think it's important for kids to feel respected as the primary agents of
change in their lives and know they can say, "I don't care about that anymore,"
without my assuming they're being "resistant." For me, the more interesting
conversation becomes, *Hey, how does something that meant a lot to you last
Thursday not mean much at all to you today?* asked always with curiosity, not
derision.

   By un-coupling an issue or topic from the commitment of therapy, clients
are freer to talk and emote. Without the ability to retreat or reconsider or back
out altogether, therapy can, for some, feel like too big of a commitment. And if
"in or out" is the only option, most kids are going to play a conservative game.

## *When Fixing Things Becomes Too Important to the Therapist*

One way that this principle of respect is unwittingly undermined in therapy is when therapists jump on something a client has said, making it a bigger deal than he or she ever intended or anticipated or needed it to be. Cutting and other self-harming behaviors are good examples of where this sort of thing happens. It's possible the therapist doesn't want to miss the opportunity to address it, or becomes frankly anxious about safety concerns. As a result, rather than allowing a teenager some space to expand on the topic on her own, or following up patiently with thoughtful inquiry, a therapist responding with only alarm will pounce on the matter too quickly and urgently. One consequence of this may be that the teen becomes reticent to bring up the topic again. When therapists come off as more eager than their clients to talk about their clients' issues, they risk them running for cover, as well as taking over their responsibility for reflection and change.

## Accountability

Accountability, powerful both as a philosophy and intervention, refers to a therapist's willingness and ability to hold clients responsible for the choices they are making and the impact those choices have on the people around them. As mentioned earlier, it refers to the therapist's commitment to understanding a teenager's actions as *functions of choice*, and not things that he or she cannot help. It's important, though, that no criticism or judgment is passed on clients or their behavior; it just means that the therapist attributes to the behavior choice, meaning, and responsibility. Moreover, there's never any arguing or challenging the teenager in order to get him to see it the same way. It's important only that the teen understand he can't control how the therapist is going to define or understand his actions. It's a preview for a teen of what would happen were he to lose the family safety net, the patience or oblivion of his friends, and general good will afforded kids in society until they become adults.

The role of accountability in adolescent therapy is never a matter of getting the teen to "own up" to problems or agree to work on them. The therapist is simply ascribing *intention* behind the client's actions or choice. Accountability is valuable for its ability to *dis-illusion* the teen, that is, reinforcing the idea – without confrontation – that you cannot control how people are going to see you or the judgments they will make about you.

Because of that, sometimes bringing matters of accountability into a therapy consists only of a therapist's quiet, understated refusal to go along with a party line that no one ever really believed in the first place (e.g., that she couldn't help it, that he didn't mean it, that it was just a joke). Importantly, it refers to a therapist's ability to speak to the truth in the room. These twin clinical tasks – that of demonstrating compassion for your clients on the one hand, and of holding them accountable for their choices on the other, create a very subtle but active tension for therapists throughout the course of therapy.

**These twin tasks of demonstrating compassion and holding adolescents accountable for their choices and behaviors create an active tension for therapists throughout the course of therapy.**

That said, there is a big difference between *not having to pretend you don't notice something* (in other words, not turning a blind eye), and actually *confronting a client.* The first one doesn't challenge the client in any way, it simply ascribes intent behind a particular behavior or comment. The second, however, asks the client to account for the behavior to you, and possibly change it. One is *I'm aware that your comment was meant to unnerve me but, anyway, go on, what were you saying again...?* (can even be expressed through a facial expression, as in, *Nice try...*), and the other is *Why did you just do that? I think you're trying to get me to react to you.* Their respective application in the therapy depends on a collection of factors, including but not limited to, the quality of the therapeutic relationship, where the two of you are in the therapy, your clinical intent/purpose, the personality and reactiveness of the client, and what the clinical task at hand is in that moment, among other things. In most cases, however, it is the first application that will be most useful in your work with teenagers, especially if you are in the beginning stages of therapy.

Now, here's what I find so remarkable about this: You don't wait until you have a therapeutic relationship with the teenager to do this; a therapeutic relationship often will develop *because* you've done this.

## *Addressing accountability in a therapy session without letting it take you off topic*

A teen disrespects his parents in session and the parents don't respond. You don't want to derail the conversation, but because of the risk of it setting a precedent for pushing boundaries, you also don't think it should be ignored. Let's think it through:

By not saying anything, I would become as passive and appear as intimidated by what the boy said as the boy's parents. My choosing *not* to respond becomes a vote of complicity, and I lose the respect of the teenager who would see my ignoring this as an attempt to avoid any conflict or "getting on his bad side."

This does not need to become a point of confrontation. In fact, it's important only that the comment, and its intention, be acknowledged by *someone* in the room – it doesn't even have to be me.

"How often does *that* happen?" would do the trick. Maybe the dad would say, "Too often," and I'd say, "Oh, that's too bad," before continuing with whatever the discussion was prior to the boy's remark. You want to make sure the parent doesn't use your question to launch into a litany of all the problems the teenager causes at home or at school. If the dad in this case were to do that, you could say, "Oh, we'll circle back to all that in a bit, I was just curious about Sean's comment, but go on, you guys were in the middle of talking about last weekend ..."[2]

By now, the boy is already feeling a little uncomfortable; he hadn't expected there to be any commentary, as most adults, being uncomfortable with the possibility of friction, typically ignore what he says. Usually, when kids say something provocative in session they're not looking to mix it up the way they do at home; it's more of an underhanded missive. They don't anticipate the therapist addressing it because most will not, preferring to stay "on task" with the conversation. But the therapeutic task has abruptly shifted, even if momentarily.

Another comment I might make is, "Are any of you guys uncomfortable with what just happened in here, or is it just me?" I might say this in a session where I've noticed the parents tend to downplay or ignore their teen's inappropriate remarks. I'd do that in order to begin giving the parents some structure or gauge (for example, their comfort level with a particular remark) to use when trying to figure out which ones their son says are response-worthy and which are better left alone. *What's important here is only that the question get asked*, which makes its own point and stands by itself as an intervention by bringing unexpected attention to the teenager's behavior. The answer to the question is pretty much irrelevant.

To summarize, the only thing my comment (or question) has to do is communicate the following:

- I heard it (the teenager's rude or inappropriate remark).
- I'm pretty sure everyone else heard it.
- I'm not sure why no one is saying anything about it, but I can't let it go unacknowledged.
- No one really needs to do anything in response to my comment.
- Let's continue with what we were doing/saying.

Kids try to intimidate adults who attempt to hold them to a higher standard of relating than they are accustomed to having to meet. The fact that we're talking about a therapeutic relationship rather than a "normal" one shouldn't change anything; a therapeutic relationship is still a relationship, with many of the dynamics present that exist in non-therapy relationships (and a few extra ones). Remaining warm, empathic, and nonjudgmental while communicating that you're not going to placate or pretend you didn't hear a caustic remark is how that teen will come to see you as someone to believe in. As soon as you join in on the farce that everyone else has chosen to play into, you lose both your credibility and the teenager's respect.

No one said it better than the four-year-old girl I saw briefly for her temper tantrums:

Ally regularly wrecked her room by throwing things. She told me in one of her sessions how the weekend before she threw her Barbie against the wall and broke the curtain rod and her parents had to buy paint for the wall where Barbie's foot had made a chip in it.

"Wow, what was that about?" I asked.

"My mom said I couldn't go to Nina's house (her best friend) because my grandma and grandpa were coming over for dinner."

"I'm curious, do you ever smash things at Nina's house?"

"No! Of course not! If I smash things there, they might not let me come back for another play date. Because it's not nice."

Ha. And we think young kids don't know better or can't control themselves ....

### Addressing accountability in family therapy versus ignoring it, and its effect on a client's emotional health

Here is a case illustrating how bringing issues of accountability into the therapy of an anxious and depressed fourteen-year-old girl with unregulated emotions can move the therapy forward, and how *not* addressing them holds back both the therapy and the girl's emotional maturation:

Courtney had been coming to me intermittently for therapy for close to a year. She had a history of being temperamental and took her frustrations out on everyone at home. She would get very defensive and belittle her sisters and was extremely rude to her mother. Like so many teenagers, Courtney didn't exhibit this behavior anywhere but at home.

Courtney's mother had tremendous difficulty setting limits on her daughter's behavior and over time it got worse. The more depressed her daughter got, the less the mother insisted on appropriate behavior. The more Courtney was allowed to act out, the more depressed she got. Then she'd feel guilty and cut herself. The whole thing was a formula for self-loathing. Kids get entrenched in their depression or anger when their mistreatment toward the people who love them and look after them is tolerated. And because Courtney's moodiness had been indulged at home for years, she had shown little interest in reflecting on her inner life in ways that would help her understand and better manage her feelings.

I was meeting with Courtney's mother when she told me about an incident over the weekend prior. Apparently, the mom had suggested that she and her three daughters – Courtney and her two sisters – walk into town to get ice cream. Courtney once again was in a bad mood and taking it out on everyone. She became rather mean. Eventually, Courtney's mother got so frustrated with her that she told her, very angrily, to go walk back home by herself while she and Courtney's two sisters continued into town.

With regard to this incident, Courtney's psychiatrist had advised Courtney's mother as follows: "Don't point out the fact that she's yelling or in bad mood or hurting people's feelings because she already knows it (this is true) and cannot stop it (this is not true) and then feels guilty and cuts (this is true)."

I know about the advice from Courtney's psychiatrist because the mom was telling me about the session she and Courtney had just had with him, and her ensuing confusion about whether to follow his advice or mine, each reflecting a very different approach to working with acting out, dysregulated teenagers.

I told Courtney's mother that I believed following the psychiatrist's advice of "protecting" Courtney's feelings at the expense of everyone else was counter-productive and would put even more of a strain on the relationships Courtney had with her mother and her sisters. I added that his approach provided no opportunities for Courtney to learn to manage her frustration in ways that didn't turn people off.

This is too important a social/emotional skill to be pardoned and passed over – that is, learning to express your problems in ways that draws people to-ward you rather than pushes them away. Kids need their parents to thoughtfully and kindly show them what that kind of emotional regulation and intelligence looks like, and encourage them to begin employing it, building it up over time. Otherwise, they go into young adulthood continuing to impose their bad moods and frustrations on others and then complain that no one cares.

ME:    This is why I think it was important to hold Courtney responsible for how she handled her mood during the walk into town. Court-ney needed you to intervene as soon as she started with her sisters, and say, "Courtney, stop. I won't let you keep imposing your bad mood on the rest of us. I've done it for too long. You can turn around and walk home and we'll bring you back something, or you can act pleasant while we walk, even if you don't feel pleasant." Is that something you could see yourself saying to your daughter in the future?

MOM:    I was just hoping she'd get it all out of her system and feel better.

ME:    Courtney will never "get it all out." Her feelings are not a finite thing. Her anger feeds on itself and gets bigger. As long as Courtney is allowed to treat her sisters and you like crap, I don't believe she'll ever really feel good about herself or be able to exit her depression. That is *not* a formula for feeling happier, or for developing the self-control she needs in order to regulate her emotions. Courtney needs you to do whatever you can to stop her from doing things that leave her feeling guilty. She'll gradually internalize some of the external controls you'd be exerting on her, plus she'll be more incentivized to do so once she realizes it helps her feel better.

I met with Courtney by herself for the next session and talked with her about the things I'd suggested her mother change regarding her handling of Courtney's moods and behaviors.

ME:    Courtney, your mom lets you treat her and your sisters badly because she feels terrible that you've been so depressed this past year. But I don't think it will ever help you to feel better, only worse. I can see where it might feel good in the moment because you're angry or sad, but I doubt you feel good afterward.

C:    (shaking her head slowly) I don't.

ME:    I know. Like a lot of parents in her situation, your mom doesn't want to upset you, so she gives you a lot of slack. But I think you need her to say, *Stop. I'm sorry you feel so bad today but what you're saying is not okay.* And then hold you to that. That's what she and I talked about last week and I wanted you to know that. You and I can work here on ways to help you hold back when you feel like cutting loose on someone. You okay with that?

C:    (nodding her head) Yeah. Okay.

I may be biased here but a part of me felt like Courtney had been waiting for someone to be firm with her and tell her *Enough, you need to stop.* It reminded me of working years before with another depressed adolescent girl, a few years older, who was verbally abusive at home and whose parents also felt so bad for her that they allowed it, serving only to feed their daughter's depression and self-loathing.

"Jeez, Dana," I said to her one day, "someone at home's got to tell you to knock that shit off …"

"I know!" Dana said, with enthusiasm and a glimmer of hope that someone actually might.

It's so important to remember that addressing issues of accountability in families should never be done in a spirit of control, or punishment, or shaming, but as a reflection of how healthy, respectful human communities operate. It's uplifting when you talk about it that way, rather than being just more rules to follow. That's part of the reason why I believe accountability to be an integral part of doing therapy: *It directs us toward being our best selves and emphasizes that belonging to something (a family, a community, a nation) carries with it a set of obligations.*

Another reason why I believe addressing issues of accountability with families to be so critical is that it plays a pivotal role in reducing parents' resentment toward their (over-accommodated or boundary-pushing) teenager. In families where accountability for behavior has been absent, there is often a great deal of bitterness and anger on the parts of parents and siblings who have long felt at the teenager's mercy. Accountability as a practice serves to bring down the emotional temperature in the family, clearing the way for healthier, less embittered bonds to form.

## We are accountable, too

Parents are always told to not take their kids' anger or complaints personally. Therapists are often instructed to do the same. I think this is crazy advice. How can we possibly show up in these relationships authentically and fully if we don't take the experience that others are having in our company seriously, at least for starters? If it turns out that our own kid or our client is voicing a more general or impersonal complaint not specific to us, we can then respond differently. Otherwise, we are simply dismissing what they're saying to us right out of hand.

"Therapy is a waste of time," Layla says, and you immediately wonder if she's referring to *all* therapies, or only *your* therapy. So you ask her:

THERAPIST:     "Do you mean all therapy, or just this one with me in particular?"
LAYLA:         "All of them. They're just stupid."

Okay. Layla is painting with a pretty broad brush here, and her comment appears less personal than it is a sweeping commentary of the state of therapy. You can move the conversation forward by being curious about how she finds the *institution* of therapy to be a waste of time. This is characteristic of clients' comments that are directed *toward* you as a representative of the mental health community, but not *at* you, as a distinct person apart from other therapists.

But maybe your client's questions do have to do with you specifically, and it *is* personal. Consider, for example, the following situation:

**"How come you never know what to say to me?"** says a saucy teen client who has been reacting aggressively or provocatively to anything you've said so far in the three sessions you've had to date.

*"I don't know. I've been wondering the same thing …"* is one way I might respond if, in fact, I've been similarly baffled by my own lack of spontaneity in speaking or unusually measured countenance in the boy's presence. I'd probably continue with something along the lines of, *"So much of what I say comes right back at me, with a vengeance, so now I think about everything I say before I say it, which is really no way to have a conversation. I actually don't have a problem with you pushing back on what I say to you; I just want to figure out how we can talk about it rather than get stuck there …."*

The last thing I want to do is react defensively. If I am really struggling to bring forward a fluid, un-affected conversation, then I *should* be trying to figure out a workaround, and that's something I can invite my client to do with me. He may scoff at the idea, but my lack of defensiveness and the collaborative framing of problem solving is likely to be pretty disarming to him. He might have been prepared for a prickly response such as, *What do you mean, never know what to say?* or *It's hard to have a conversation with someone who isn't interested in talking about himself,* but my saying, basically, *Yeah, I see it too, I don't know, wanna do something about it?* takes whatever fight he was looking to have with me right out of it.

Here are two other situations that pop up in therapy, requiring a thoughtful response on the part of the therapist:

**"You're not Latinx/gay/from the borough/an immigrant …. You couldn't possibly understand me or my life."**

Options for responding:

- "Tell me what you think you'd never be able to explain to me. Or what I wouldn't be able to get."
- "Oh child of such little faith…!" (to a teen with whom I already have a really good relationship)
- "Sounds like you want the person helping you to be just like you, or like you in some way that's really important. You may be right, maybe I wouldn't be

able to. I don't know. I'd like to think that I could. You okay talking about this with me more until we figure it out?" *No problem, no argument, who knows, let's discuss.*

**"My dad says you guys all have such messed up lives, says you have no business messing up other people's lives..."**

You might respond:

- "Yeah I've heard people say that before .... I have no idea what to say in response. But here's what matters, really: Am *I* messing up *your* life? Or do you worry that I could?" *Again, no fight. This, too, we can talk about.*

What's the **worst response** we could give when asked a question that's personal but not inappropriate, or that challenges our work? It's this one: "We're here to talk about you, not me."

Telling our young clients that we're here to talk about them and not us comes off as withholding, academic, and aloof. How could it ever lead to a constructive conversation? It's not like a kid is going to respond by thinking, *Oh, right, this is supposed to be about me, never mind. I'll drop the questions.* Instead she's thinking ... *"Uh, you may be here to talk about me, but I'm not. I wasn't sure I wanted to talk to you in the first place. And now I'm sure I don't."*

For clinicians who aren't comfortable revealing too much about themselves, I think there are better ways to respond to personal questions than with the response above. Possibilities include,

- "I don't want to be too mysterious here or anything and you're always free to ask me stuff, but I probably won't answer too many questions, at least not the more personal ones. I've discovered over the years that I'm a pretty private person. But it doesn't mean I can't be a good therapist."
- "I understand you're curious about me. Here I am asking you all these personal questions and maybe you're thinking, like, *Okay, my turn now!* But it's a different kind of conversation here than you have with your friends or family, and it can feel kind of one-sided. Are you game to try it out for a while, and see if you start feeling more comfortable? I have some ideas already that might be helpful, if you want to hear them ...."

I encourage my trainees to be thoughtfully open to answering clients' questions about them. Most of the questions are simply expressions of a natural curiosity and an effort to turn what could have begun to feel like an interrogation into a real conversation. I like to think of clients' questions as an opportunity for a therapist to bring more of their own self into the room in a natural way, so that clients feel they have someone not only to talk with but to connect with, as well.

## Notes

1  "Mister Rogers defending PBS to the US Senate." (Fred Rogers's 1969 appearance before the United States Senate Subcommittee on Communications), www.youtube.com/watch?v=fKy7ljRr0AA, accessed February 2008.

2  There are ways, too, to indicate that a question you're raising is more to make a point than it is an invitation to start a new conversation. In this case, you'd say How often does that happen? quickly, ending the question with a rising inflection of your voice (uptalk) in contrast to saying it with an emphasis on "that" (How often does *that* happen?), which invites a very literal response from a parent and gives off the uneasy feeling now of talking about the boy as if he weren't in the room.

# CHAPTER SEVEN

# Mistakes in Therapy with Teens That Stop the Conversation, and What to Do Instead

In the very first chapter of this book, I mentioned that counseling adolescents is not for the faint of heart. Seven chapters in, and I'm doubling down.

I've talked about some of the things that can get therapists trying too hard to make connections, get conversations going, prove their ideas useful, appear competent, etc.; the list goes on. Other rabbit holes include ones resulting from those lively but largely obscured dynamics frequently at play between therapists and their teen clients discussed in Chapters 4 and 5. Let's look at five of the more common impasses that show up in therapy, almost all of which are triggered inadvertently.

## Five Things That Stop Conversations

### 1. Trying to motivate the teenager to change

Sometimes we're the only one of two people in the room who cares about what happens. This is enough to make us work twice as hard.

Can we work with someone who comes into therapy as a disinterested consumer? In many cases I think we can. The idea that clients must be motivated for therapy in order to benefit from it hasn't been true in my experience, but it does require the therapist to offer something (conversation, experience, self) intriguing enough that the teenager engages apart from any therapeutic agenda.

I think the first clinical task for us as therapists sitting with a new teen client is to generate a conversation that interests her enough to want to come back (or at least be 'okay' with coming back) a next time. Then maybe that next time or over the next couple of times the teenager gets enough out of the

DOI: 10.4324/9781003257080-7

conversation that the relationship itself starts to matter a little bit. And then with the connection you've been developing, the teen starts to genuinely care about the therapy, which means she's starting to care about herself.

If I were to consciously set about trying to motivate a teen to work with me in therapy, I'd worry that whatever I said to entice her would end up sounding like a sales pitch. Chances are, that would make her run in the *other* direction, which of course makes therapists try even harder to attract the client's interest. Which spooks her even more. Over-eagerness is universally unappealing, whether we are talking about dating, interviewing for a job, or doing therapy.

Motivation, or the lack of it, becomes an obstacle to therapy only when we make it a necessary condition. What if we focus less on how to motivate clients and more on how to create interesting discussions that intrigue and draw our clients into therapy organically? If the therapy is *in the conversation*, then it doesn't matter what attitude our clients have toward therapy as long as we can keep them engaged in conversations that address the things that matter to *them* – not their parents, not their school, not their case manager or probation officer. There may be overlap in the things that matter to everyone, but unless our conversations have relevance and application to the things that keep these kids up at night, we can too easily lose them.

Think about the following exchange:

| THERAPIST: | I can't help you if you don't talk to me. |
|---|---|
| CLIENT (reluctant fourteen-year-old girl, depressed): | I don't need any help. |
| T: | But don't you want to feel better? |
| C: | Yeah, probably, but I don't think it's gonna happen here. |
| T: | Why don't you just give it a try? |

There is not very much that's appealing about this therapist's invitation to her client to "give it a try." Give *what* a try? All that's in the room is a therapist asking her client for blind faith in her ability to help, and she's already not making a particularly good impression.

Here's another exchange in which you can spot the seeding of a power battle between a therapist and a high school truant:

| T: | I'm worried that if you don't do something that tells your school you want to be there, they're not going to want to keep investing in you. |
|---|---|
| C: | Well, how about I just don't go at all …? |

**When we dig in, they'll always dig deeper.**

This therapist made the mistake of 1) assuming the client's school refusal was ego-dystonic, meaning that it bothered her, and 2) assuming that the prospect of being suspended or expelled would prompt the girl to go back to school. It didn't. The best way to get this conversation back on some solid footing would be for the therapist to acknowledge that she jumped the gun …

T:   Okay, I really jumped the gun there. Sorry about that.
C:   What do you mean?
T:   Oh I don't know, for some reason I thought telling you that the school might not let you come back if you stayed out too long would be a way to get you back to school. It was so off the mark.
C:   Yeah, kinda.
T:   Yeah, sorry. I think I can do a little better … like, for starters, is there anything that would make enough of a difference to you about your experience in school that you'd be willing to return?

And here's the thing – *when the basis of our impact on others is through influence rather than control, then whether our client is motivated for change doesn't really matter.*

Clients change because they allow us to influence their way of thinking about something, or about doing things, or about responding and relating to others. We don't need their motivation. We need their *interest*, so that we can get an "at bat." Think about the clients you've been able to help. Was it their motivation that did it (something over which we have little control), or was it their degree of engagement with you and your work (something over which we do)? *Don't worry about getting your clients motivated; instead, think about how to get their attention.* If you get their attention, and they think you can help, they'll be plenty motivated enough.

## 2.  Appealing to logic or a teen's more "rational" manner of behaving

One of the best things we can do as clinicians is to distinguish ourselves from the scores of parents, relatives, school counselors, and teachers who are hoping to get troubled teenagers to see the fallacy of their thinking in favor of a more reasoned and logical choice.

Here's an example of a therapist imploring her client to think more "rationally" by suggesting she look at herself from the perspective from which she saw others. It drew not the "Oh yeah, I guess that's true" the therapist had expected, but rather a dismissive shrug and change of topic.

"I feel responsible for everything," said Gemma, when asked by her guidance counselor about the stressors she experienced at school.

"If I'm involved in a group project, and we get a bad grade, I feel that it's my fault.

"What would you think if a friend told you that same thing – that she felt totally responsible for the other students in a group project that she was part of? Would you hold her responsible?"

*"Of course not. But that's different,"* Gemma replied, and indeed it is. There's *Gemma's friend,* and then there's *Gemma.* People have different rules for themselves than they do for their friends. For that reason, this is not a very helpful intervention.

The temptation for therapists to *push back* against a client's (seemingly unreasonable) idea is often strong. You want to say, "C'mon, really? What makes you the fall guy?" But therapists are rarely that forthright. Painting broadly here, I'll say that instead, many therapists soft pedal their point, so that it comes out as a more tentative proposal, that is, "What would you think if a friend told you ...?"

I believe there's something about the frankness and candor of the first comment *(C'mon, really?)* that cuts through a person's stylized/default defense and invites them to respond in kind: "Oh I don't know, I just worry about getting a bad grade ..." or "I don't want anyone to think I'm just leeching off of them ..." which at least gives you a little more to work with than *"Of course not. But that's different."*

All that said, there is a big difference between asking a client if she would feel differently if what was happening to her was happening to a friend, and inviting your client to see things from *another* person's point of view. In the latter, you're inviting someone to suspend judgment on something – an event, a belief, a behavior – that, let's say in this case, is *outside* the dyad of Gemma and her friend. And while Gemma has rules for how she handles her friendships, for example: *I always treat my friends better than I treat myself,* or *I never want to do anything that makes my friends mad at me,* Gemma is unlikely to have rules for other events or people with whom she does not have a relationship. That's why Gemma could more productively answer a hypothetical question about other people than one about herself or people she knows.

I think a more helpful approach for this therapist to take would have been to ask, "Hey, how do you end up holding the bag for all these group projects? And *what if* you got a bad group project grade? Let's go there ...."

## School counselor tries to get student to be "rational" and bombs

Nadya is recounting to me a miserable exchange with her high school guidance counselor. "She was in her office," Nadya tells me, "and — you know how some people do this thing with their hands when they're nervous, as if they're going to pull their thumbs off …? (gesturing with her hands). Well she's doing that and says to me, 'Hey, I heard you might be thinking of cutting.'"

"I told her, 'No.'"

"So you're not thinking of cutting?" the counselor responds.

"No."

"You've never cut?" she asks.

"No, I didn't say that – I'm just not thinking of it now," says Nadya.

"Right," retorts the counselor, sarcastically.

Nadya asked me, "Why didn't she just come out and say, 'I heard from the prevention specialist that you started cutting again and was hoping we could talk for a few….' and I'd be like, 'Uh I guess….' I'd be totally disarmed by her question…."

A nod to the power of honest inquiry.

Same kid, same counselor, two weeks later. Nadya had just thrown up in the school bathroom from the oxycontin she had taken earlier that morning. Her art teacher brought her to guidance, where she emphatically denied being upset, despite her pale face and bleary eyes. No one knew about the oxy.

"You're being irrational," her counselor says "If you're not upset, then why are you crying?" Rarely is it productive to press a kid to reconcile how they look with what they feel, especially when they are upset.

"I don't know," Nadya replies. "I just want to go to history class now," trying to leave.

"It doesn't make sense – you going to history class if you're crying!" asserts the guidance counselor, before adding, "Obviously something upset you! You need to tell me."

"No, I just want to go to class," says Nadya.

"Well, go then!" the counselor replies frustrated at her inability to get Nadya to open up to her about what she was feeling. "I've got things to do!"

*I've got things to do?*

It doesn't really matter if how the kid looks doesn't match up with what she's saying. Life is like that sometimes. Nadya just needed someone to say, "I can see you're upset about something and I'm all ears if you want to tell me about it. If not, do you want to sit here a while until you feel ready to go back to class?"

Or, if you realize you're bombing in the middle of an interaction like this, an awesome thing to say would be, "Hang on, Nadya, I'm sorry. I shouldn't say you're being irrational. I have no idea what's going on for you so how could I possibly know what's rational and what's not. And it doesn't matter anyway. I can't believe I even said that ... apologies, kid." Teenagers will respond so much better to this than to someone doubling down on something they mistakenly thought was true.

## 3. Ignoring the Forces of Natural Law

For the most part, therapy operates under an unnatural set of principles. Almost everything about the way we meet our young clients, talk with them, tell them about ourselves, and direct the discussion is different from how conversation is experienced in real life. As a result, therapeutic conversations can feel and sound unnatural, which contributes to some of the difficulties some therapists and teenagers have connecting, especially in the beginning.

I think that when we depart too much from the ways in which people naturally come together and share stories, as well as share themselves, it's harder for a relationship to get off the ground. Natural law (or the laws of nature) refers to that set of universal and natural (unlearned) laws governing the ways in which people meet, relate, and allow themselves to be influenced.

A therapeutic approach that appreciates the influence of natural law on human relationships tries to guide and configure therapist/client (as well as parent/teen) relationships somewhat along the lines of what would be the most natural human dynamic in that situation. Ignoring these laws, or not being aware of them, is a major contributing factor in a lot of derailed relationships between adults and kids. That same lack of awareness can also turn out to be a primary trigger for displays of anxiety, aggression, defensiveness, or one-upmanship between therapists and teenagers, as well as between parents and their teens.

One of the most recognizable laws of nature, and the most disregarded one in therapy with teens, is the Principle of Least Interest. This dynamic was coined by sociologist Willard Waller[1] in the 1930s to describe one of the indicators of power in a relationship. It says, basically, that the person with the least interest or investment in the matter at hand, or in the relationship, has the most power. Pepper Schwartz, in her book **Love Between Equals: How Peer Marriage Really Works,** [2] showed how this principle applies across human affairs from international diplomacy to used car lots to who does the dishes. If you're willing to walk away and the other person is not, then you hold the advantage.

Let's apply it to doing therapy with teenagers. In many cases, the therapist is the person more interested in getting a conversation started and having something therapeutic take place. Teenagers understand this dynamic very well and can exploit it spectacularly by holding back on their expressed interest in the therapy or the conversation, or their endorsement of an idea the therapist raises, or their active participation. It's not even malicious or premeditated; it's just how people unconsciously position themselves in relationship to another in order to reserve a measure of control. You'll see this dynamic highlighted in couples where the two parties won't allow themselves to be vulnerable and wind up each pretending to be less interested in the relationship than the other.

Going back to therapy, what often happens is that a therapist, faced with a tepid response from her teen client, might try to compensate for the teen's disinterest/skepticism/rejection/circumspection by trying harder, that is, by being *more* empathic, making *more* attempts at joining, exerting *more* effort to make something happen, therefore creating even more of an imbalance in the relationship. Now it feels really weird to the kid, who is probably looking for a way out of this awkward experience.

It's a little different with adolescents who come into therapy eager for the help and anticipating a positive experience. They may have sought the therapy out themselves or have played an active part in selecting the therapist. As long as the relationship remains relatively balanced, in terms of mutual engagement and commitment, everything usually rolls along just fine. But that can change if, let's say, the teen becomes disillusioned with the process or with the therapist, or if the therapist becomes overly committed to the outcome of the therapy and starts either pressuring the client for change or becoming judgmental in the face of the client's ambivalent commitment, noncompliance, or unhurried timeline. Being an agent of change in a someone's life while allowing that person to freely make the ultimate decisions about what they're going to do is the gold standard for service to others.

## 4. Suspending common rules of decency and courtesy for the sake of keeping a false peace

Teenagers always pick up very quickly on adults' attempts to appease or over-accommodate them for the sake of keeping the peace or "gaining" rapport. When it happens in the context of therapy, the teen learns that alliances between therapist and teen will be forged through consensus or agreement or placation, rather than through mutual respect. This makes any eventual confrontation problematic, in addition to bleaching respect and credibility from the relationship at large.

I gave an example of this in Chapter 5 with the boy who disrespected his parents in session in my presence. It happens even more often in individual therapy, where teens are less inhibited about acting out, given that it's "only" the therapist in the room with them, a therapist from whom they anticipate an unearned bye on civic decency.

So maybe this time we have a teenage boy who begins picking up personal items on your bookshelf or taking out his phone to casually scroll, or says, "I'm bored as fuck here – how long do I have to stay?" Okay ... how do you respond to that?

The most important thing is that you respond, somehow. You might be tempted to ignore it this "first" time or to respond to the behavior at face value, meaning, as if the kid didn't know it was inappropriate to do any of those things, something along the lines of, "Hey, Cole those things on the shelf are kind of more to look at than pick up ...." But the kid knows that what he's doing is wrong, and he's waiting to see what you're going to do about it. Almost like a toddler. (An exception to this would be that ADHD kid who's wandering around in your office, impulsively picking up this and that .... You still need to say something but, in most instances, it's not a provocation.)

My choice of response to the kid who scrolls or otherwise pushes the envelope is always decidedly low key. "You're kidding, right?" or "Seriously?" It says that I know that he knows he shouldn't be doing whatever he's doing, but I've stopped short of becoming the teacher in class who says, "Put your phone away." And then I just look at them and wait. If a kid says, "What?" I'll respond with "That," pointing with my chin. Or I might say, "Tell me you're not really going to scroll through your socials right now ...."

"Oh, no, sorry, I was just checking something," is typically the response I get, and I just say, "Cool."

Here's an example of a school counselor I was supervising who got really stumped when one of her students asked to call her mother from her office and then, in the counselor's presence, became very disrespectful over the phone. With her mother on the line, the girl started ranting about something that had happened that morning and ended up screaming and cursing at her for more than ten minutes.

"I didn't know what to do," the counselor said. "I was not okay with what she was saying – I mean you could hear her in the hallway, and it was really rude – but I thought that if I said anything about her cursing, she'd blow me off too or see me as taking her mother's side. So I didn't say anything, but I feel like I should have."

I said to the counselor that she was smart not to address the matter by getting into a battle about cursing or school rules. "She has other adults in her school to do that," I explained. "But it's not always easy to think on your feet like that. Here's what I probably would have said, along with a slight smile on my face, *'I can't believe your mother actually stayed on the phone with you that whole time ....'* And I'd have left it at that. What you want to do in moments like that is to speak to what's true between you and your client, but without the disapproving look she'd have gotten from, say, her principal."

In my view, that comment says everything you want to say to a teen who's acting inappropriately in your presence, without engendering a defensive response. There's nothing to fight, because you're not saying it was wrong (although you're intimating that it was inappropriate) and you're not telling her not to do it again (although she'll be a little more self-conscious the next time, especially if it's in your presence). You're implying that the only appropriate response to her rant would have been for her mother to have hung up on her.

If you are experiencing anxiety about saying something to your client or are worried that you don't yet have the connection to address anything even mildly controversial, you can consider saying exactly that. For instance, let's say you go to retrieve your (relatively) new client in the waiting area and she's on her phone texting. She sees you, and nods, as if to say, "Okay, hang on," so you … hang on. And hang on some more. She gives you another nod of her head; clearly, she knows you're waiting. But she's still texting and occasionally laughing to herself and finally after about three minutes she gets up and says, "Okay."

Your client follows you into your office and when you go to sit down you realize that you're kind of offended and a little angry at your client's casual dismissal of your coming to get her and then expecting you to wait while she finishes her chat. But you have no idea what to say.

Think *be kind*, think *be honest*, think *no agenda, no point to be made here*, and give it your best shot:

T: Hi Mollie, how are you doing?
C: Oh I'm okay. I just came from school, where me and my friends on Student Council just had a big meeting about Homecoming.
T: Yeah, it seemed like something big was going on …
C: Oh, you mean out there, when I was in the waiting room?
T: Yeah, well, it was weird, actually … cause when I came out to get you, you were texting and I get that but then you kept texting and then it was like

okay we're now *both* in the waiting room, but I'm waiting and you're not, and I don't know, it just felt weird. Like, should I go back to my office, or should I just wait, but then I felt sort of stupid waiting, like, *What is she doing? And what am I doing? And what exactly is the right thing to do here? And then I'd just smile at the kid and wait to see what she says.*

Another example could be something as commonplace as a therapist and client who are having a tough time getting any kind of conversation going in the beginning of a session. There's always the option of deflecting the awkwardness by pulling out a game to play or some art supplies. Another option is to address the mutual self-consciousness or discomfort as something you're both experiencing together. This would sound something like,

"We're having a heck of a time getting a conversation going today, don't you think? I have no idea why, but I figured we're both thinking it, so I might as well say it …. No worries, it's not like it's a problem. I'm more curious about it than anything … I'm sure we'll figure it out …."

I think that feels a lot better than pretending that you and your client were simply "taking time to establish rapport," which is often just a euphemism for "we can't find anything to talk about."

## 5. Being reluctant to follow the negative affect of an individual or family in favor of (prematurely) bumping it over into something more positive

"Think of one positive thing about each person." This is a question I occasionally hear therapists ask family members in a therapy session. They are trying to help family members recover some positive affect or memory in relation to the others in an attempt to rekindle relationships that have soured or are fraught with too much resentment to heal on their own.

At the same time, however, such a question/intervention tells your clients that they cannot count on you to travel with them into the darker recesses of their family's history and emotional life. People who have been angry at one another for years or who are just too depressed to nurture their attachments are not interested in the one positive thing they can say about anyone. Feeling pressured to vacate their emotional habitat and come up with something "nice" to say about everyone, clients, resenting the empty exercise, will simply become annoyed.

Instead, go to that dark(er) place with them. Show them that you can go there, even lead them there if you have to. "How'd you all get here?" is a good question to ask, *here* referring to the ugly or uncomfortable emotional place in which they co-exist. It honors the truth in the room and the truth inside each person without placing blame. And if it is asked calmly, warmly, and patiently, the question serves also to normalize the family's experience, to let them know that, *Yes, sometimes people who love one another very much end up in places where they can barely tolerate to be in the same room.*

Making mistakes with my clients and correcting them doesn't worry me as much as making mistakes and never knowing that I made them. I comb through my cases that had unsatisfactory outcomes for misjudgments, assumptions, anxieties, countertransference, or things I said that were just weird. I do that for my successful cases, too. There are plenty of times when I think to myself,

* How could I have forgotten that she said she was adopted!
* This would have been a good time to mention XYZ instead of ABC …
* God that was clumsy.

Clients may not have paid it any attention and it may not have affected the outcome of therapy, but it's still a good exercise to be mindful of where you could have made a better decision. Kind of like chess.

What's even worse, though, is being in the middle of a case presentation and, *as you are talking about a case*, you start to feel a little self-conscious about how you handled something or responded to a client. There's nothing like the "light of day" or the specter of public opinion to make you suddenly aware of what you now wish you had done differently, or what you wish you had had the sense to think of. Rarely does anyone say anything and if they do, they're really, really nice about it, and I always appreciate that.

But what's worse than *that* is the eleventh-hour cold feet feeling you get (or at least I get) when you're about to release an entire book of your stuff and you start wondering, *Oh my god, people are going to read this and what if there are parts that make me sound silly, or arrogant, or dated? What are my blind spots I'm unknowingly broadcasting to the world?* It's kind of like when you go to bat for a kid whose parents are all up in his grill about smoking marijuana and then you find out he's been stealing money from them for months….

None of this should ever be anything that stops us from sharing our work. Our profession is already enshrouded in enough secrecy – I mean, can you think of any other occupation where you can go your entire career with no one seeing how you do your thing except for your clients or customers? Carry on and share, I say, mistakes and all.

## Notes

1 Willard Waller, The family: A dynamic interpretation, Cordon, 1938.
2 Touchstone, 1995.

# CHAPTER EIGHT

# Helping Teenagers to Emerge
## Strategies for Bringing Forward Conversations That Matter

Years ago, I reconnected with an old friend and made plans to have dinner with her at her new apartment. My twin sons, sixteen at the time, remembered this friend fondly, and asked if they could come along.

Over dinner, I watched as the three of them talked easily about school and work, politics, adolescence, and their respective interests, among other things. I noticed that each of my boys answered my friend's questions eagerly and thoughtfully and asked interesting ones of her in return. They seemed to enjoy the process of becoming known by her, and of getting to know my friend in a way that was different from how they had when they were younger.

All in all, it was a beautiful conversation – balanced, respectful, revealing, engaging. It had none of the self-consciousness, awkward gaps, or stilted timing that so often plagues conversations between therapists and their teenage clients and, honestly, between many adults and adolescents. Its patterns and rhythm were like conversations that take place between any two people, including two adults. I suppose that's why it flowed along as well as it did.

Conversations in therapy are never going to be the same as the ones we have with our friends, family members, or co-workers. For one thing they have a distinct purpose and need to be shepherded along those lines. For another, the initial setting in therapy is contrived and the relationship brand new. In addition, one party (invariably the therapist) usually cares about the conversation (having it, sustaining it, utilizing it) more than the other party does (at least in the beginning), creating an imbalance in the interest level between the two. This leads to a fourth difference which is, especially in the very early stages of therapy, the *unshakeable awareness on the parts of both therapist and client that a conversation is taking place*, which sometimes is enough to derail it. This mutual heightened awareness about the conversation underway is normal in the

DOI: 10.4324/9781003257080-8

beginning of therapy; it's very much like trying to fall asleep and you suddenly become aware it's about to happen, and – it's "ruined." You've woken up, and have to start all over again.

But eventually, clients settle into the therapy and what materializes are dozens of conversations or shorter exchanges, snippets and snatches of stories and memories, reactions in real time, tears, a figurative arm wrestle, a concession, an expression of care. Neither therapist nor client are self-conscious about them anymore, *unless* they start to depart too much from the rhythm and cadence and flow we see in "regular" (outside of therapy) conversations, or at least in the conversational pattern that the therapist and client have established as their norm.

Here's a funny thing, though: In our "regular" conversations outside of therapy sessions, we will frequently and casually talk over each other, cut each other off with something too important to hold back, or interject quickly to add something to the discussion. It's not the tidy *You speak, then I speak* template you see in moderated debates and the like.

However, I've noticed that many therapists avoid doing anything of the sort. Not wanting to appear rude or overbearing, they will instead contort natural conversational patterns to fit their felt need to give a teenager all the space she wants to complete her thought. The teen, now feeling waited upon to complete an offhand thought of no particular significance, once again becomes self-conscious and uncomfortable. Teenagers recognize this break in the flow of conversation as their therapist's effort to get any last bit of content from them, which reinforces the (usually accurate) feeling that the therapist is always eager for them to speak and at the ready to facilitate that. It's not a big deal, and the moment passes but, again, it is a departure from how two people normally converse, and is noted somewhere in the teen's unconscious impression of therapist~teen relationships.

I think of good conversations as talks that are built up one sentence at a time. As soon as you start thinking about them as big, long *important* discussions, the task becomes overwhelming. Essentially, all you really need to do to keep a conversation going is add another sentence. Just one, and it moves everything forward by a step. Again, just like a chess game, but without a winner or loser.

## Strategies for helping teenagers and conversations emerge

### Remove pressure for the teen to speak.

*"Tell me about yourself"* – is that question most of us dread when interviewing for a new position. Some people love it, and jump at the chance to tell their story; others, not so much. It's too broad, it's too unstructured, there's so much tell, and you're trying to hit all the points you practiced at home.

It must feel like that for our teenage clients, in those early sessions. Even if we're not directly asking that kind of question, they probably anticipate our expectation that they will speak, answer questions, tell their story.

I don't like to start off therapy by putting pressure on my clients to speak. Often enough they're not the ones who initiated therapy, so there's even less reason to expect that they have something significant or personal to say at the outset. The two defaults for most therapists are a) asking a bunch of questions about the reasons why they're there, and b) asking questions about non-clinical topics such as school, hobbies, sports, and the like. Neither is necessarily a terrific way to get started.

The first default brings forward an uncomfortable exchange that often feels to therapists as if they are pulling teeth. The second one leads to a casual discussion that stops as soon as the teen has answered the question and begins again only with the therapist's follow up question. I think any therapist who's worked with children or teenagers knows what it's like trying to break the ice by asking them about their favorite shows, sports or video games. Kids know that's not the conversation we're really looking for, and that it's our attempt to get them to "open up." Interestingly, I don't think that us fumbling around for something to say in the beginning in an attempt to find common ground is the problem we think it is.

The problem is *when we try to finesse it* by asking about things other than what we really want to ask about. We think we're easing into a conversation, but what kids see is a therapist who is tentative, and afraid to say the wrong thing. We don't need the warm-up as much as we think we do, and I believe kids are relieved when we come out and, with discretion and sensitivity, ask about the things we really want to ask about, without the rat-a-tat-tat of an intake.

Martha Straus[1] reminds us that the old standards of engaging kids, things like active listening, supportive reframing, and miracle questions, often provoke a furious silence, monosyllable responses, withdrawal, contempt. A clinical language that depends less on words and problems in favor of connection and competence is how she has navigated this part of therapy. Something I often do is just start talking myself, casually and invitingly, which takes the pressure off the teen to fill in all that blank space. Or I'll ask something specific about a teenager's interest area, but one that I can build from myself without having to depend on the teenager's expanding on the topic in order that the convo doesn't die off. An example would be if a star athlete in the kid's sport of choice was in the news, and I was familiar with the back story, or if his dog breed of choice had just placed in the Westminster dog show, which I often will have watched. Makes for lively convos.

Back to my starting us off. Let's say my new teenage client, who suffers from copious amounts of social anxiety, comes into my office for first her session accompanied by her mother, who happens to say something about how cold it is outside. I might say, "Oh my god, the winters here are the only thing that could ever get me to consider moving back to San Diego – I lived there for three years and never felt so out of place in my life. Beautiful place. And all I did was feel homesick. Go figure …."

Traditionalists might say, "Oh, be careful about introducing material into your client's therapy." But – no surprise here by now – I feel differently about such things and am comfortable sharing a piece of my history like that. (See Chapter 4 for more on self-disclosure in therapy.) It's not random, and it's nothing too personal. That brief San Diego story, however, sets the stage for other conversations down the line that easily could relate directly to my *client's* material. Consider the conversations it seeds: feeling out of place and all its iterations; feeling like a stranger; feeling like you don't belong; homesickness, among others. For a kid with social anxiety as the primary complaint, it would be surprising if there was no derivative of my story that bridged to something we could at some point talk about.

Here's another occasion where I'd haul out my San Diego story. Let's say I'm meeting with a teen client who just started going to the new 6th grade center that her local school district opened. Everyone loves it – except for this girl.

"I hate it," Carmela says. "It's the worst. I'd almost rather be in elementary school again."

"I know you would," I replied. "We all were hoping that after a few weeks you'd feel better about it, but that's not happening."

"Everyone else really likes it. I don't know why, but they do."

"Doesn't it feel weird to be the only one who doesn't like something that everyone else is crazy about?" I'd say. "I lived once in San Diego, California. Everyone loves it there. Beaches, sunny weather, palm trees. But I didn't. I missed the east coast, missed New York. I actually felt homesick…."

"Really?" Carmela replies, with not a lot of interest. That's okay. I wasn't expecting her to be particularly interested in it. I used the story to join and as a bridge to my next question:

*"Carmella, what do you think is different about the other kids that they like the 6th grade center so much?" I might ask.*

Or,

*"Does it make you hate the 6th grade center more because everyone around you likes it so much?"*

Or,

*"I really missed the east coast vibe when I was in California. What do you miss about elementary school?"*

And soon enough, we're having a little conversation, or beginning one, and my client relaxes. She knows that I'm not going to expect her to just start telling me about herself, and that I am not going to remain a stranger to her, and that I will always help get things rolling.

## Avoid asking a lot of questions about feelings

The only thing more boring than having to listen to the same old questions from your therapist is having to answer them. We are all so much more than what we feel.

> "How do I get her to talk about her feelings?" asked Jean, a counseling intern about to meet thirteen-year-old Hannah for an initial appointment.[2] "I'm not sure what to say to her." Hannah was going to be the first client Jean had ever seen without a more experienced co-therapist by her side, and she was very anxious about it.
>
> *Oh boy,* I wondered privately. *Are grad schools still teaching students that good therapy means getting kids to pour out their feelings?* I was suddenly reminded of a teen client I'd seen years ago who, when asked what hadn't worked in her prior therapy, began a mocking singsong of her therapist: "So, Cindy, how does *that* make you feel? How *does* that make you feel? How does that make you *feel?*"
>
> "Ugh," Cindy continued, "enough already with my fucking feelings. It made me feel like I just wanted her to shut up! That's how it made me feel!"
>
> "Don't worry about getting her to talk about her feelings," I said to Jean. "If you're doing anything close to what Hannah needs you to do, you won't have to. Her feelings will show up in the conversation, on her face, in her body."

Asking questions about feelings might seem like a natural thing for therapists to do. But too many direct questions about feelings are a source of irritation to kids. Kids *will* talk about feelings, but not in a discussion that's isolated from the conversation at hand.

Questions will always be part of therapy, there's no getting around it. But that's okay, because if we're mindful about how we ask them and about how many we ask at a time, they don't have to become annoying prompts but appealing invitations to reveal oneself. Another thing we can do is to consider asking *different* questions than the ones from the standard playlist – something unexpected, thought provoking, but without being provocative or gamey:

- Are you different around animals than you are around people?
- What do you think our first disagreement will be about?

- What used to matter more to you in the past than it does now?
- Are there things that you wish mattered more to you than they do?
- I talk a lot, is that ok?
- Who has a harder time apologizing – you or your dad?
- How come you pick fights with everybody but me?

With Covid-19 and the pandemic came new dimensions to mental health in children and teenagers. Asking your clients how they and their loved ones fared during that time period and how their experiences during the quarantine impacted them offers opportunities for kids to talk about issues that others in their lives may have long shut down. "Covid was three years ago, Amanda!" says Amanda's grandmother and guardian. "It's time to move on. Everyone else has."

But Amanda hasn't, and probably won't as long as she has no one willing to process her experience with her. Amanda lost her beloved grandfather to Covid-19, and things in her home have never been the same since, and nor has she. You'd have only to say to her, *Tell me what it was like for you going through Covid and losing your grandfather ...* before she'd probably melt into tears at the invitation to share her sad story. A lot of stories will come out of asking about the Covid years – stories of finding out who your real friends were (*What was the most surprising thing you discovered during quarantine?*), of finding out you really like your own company (*What's something new you learned about yourself during the pandemic?*), of sweeping disillusionment (*You mentioned a loss of faith – in who or what?*).

When sitting with a family, consider some of these questions:

- "What used to matter to your child that doesn't seem to matter anymore?"
- "You argue with your son a lot about his screen time. How do you think he would be different if he had been raised without electronics? What are the other things that would be filling his life instead?
- "How have you tried to inoculate your daughter against the perils of social media?"
- "You blame Covid for your son's disrespectful attitude toward people in authority – make that connection for me, please."
- "How does your family play?" "What?" "You know, play ..." "I don't know, I don't really understand the question ...." (You have all the information you need on that one now.)

And finally, if nothing else, at the very least avoid these:

- So, what do you want to work on today?
- How do you feel about that?

- Why do you think you did that?
- Why are you getting so upset?
- What do you think will happen if you continue doing what you're doing?

## Be careful to not withhold your own emotional expressiveness from clients: You can be professional and real at the same time

Seventeen-year-old Courtney met a boy and they both rode the wave until it came crashing down onto the shore two months later. "I really let myself like him," said Courtney, in the aftermath. "I felt so good all that time but now everything just hurts, so much." She looked up at me, her eyes hardening as she declared, "Well, you know what? I'll never be that stupid again!"

This is a beautiful remark, with innumerable possibilities for carrying the conversation forward.

What responses from a therapist are going to open things up, and which will close things down and make it a smaller conversation than it could have been?

These make it smaller:

- Why would you say that?
- Why do you say that?

These are very *cognitive* responses; they ask Courtney to explain herself, which would then dampen her emotional processing and expressiveness. The two questions direct attention more toward the reasoning behind her decision than her feelings. Courtney offered up an affective statement, and it warrants an affective response in kind.

Then, there's:

- No, don't say that.
- I'm sorry to hear you call yourself stupid.

This tells Courtney that the therapist needs everything to be nice and positive. With this remark you risk introducing a Pollyanna-like tone to the therapy, as in, everything people say about themselves should be positive, a *focus on the good* kind of approach. This just ends up discouraging kids from being honest.

An exception to this would be with a kid who is very self-deprecating, in which case the opportunity to address the self-deprecation trumps the opportunity to discuss risk and vulnerability in relationships because the clinical task or priority has changed.

What about:

- *What would you differently next time?*

Unfortunately, this tells Courtney that she's on the right track by trying to avoid being "stupid," and affirms her belief that you can actually accomplish such a thing, perhaps by being more careful/perfect/self-protective. But is that really what we want to tell a seventeen-year-old girl who was charmed over and subsequently dumped by her first boyfriend? This is where a therapist's values may come into play in terms of the direction or accent or tenor of the therapy. This isn't an issue of right or wrong; it's a conversation about whatever you think is important for this girl to hear and for you two to talk about.

I personally would want to move Courtney in the direction of continuing to accept the risks and vulnerability that come from taking a chance on connecting with someone special (discretion and judgment in picking boyfriends notwithstanding). Asking her what she would do differently next time suggests that she *should* do something differently next time, which Courtney could easily interpret to mean, *Be more vigilant* and *Be more guarded.*

And what about:

- *"You won't look stupid. Everyone makes mistakes."*

This is like when a kid says, "I'll never be able to do it" and a therapist or parent says, "Sure you will, keep trying, no one gets anywhere without hard work!" You think you're being encouraging but,

- You are saying, *I'm not listening to you.*
- It gives the person something to push against. (*I won't, mom. Just forget it.*)
- You lose the opportunity to model and talk about facing negative thoughts, self-doubt, etc.

All these responses above on the part of the therapist are likely to shrink the conversation rather than open it up. What I want to do here is *expand* the conversation by saying something that keeps the focus on Courtney's story. To that end, what might I say?

- *"Are you kidding me? Of course you will!"*
- *Oh my god I* hope *you give yourself the chance to be - as you say - stupid again!*

Here, I'm normalizing the experience of getting your heart broken and suggesting to Courtney that there's more value in taking a chance like that again than in spending your life defensively guarding your heart. Normalizing it means she doesn't have to react so aversely to it, and introduces a kernel of humanity (meaning, *It's happened to all of us, kid*) that sweeps the story forward in the direction of a larger theme: **Letting something matter enough to you that you are forced to deal with the anxiety of losing it.**

Other things you might do here include,

- *Telling a story about someone you knew who lived a "too careful" life and the emotional price she paid.*
- *Telling a story about someone who overcame her defensiveness and decided to risk again.*
- *Asking your client if she knows of someone who promised herself she'd never be "stupid" and ending up feeling as if she gave up something important for the sake of feeling "safe." And what's "safe" anyway?*

And in case you're worried that you'd have missed the opportunity to address what Courtney said earlier about feeling stupid, well, you can always circle back to that. And because you've put some distance between her comment and your return to it, chances are that she will be less defensive than if you were to ask her about feeling stupid right after she said it. Going back to it later allows you to use your voice and (a softer) facial expression to change the tone of the conversation:

> *"Courtney, you said the other day that what happened between you and Jason made you feel stupid. Tell me what about all that felt stupid to you …."*

This is an example of how I think about therapy with teenagers as being less about understanding BIG issues and dynamics, and more about helping them make sense of their feelings and choices. This is what makes therapy feel relevant. They can often put the pieces together from there.

### Can you figure out what it means to your client for her to speak with you and help her get past any misunderstanding or bias?

For example, is your client thinking any of the following?

- *If I talk to her (the therapist), my parents will think I actually want therapy.*
- *If I talk to her, they'll think they were right.*
- *If I talk to her, I'll never get out of this freakin' place.*

Maybe during the session with a new teenager, the dad makes a point of telling you how his son had sworn not to speak during the appointment. And so you say, "That's okay, not a problem," and continue the conversation you're having with the father. But about twenty minutes into the session, the boy twice starts to say something and then abruptly stops, as if remembering his pledge to remain silent. What can you say to encourage him to join the conversation?

Nothing that is sarcastic, provocative or that sounds like "I gotcha" such as

- *I thought we might hear from you when the conversation turned to school ..."*
- *"I thought you weren't going to talk to me ..."*
- *"Hmmm (turning toward the father,) I think he's changed his mind ..."*
- *"How's that working for ya?"*

What's better? A comment that refers respectfully to his earlier pledge to not say anything while acknowledging that he might now have found himself in a dilemma, meaning, he has something to say now but had already sworn he wouldn't talk. You're trying to help the kid save face here, in part by communicating that you understand that if they were to say anything it wouldn't cancel out their prior point of non-consent. For example:

- *"I know you swore you wouldn't say anything in here, but maybe the conversation is going in a direction you didn't anticipate, and now you do have something important to add. It's fine. I still understand that you're not keen on this whole thing."*
- *"Some kids worry that if they do join in the conversation here, it means they agree to therapy or think they need it. I don't do that. I just figure you have something you want to say, and that's it."*

## Name the ambivalence that's holding a client back

ME: There are times you talk about stuff that bothers you and I can't tell whether you want me to help you with it or not ....

C: Why would I bring it up then?

ME: Well, some kids bring stuff up just to find out whether I'm going to jump down their throat in an attempt to solve their problem. Others aren't so sure they're ready to work toward resolving problems or giving up a bad habit – they're kind of testing the waters.

C: That's dumb.

ME: That's what we do as people. One foot in, one foot out. Having two different feelings about one thing is as common as rocks.

C: Still sounds dumb.

ME: For example, some kids actually want to move forward and make changes, but they're worried that if they're no longer stressed, everyone will think they're fine and move on to the next kid.

| C: | (Looks up at me before turning away) |
|---|---|
| ME: | And some kids just like to make us adults feel stupid for responding to an SOS call that was really a false alarm. So … which kid are you? |
| C: | Not any of those, all that shit's just stupid. |
| ME: | Tell me something, anything, that you have two different feelings about. |
| C: | I don't know. Nothing. |
| ME: | (Softly now, with curiosity and not as a challenge) Well, how about you coming here? You say it's stupid but you still come…. |

## Normalize behaviors that embarrass your clients

Nine-year-old Liam sheepishly describes to me his habit of touching his butt and then bringing his hands to his mouth, which freaks his father out. I want Liam to talk with me more about this habit – specifically, what's fun or appealing about it and how he thinks about it, but *not* "How often do you do it?" I realize that if anything about this conversation tips in favor of him feeling embarrassed, it will stop. If, however, I can get him to feel like this is something other kids do, too, sometimes (which they do), then we have a conversation. "Yeah, I get it, buddy," I reassured Liam. "Some kids really like the smell of their own body. Sometimes they're just curious. They smell their skin, their toe dirt, their farts, and even their poop!" You can always see the relief in a client's face when they realize that it really is okay to talk about *anything* with you.

## Don't abandon dead end conversations too early. With some playfulness and creativity, you can discover avenues to keep it going.

| THERAPIST: | Off from school? |
|---|---|
| TEEN: | Yeah. |
| THERAPIST: | What did you do? |
| TEEN: | Nothing. I was bored. |

Okay, what's your response? Can you find a way to be interested in this kid's boredom? Clients say these things either because they really are bored or they're trying to shake you off their trail. *So, make boredom the topic of conversation.*

Here are some ways to do that – just be sure not to ask them all at once!

- *How can you tell when you're bored?*
- *Would anyone else be able to tell that you're bored just from looking at you?*
- *Good for you. I don't think enough people really let themselves get bored these days.*

- *You know, sometimes I miss being bored. I used to be bored all the time and now I'm too busy.*

Here is the exchange I had with the daughter of two philosophy professors who was trying hard to avoid getting into any kind of conversation with me:

ME:          "What's dinner conversation like at your home?"
LANA:        "Nothing deep."
ME:          "Do you ever wish it were deeper?"
LANA:        "No, I hate deep!"

What can you do with this concept of *deep*? Well, instead of asking Lana why she doesn't like "deep" (which is a boring question and unlikely to lead to anything broader), you might ask her:

- *"Does anyone else at the table object to deep conversations beside you?"*
    or
- *"What do you do when the conversation starts getting deep? Do you get up? Do you ever just groan?"*
    or
- *"If you do groan, will your parents stop or does it just make things worse, like they get mad at you?"*
    or
- *"Do you ever find yourself in a conversation and then realize, 'Holy crap' this is way deeper than I meant to go?"*
    or
- *"Do you have any allies at the table to steer deep conversations back to shore? What about your brother? Does he help make the conversation lighter again?"*
    or
- *"Have you ever bailed on a dinner that got too deep?"*

The point isn't to ask all these questions. The idea is to select one or two that, based on Lana's personality, you felt stood the best chance of jump starting a conversation with her. For example, if you knew her to be contrarian by nature, and always one to push back on her parents, you might opt for the questions about groaning or getting up and leaving. If you wanted to talk with her about her relationship with her siblings, you would ask about whether she can count on her brother at a time like that. If you understood her to be someone who had trouble owning aspects of herself that she didn't think were cool or she wasn't comfortable with (for example, her intellect) you could ask her about finding herself lost in such a conversation before realizing that she wasn't supposed to be enjoying it. The question acts as a bridge, in addition to an extender.

## Demonstrate curiosity about your client's world views, even if you find them politically "incorrect"

I'm talking with fifteen-year-old Teagen about how easily important matters and topics are simply dropped and forgotten about in her family.

"Do you ever wish they wouldn't get dropped so quickly?" I ask.
"No, not really. I don't think anyone in my family wants to talk about that stuff," Teagen replies.
"It sounds like it's really hard for your family to talk about sensitive topics."
"Yeah, we never do. I don't like to either."
"What about with your friends?"
"I don't know, not really."
"Your boyfriend?"
"No, boys don't talk."
"Really? Get out!" I say, with interest, and no challenge. Teagen looks up and smiles.
"Tell me more!" I say.

Here, I want to encourage Teagen to tell me more about how boys don't talk because *I want to understand how, in her world, boys don't talk*. And she lives in *her* world, not mine (where boys *do* talk). And even if the boys in her world do talk, I want to know why she doesn't hear it. But I'll never find out if I tell her outright that she's overgeneralizing or that I know plenty of boys who talk. A slight glimmer in your eye will tell her that you don't necessarily agree, but that it's not about agreeing.

What if I had said:

• "What do you mean, 'Boys don't talk'"?

The judgment I'm communicating in that response is enough to put the kibosh on the conversation. A lot of kids would probably issue a generic, "Oh I don't know, never mind," and it will be hard to get back to. It's just not an inviting remark.

• "Where did you get *that* idea?" sounds even more judgmental, like you might get a lecture about gender stereotyping.
• "Do you really think that's the case with *all* boys?" is leading the witness.
• "They don't?" Ditto.

Your goal is to get the conversation out there, and the more it's filled with how this teen thinks and chooses and loves or doesn't, the richer the texture of therapy will be.

## Engage in banter

Banter – that witty, good-natured and animated exchange between two people – has a place in therapy as much as does any other way in which we communicate with our clients. It's a lovely way to reveal your more playful side and to relate more informally for a few moments.

In addition, bantering with your teenage clients is a helpful means of keeping conversations moving forward with kids who get balky whenever anything "important" comes up. The flow-y, mosaic quality of banter, where you and your client can have conversations about several different things all at the same time stands in contrast to linear conversations where the emergence of an "issue" stands out in bold relief, commanding everyone's attention.

Here's fourteen-year-old Cassidy, an aggressive, sarcastic, and impulsive eighth grader who loves being the center of attention and mixing it up with her teachers and principals at the small private school she attends. In addition to being depressed, Cassidy suffers from pretty severe OCD. She does not get along with her family and speaks frequently of wanting to die. According to her mother, Cassidy has "no desire for the long game."

Cassidy has been to a bunch of therapists in the past but no one ever got any traction with her. They took her comments about wanting to die at face value and were overly sympathetic about her dislike for school. To Cassidy, everything was a big joke, and she dismissed their help immediately.

In this session, her fourth with me, Cassidy is explaining that she's angry with her teachers for trying to teach her.


I smile and ask, "What should they do instead?"
"Leave me alone."
"Then you'd get mad at them for ignoring you."
Cassidy smiles and tells me that's probably true.
"Maybe you're just mad," I say lightly.
"I fall asleep in all my classes," is how Cassidy chooses to reply.
"What, you don't like what I said?"
"What'd you say?"
"That maybe you're mad no matter who's doing what."
"Oh. I already know that."
"Oh my god," I say, "it's impossible to tell you anything about yourself you don't already know …."
"My teachers are always playing these power games." (Interesting here how Cassidy, given her remark about power games, might have experienced my comment about never being able to tell her something about herself she doesn't know as a power play….)

"What are they trying to win?"

"I don't know, but my English teacher told me she really liked my essay. I wrote one about how much pain I feel inside and, like, how it makes me not want to live."

This is something worthy of more conversation, but I also recognize it as a topic that Cassidy tends to avoid discussing. Were I to have jumped on the opportunity to talk with Cassidy about it, she'd have learned to park at the door issues she didn't feel like getting into, and I'd never hear about them. I wanted Cassidy to know that were she to bring things up like that, she wouldn't lose control over the topic or the conversation, and I wouldn't press her to discuss it with me, citing "safety" reasons.

I felt comfortable with this as my response because I'd known Cassidy long enough to have learned that she, like many other teenagers who spent the Covid-19 pandemic isolated, depressed, and withdrawn from all meaningful activities, used the fantasy of "not being here" as a way of coping with their despair, loneliness, and/or uncertainty about the future. For some kids it offers a measure of relief from worrying that they would ever have to be at the mercy of their sadness for the rest of their lives. It's like they could say to themselves, *Well, if it ever gets really bad, I can always just bug out*, never having to seriously entertain the idea of taking their own life. But enough kids do take their own lives, so this is not the place to get cavalier and disregard signs that your client may be in serious trouble. Cassidy, however, was not.

I decide to respond to Cassidy's story about her essay by saying something that references her comment about her pain, but only indirectly. That way she could leave it behind if she wished, but also would have an easy way to bring it forward it she felt it were time to do so.

"I'm glad your teacher was able to appreciate your essay," I say to Cassidy. "It would have been alarming to some …"

Cassidy ignores my remark about teachers' responses but picks up on her theme of emotional pain. "When I don't feel like doing my homework, I just go on YouTube and watch videos of toddlers getting hurt because it reminds me of my own pain."

Cassidy now hangs her head upside down and talks to me through her long, thick hair. She stays like that for the remaining ten minutes of the session. Because she mentions her pain a second time in a matter of minutes, I decide to expressly invite her to tell me more, even though I knew I'd have to end the session shortly.

"Tell me more about your pain."

"I don't know. It's just there," she says, before growing silent and, still upside down from her neck up, folding her hair into braids.

I choose not to push, confident that Cassidy and I will be able to circle back to the topic of her pain in future sessions. I say that because the topic is already out on the table, so to speak, by Cassidy's own voluntary admission (meaning, I didn't have to "pull" anything out of her), the result being that I'm not likely to run into too much resistance when we do.

Cassidy and I sit together quietly and easily for another minute or two before I close with, "Hey, Cassidy, I have to wrap up but maybe we'll circle back to this another time …"

"Yeah maybe," Cassidy says.

In her next session two weeks later, I find out that Cassidy and her family are moving across the country to San Francisco. She had gone to visit one of the private high schools out there and told me they kicked her out before she even was accepted.

They didn't like me at that school and told my mom I couldn't go.
Oh my god, you are unflaggingly provocative.
What's that mean?
It means you just love to mix it up with school people.
Cassidy smiles.
I don't know whether you're trying to make a point, or get a bit of attention, or make them mad, or maybe all three, or maybe something else altogether, but you do love being *that* girl. So, what'd you actually do?
I made a joke!
Uh, not a good one, I guess.
No, it was really funny! It was a great joke!
Timing is everything, kid.
I had perfect timing too!
(A few minutes later…)
I resent people who are really happy.
Did the kids at that school all look really happy?
A lot of them.
It's hard to tell from the outside sometimes.
I'm sure they all have perfect families.
I don't know about that.
I like watching The Simpsons!
Of course you would. The pessimism! The anarchy!
My tooth fell out today in school!

Fell out? Like a baby tooth?

Yeah.

Wait, how do you still have baby teeth?

I don't know but I pulled it out.

You *pulled* it?

Yeah. You know it was hanging there.

Oh god, I know. Ugh, like when it's hanging by the corner …

Yeah.

Are you putting it under your pillow tonight?

No. I'm not a kid anymore.

What does that have to do with it? I'd put it under my pillow if knew someone would exchange it for some cash.

I used to but then I found out the tooth fairy wasn't real.

Well, yeah, but still …. How'd you find out?

I'm really good at fake sleeping and I saw my dad come in and take my tooth and put a dollar under my pillow. That's when I knew. I had tears coming down my face, but I didn't say a word. He left and I cried and cried …

That's a beautiful story, Cassidy. Sad, but beautiful. The moment when everything changed. *I found out the tooth fairy wasn't real. I found out my parents have let me believe things that aren't true. What else isn't true?* You told that story so beautifully I think you should write about it ….

Cassidy starts talking about the impending move out west.

Who are you going to miss the most, I ask.

Jack (her boyfriend), my grandma, Abby …

Who's Abby?

I know her from the Mommie and Me group when we were babies.

No way!

Yeah. We've been together since we were two weeks and three weeks old! We're still best friends!

So cool.

Not like my friends from camp, I hate them.

*What?!* I practically yell. "They're the *best* kind."[3]

No, they're not. They're stupid friends.

Oh you are so wrong on this one, Cassidy. Camp friends are the best. I've known mine for fifty years!

Really? You're still friends?

The best of. Super friends. For a super long time. Longer than Mommie and Me!

That *is* longer, Cassidy says, smiling. She throws her legs up onto the back of the couch and closes her eyes.

Are you going to sleep on me?

I don't know. Maybe.

Am I especially boring today?

No. Cassidy keeps her eyes closed.

If you're gonna sleep let's get your mom in here then so we don't waste her money.

She left.

Where'd she go?

Target.

Oh god. Every parent goes to Target after dropping their kid off here. They never come back in time.

I won't look at any pictures of the (new) house in California.

I think that's your way of protesting. I know you don't want to go.

I'm gonna chain myself to my house here. Where can I get a chain? Hardware store?

I can't believe you answered that!

Me neither! For a second I thought, *Could I get in trouble for saying that?* And then I thought, Oh my god, that's ridiculous, like the kid doesn't know where to buy a chain?

I'm gonna chain myself to the fridge.

Oh god.

Yup, I'm staying here. They can all go.

Well, at least you'll still be able to eat. Cassidy smiles a big one.

Cassidy left for California a few weeks later so we never got to finish working together. But I include this example because it illustrates the ease with which many topics or issues come out unexpectedly while bantering that might never have come out otherwise. Among them are:

- Cassidy's fractious relationship with teachers and other school personnel.
- The undercurrent of anger in her dealings with people.
- The pain Cassidy feels inside, and how it sometimes makes her feel like not living.
- Her seeming ability to write about this more easily than she can talk about it.
- Her unrelenting and self-destructive provocation.
- Her resentment of kids who "have it better," who "look happier."
- Her aversion to doing something so childlike as play the tooth fairy game.
- Her decision to stay silent when her dad took her tooth from under her pillow.
- Her reluctance to move to California.
- Her strategy of tying herself to the house.

Had we more time, Cassidy and I could easily have picked up on any of the topics above. They were already "in the air," in the room. I don't think she'd have had any problem with me just saying, "Hey, talk to me about all those kids who you think have it better," or "What's your end game, girl, with all the egging on you do with school principals?" I imagine she'd laugh, a little proud to have been seen as one who can get under the skin of all those adults at school.

I don't think Cassidy was as hard-hearted as she liked others to believe she was. I found her quite likable, plus she was funny. Kids who are truly anti-social don't have the easy, unguarded sense of humor that Cassidy carried around with her and that attracted so many different kids at school who wanted only to be in her inner circle. I think they felt safer there than outside of the circle, where anything went in the service of a good laugh, and no one was really safe.

When thinking about how to help your teenage clients get started in their therapeutic work with you remember that, even with all the compassion and support and guidance we offer these kids, we do ask for a lot in return. We ask for their feelings, their thoughts, their stories. We want to know their reactions to the things we say and whether they followed through on some of the suggestions we made. If nothing else, we ask for their attention, their trust, their confidences. Remember that many didn't ask to come. It wouldn't hurt for us to give a little something up front – a vignette from your summer, a funny story about yourself, maybe your personal reaction to something like a recent movie release or a season-ending show or the opening of a new taco place. Yes, something personal. Something warm, inviting. You don't have to do much. Here, more than in many places in life, a little does a lot.

## Notes

1 Martha B. Straus, *No-talk therapy for children and adolescents*, W.W. Norton & Company NY, 1999.
2 A version of this was first published in *Psychotherapy Networker*, Why teens hate therapy: Mistakes therapists should avoid, Sept/Oct 2012.
3 Just for the record, I spent practically all my summers from the age of 3 up through 15 in an overnight summer camp in Maine, my favorite place on earth. I sent my three sons, too, who waited ten months out of the year for those two months in Fryeburg, Maine.

CHAPTER NINE

# Counter-Intuitive Strategies to Keep Teenagers in Therapy Talking

You've been there: You and your teen client are rolling along in a session, having what you think is a good conversation that you're sure is going somewhere, and then you notice it's gone nowhere at all and can't even be found anymore. Nothing really happened; it just kind of died.

If we pay attention to what derails our interactions with young people, we can learn a lot about how to bring about more engaging ones. Asking too many questions and engaging stiffly are obvious conversation killers. Harder to discern are the ways in which we leave clients feeling self-conscious, pounced upon, misunderstood, or mischaracterized. We don't always recognize this and our clients infrequently tell us. All we know is that neither we nor our young client has much to say anymore.

Here is where an appreciation of character, and of the individual psychology of your teen client in particular, can make the difference between conversations that go places and ones that don't. Some teenagers need their therapist to be very animated; others want them to be more chill. Some need their therapist to conspicuously endorse their better decisions or behavior, while others would shrink under such frank accolades, feeling embarrassed, maybe even a little patronized. Some teens want their therapist to stand with them, shoulder to shoulder, and attack problems head on and together, whereas some will accept help only if their therapist works from the other side of the room. *We can be any and all of those therapists*; the differences are subtle and within range of any emotionally flexible individual, but the differential effects are huge.

This chapter is all about clinical refinement. You are using your understanding of the person of your client as a guide to intervention rather than the particulars of their clinical situation, their diagnoses, or what your training indicates you do. Responding counterintuitively as a therapist means showing restraint when

DOI: 10.4324/9781003257080-9

everything about a situation calls on you to act or to say something, because *your* understanding of *that* person sitting in front of you tells you to check yourself. It means resisting the urge to prematurely seek solutions to what appear to be urgent problems, because you understand that what your client really needs in that moment is *to accept the discomfort of uncertainty and ambiguity.* It means that even though Therapy 101 taught all of us not to challenge teens when they're agitated, you recognize that for *this* agitated teen sitting in front of you, it is only by being held accountable in the moment for his questionable behavior will he settle and begin to relate genuinely. Counter-intuition is nothing mysterious or otherworldly or reserved for a special few. It's there for anyone who knows when to suspend conventional responding in favor of something that better suits your client and the therapeutic process.

Sometimes, all you have to do to keep a conversation alive is avoid doing the things that tend to stop them.[1]

## #1 Unhitch the act of talking about problems from having to fix them

Some therapies with teenagers veer off the rails before they've even begun. Here's an example: A therapist invites a teenage client to open up to her, and she does. But at the first mention of a problem the girl is having, the therapist makes that the focus of attention. The active conversation the two of them had been having vanishes and in its place is a stilted question and answer exchange. Unfortunately, this therapist had assumed that the client had brought up her problem in order to get help for it. She hadn't.

Teenage clients often bring up or refer to problems they're having before they're ready to actually do anything about them. That's because ...

- *...sometimes a problem just slips out, or*
- *... sometimes they're troubled enough by their problems to want to talk about them, but not ready to make changes that would help the situation, or*
- *... sometimes they don't want to lose control over what they feel is their problem, no one else's.*

When we jump the gun on this, two things happen: a) We lose our credibility as someone who can discern a person's readiness for change, and b) We lose the quality of restraint (temperance) in our work, rendering it urgent and more about what the therapist needs to have happen than what the client is ready to have happen.

But when we are patient, when we show reserve, we are telling our clients this: *I don't have an agenda separate from one you might have; I don't need anything to happen here; and I'm open to the idea that what really matters to you may have nothing at all to do with the problems listed on your intake sheet.*

## The Middle Space in Therapy

There's this vital "middle space" in the unfolding of a therapy that many therapists often hurry through or neglect altogether. It's that space where a young person's problems finally come to light without the need to immediately shift into problem-solving mode. Typically, therapists use the term safety to refer to a client's sense of comfort regarding distinctive features of the therapy relationship such as confidentiality, unconditional regard, and the absence of criticism or judgment. While all of these are important, I think safety also has to do with a client's freedom from worrying about having a conversation hijacked by a therapist's need to be helpful, make a point, or send a client home with "things to try."

When adolescent clients open up in therapy, especially after not having said much to begin with, some clinicians respond very eagerly, trying to expand the conversation about the client's problems or issues that just came forward. They might be worried that they won't have another opportunity to address them, and so they rush right into problem-solving mode: *Write in your journal. Try deep breathing. Think about a positive memory. Envision a safe place.* This may make the therapist feel better, but it's not necessarily what the client wants.

Teenagers need a place where they can think out loud and trust that their ideas and opinions won't be immediately dismantled in favor of a more "logical" or even more "healthy" line of thinking. Besides, there is nothing about those suggestions that says, *These are things I believe will help you, as opposed to another client of mine with a similar problem.* They're uncreative and un-tailored and, as a result, largely unappealing.

## Teenagers' more alarming symptoms

This approach to therapy has special relevance for working with adolescents because their presenting problems can easily alarm a therapist. Anxious to get a 15-year-old kid to stop cutting herself or drinking to the point of blackouts or failing all her classes, we may hustle in with a plan, a contract, or an assignment when all our young client wants to do is talk a bit about her own discomfort with the choices she's making. We keep saying we want our teen clients to open up to us, but if it's only so that we can "fix" their problems rather than appreciate them, they'll stay quiet.

Sitting with her therapist, sixteen-year-old year old Erin decides to talk about her cutting. Her therapist knows that Erin cuts herself whenever she's worried that her friends are mad at her, but Erin never wants to talk about it and always resists her therapist's efforts to broaden that conversation. However, on this day Erin is talking about it *a little* bit. She says she doesn't like it, and that it sometimes scares her. "But it helps me," she adds at the end.

Erin's therapist is very relieved to be hearing this from her client. However, mistaking Erin's candid reveal as an invitation to help her with it, the therapist spends the rest of the session giving Erin suggestions for alternative activities when she feels like self-harming ("Can you think of three things you can do instead of cutting when you feel like hurting yourself?") She also tries to get Erin to review some of the coping strategies she'd used in the past.

Erin's face closes. Her reaction? *Jeez, just because I said I didn't like it and that it sometimes scares me doesn't necessarily mean I wanted you to get me to stop it. I kind of just wanted to tell you about it.*

How else could Erin's therapist have responded? A better first step would have been to find out what Erin wanted to do about her self-harming tendencies. In addition, there were probably other areas in her life where Erin "self-harmed" or sabotaged herself, and maybe one of those would be an easier way for her to begin exploring this tendency.

Another thought is that it might have been a good idea for Erin's therapist to first appreciate in some way her client's attachment to the behavior of cutting before trying to separate it from her. *Erin had a relationship with the act*, and it would have been important for Erin to know that her therapist wasn't a threat to the one thing she depended on to self-soothe.

Remember, Erin had said, "But it helps me," — that could have been a good place to start, for instance. "You said it helps you, Erin. Tell me how …" in an inviting tone as opposed to "How do you feel that helps you?" which sounds critical and judgmental.

Another way to respond to Erin's comments about her cutting without getting ahead of her would have been to address her ambivalence about self-harm, as there's almost always some degree of that. There is, for instance …

- the impulse to cut and the wish to not cut;
- the embarrassment caused by scarring and the part of Erin that thinks scars are cool or doesn't care if they show, and/or;
- the hope that someone notices while also wanting to keep it hidden.

An example of assessing the first bullet point would be something like, "Tell me about the times when you felt like cutting but didn't …. What stopped you?"

Inviting Erin to "unpack" her feelings about cutting, and its emotional benefits, would also demonstrate the therapist's respect for her client's timeline, as well as for her "proprietary rights" to the problem. The idea at first is to just get Erin talking about the problem so that the conversation expands, and she can begin to comfortably explore her relationship to the rituals surrounding her cutting. Unless it would have resulted in a devastating injury, Erin's cutting compulsion was hers to manage or resolve, not her therapist's. The bottom line: When our young clients trust us to hold the space without rushing to solutions, they're more likely to relax their vigilance and ease into more therapeutically productive conversations.

That said, it's not always so easy to do just that. Many teenage problems are scary problems (suicide, cutting, drinking, indiscriminate sex, bullying, running away), plus they're minors, so we have a large measure of responsibility for keeping them safe. A serious situation is always going to get our attention. But serious doesn't necessarily mean dangerous; and an issue being serious, without any marked danger signs, is a not necessarily a good enough reason to pounce on it.

---

**When our young clients trust us to hold the space where they can discuss their problems without it necessarily meaning we're going to go in and *solve for x*, they're able to relax into a conversation where they're less defensive, less self-conscious, and less guarded.**

---

## #2 Let A be true and not true

I once was seeing a fourteen-year-old girl in family therapy who was beyond moody – she was surly and disrespectful and mean at home, and exploited her parents' anxieties about "upsetting" her even more. For the first three sessions, Paige swore up and down that she had no problems, none at all. In the fourth session, following Paige's cavalier dismissal of her parents' sad comment about how her argumentativeness and surliness were controlling the family, I said to her, "People don't like to think their distress is causing problems for those around them, especially family, but that *is* happening and needs to be part of the conversation too." Paige's response? ***"Why should I worry about them when I'm the one with all the problems?!"*** Okay, so we have three weeks with no problems, and now Paige has not just one but all of them.

I could have chosen to point out the contradiction in Paige's statements, but what would have been the purpose in that? All I'd be doing is showing her that I was more interested in making a point than in helping her become more comfortable saying what she really felt or thought. It would have felt like I was exploiting her unguarded remark. It would have been unkind.

Moreover, I imagine that once Paige realized what she had just said, and how it contradicted everything she had been saying for weeks, she probably was already thinking to herself, *Oh shit*. And, feeling vulnerable and at my mercy, she more than likely was now waiting for me to jump on this apparent inconsistency. But I don't jump on it and instead pass it right by. I take care of her, because what this kid really needs right now is to save face, and to know that I'm not going to take advantage of her slip of the tongue.

*This* is my way of taking care of clients – less virtuous than it is practical: It's a way I can establish credibility with a kid who isn't so sure about this therapy stuff, or about me. This is where I think the issues of trust and safety come into play most profoundly in our work with teenagers. The big question isn't so much, "Can I trust this therapist not to tell anyone what I talk about?" but rather, "Can I trust this therapist not to exploit discrepancies in my stories, even if it would support a point she's trying to make?" For a kid in therapy who is undecided about her commitment level, being able to answer this in the affirmative is huge.

A second cousin to these questions includes this one: Can I trust my therapist to know when enough is enough so that I can just listen to what she's saying rather than plan my escape? And can I trust my therapist to not try to keep the conversation going just because she has my attention? Huge and huger.

## #3 Make your point and move on

Let's stick with Paige here. What did I choose to say to her after she blurted out that she shouldn't have to worry about anyone since she was the one with all the problems? I looked at her and told her gently that no matter how bad her problems were, she was also a part of something bigger – her family, her circle of friends, her community – and that if she lost sight of that, the world could become a very lonely place for her.

It was a chance for me to show Paige how her way of managing her problems and moods would ultimately leave her feeling shortchanged, but without lecturing or confronting her. I also shared with her my concern that even her sense of righteousness wouldn't be able to protect her. What I wanted to help Paige understand was that using her moodiness to get people to back off and suspend their expectations of her might at first afford her some relief from the stress she was experiencing, but that it would eventually create even more disconnection and depression.

But I don't stay there very long at all. I moved on quickly, but without rushing. The Italians have a lovely saying for this – Festina lente, meaning *Make haste slowly*. I leave my comment as something Paige wouldn't feel she had to respond to, and turn my attention to her parents.

Never in a million years would I have followed up my remarks to Paige by asking her to comment on them, or worse, "discuss" them with me. That would have put way too fine a point on something, making it an *Intervention*. I liked it better as a come-hither idea, a little ethereal and, I hoped, a little alluring. Plus, now that it was out there, I could always return to it in subsequent sessions. You can put too fine a point on something and end up losing the good will of your young client.

Interestingly, at the end of this session Paige asked if she could begin meeting with me privately – this from a kid who, when first brought in by her parents, was determined to have nothing to do with therapy. "You can talk to my parents all you want because I have nothing to say!" was Paige's opening statement to me.

I thought a lot about Paige's change in attitude and interest in starting private sessions with me. With a different kid, I probably would have just asked her: "You were so opposed to therapy just a few weeks ago and I even saw you giving me the stink eye a few times, too. What's changed?" But with a girl like Paige, who, in the beginning, had made such an urgent plea to her parents to not include her in the therapy, asking her to disclose the process by which she changed her mind would have run the risk of making her feel as if she now had to backpedal. Later, maybe, but not right away.

I believe that what drew Paige toward a connection with me was my un-willingness to placate her as had so many of the other adults in her life, plus my willingness to say in front of her and her parents what they were all think-ing but afraid to say out loud. I think of this as the authenticity that teenagers seek from their relationships with adults, where the adult is transparent, honest, non-confrontive, and emotionally responsive. It's what gets them ready for, and interested in, the bigger conversations they can have.

Kids don't change because you tell them to change. They change because you've been able to create a climate in the room where they become willing to temporarily suspend their defensiveness against …

- … a different idea or perspective,
- … an adult from whom they can learn something,
- … a feeling they thought would overwhelm them,
- … a feeling they thought they couldn't share,
- … their softer, kinder, more vulnerable side.

It's the experience of those moments, as well as what comes out of them, that becomes therapeutic – not a person's ability to muscle a point across. Good therapy consists of powerful and petite acts of transformation. By creating cli-mates like that in your office space, as well as in your personal space, you are offering clients a holding environment[2] in which they can try on for size different parts of their personality that, for much of their life, were hidden from view, left undeveloped, disdained, tamped down, or even feared. When clients begin to identify places outside of therapy that similarly offer a safe environment for the expression of these other facets of their personality, well, that's when therapy starts moving outside the four walls of our offices and into the world at large, even if the safe environment at first consists only of the bedroom of a trusted older sister or a best friend.

## Notes

1  This material was first published in *Psychotherapy Networker*, March/April 2017. In Consultation: Speak easy: Keeping it real with your teen clients, Janet Sasson Edgette.
2  Winnicott, D. (1960). The theory of the parent–child relationship, *Int. J. Psychoanal.*, 41:585–595.

# CHAPTER TEN

# Diagnosis and Treatment in Adolescent Therapy

## Figuring Out What to Actually *Do* in Session

In the American medical drama television series, *House*, [1] Dr. Gregory House, a cynic, narcissist, and curmudgeon known for his unorthodox diagnostic approaches, says this when trying to enlighten his residents about one of the paradoxes of diagnosing patients: *"The Inuit do not look for fish when they are fishing."*

I can't imagine a more perfect metaphor for talking about diagnosing mental health disorders in children and teenagers. It speaks to the need to look obliquely at our young clients when trying to assign labels to them and figure out what the therapy should look like. This, in turn, speaks to the value of generating conversations that will allow telling aspects of their psychology to come forward so that we don't end up treating all self-harming teenagers the same or all kids with social anxiety the same. How you greet new clients, how you start conversations, how you respond to urgency in clients or their push back, as well as your timing of interventions and choice of words are, ideally, shaped by your understanding not just of clients' presenting problems but of their character structure, personality, personal history, defensive system, and interpersonal style.

Clients often come with a diagnosis or two in tow but rarely do those tell us much about what the work of the therapy is going to be or what the therapeutic conversation is going to sound like. There are a million and one ways to be depressed, and as many ways to alleviate it. The facts and other data collected early in the therapy that many therapists rely on for diagnosing and designing the therapy often yield only a limited picture – two dimensional and static.

You could collect history forever if you wanted to, and it can be tempting to remain in that "phase" of therapy if you're anxious about moving forward. New therapists are especially vulnerable, as well as therapists working with chaotic, volatile families in which flash fires erupt at every turn.

DOI: 10.4324/9781003257080-10

If you consider the illuminative value of *process*, however, you'll realize that a lot of what you'll need in order to be helpful to a family or individual – certainly enough to start helping – will already be right there in the room with you.

With individuals it will show up in their relationship style with you (how open, guarded, cooperative, anxious, warm, aloof, respectful, contrarian), in the quality of their defense mechanisms (primitive ones that distort judgment and reality, such as regression or denial, versus ones that compromise one's ability to see different perspectives and adapt to new circumstances, such as rationalization and projection, versus healthier ones like sublimation), in the quality of their humor, in how they talk about the people in their lives, in how self-aware they are and accountable for their decisions and their impact on others, among so many other things.

In families it might show up in who shapes the initial narrative about what's going on and how the others respond to it (deny it, reinforce it, try to change it), in how kind a parent or caregiver is when talking about their struggles with the teen, in how easy it's been for different members to accept help from others, in the power dynamics at play in front of your eyes, and more.

None of these types of "findings" you come away with are anything you would have asked clients about directly; they are all observations you make, and impressions you deduce. But they will be rich and illuminating and instructive, and allow you to seamlessly move from assessing to intervening and back again, even if just to test the waters of flexibility, frustration tolerance, empathy, or verbal or emotional expressiveness. Who needs to be right? Who gets into fights over it? Who doesn't care?

The best diagnoses tell you,

- an approximate level of the clients psychological functioning,
- where your attention should turn or stay,
- what the problem to be solved is,
- the operative emotional forces behind the actions taking place, and
- the factors (internal, external) stopping the natural corrective forces.

Rarely will you get all that from a conventional clinical diagnosis like "depression" or "oppositional defiant disorder" or "adjustment disorder with mixed emotional features." But *descriptive diagnoses* create more of a track that you can follow. Referring to much more than a category of disorders, descriptive diagnoses give you a rich sense of that human being in front of you – what he values in himself and others; what feelings he tries to avoid and which ones he tries to manufacture falsely; what motivates him and what deflates him, how comfortable he is with anger and how well he handles or expresses it, his frustration tolerance, his capacity for empathy, how good his boundaries are and whether he enforces them kindly or aggressively, among so many other qualities and traits. These are the things that I want to figure out about my clients, because they tell me so much more than what they suffer from; **these things tell me how to help them**.

History and facts might get you to a conventional diagnosis, but it's your eyes and ears and emotional sensibilities that will guide you toward a diagnosis that is more differentiated and dynamic and, ultimately, more useful. Questions I ask *myself* while meeting with clients (but would never ask clients themselves) include,

- **What is this teenager's attitude toward her own problems? Toward therapy? Toward me?** Is she skeptical, glib, jaded, hopeful, dismissive, apprehensive, cocky? Does she present as the victim? Is she dismissive of people who think of her as having mental health issues? Is she indulgent and dramatic about her mental health?
- **How does this teen view adults?** Are they seen largely as safe? Imbecilic? Impossible to communicate with? Misunderstanding of or resentful toward youth?
- **What is her reaction toward feedback she gets from people in her home, school, and social environment?** Is she quick to get defensive and launch a counterattack? Does she use constructive criticism as a weapon to self-punish and self-denigrate? Does she punish people for their honesty by cutting them out of her life for a few days or retaliating through social media?
- **What kinds of conversation or emotional expression from others grabs her interest in session?** Does she relax when the conversation veers away from more intense topics or does she zero in when the conversation gets real? Does she shy away from expressions of care and try to ridicule the sender, or is she hungry for support and acknowledgement?
- **What vulnerabilities does this teenager carry around with her that might affect her clarity of judgment?** For example, is it important to her that she never look stupid? Feel too dependent? Not be belittled or humiliated? Not appear unpopular?
- **I also consider my own reaction to the teenager,** especially if I'm surprised by it. For example, do I find myself disliking her without apparent reason? Or wanting to rescue her? Do I feel oddly and exceedingly trustful of her? Am I wondering why I'm not feeling sorry for her when I think I should?
- **What might it mean for this teen to allow herself to participate in therapy?** For example, will she worry that her parents will then think they're right or that she really does have serious problems? Could she end up feeling as though she's giving up her right to be angry?

The kinds of questions I *would* ask clients are different ones. Take, for example, my initial (family) session with sixteen-year-old Kiera, referred for therapy because of her growing depression, which has caused her to withdraw from family members and friends, becoming snappy and emotionally aloof:

> Kiera is so dismissive about the problems her parents just described in this first session that you want to shake her and say, "Are ya *kidding*?!" But of course you don't, and instead wonder if she really is that unaffected or is she just terrifically defensive. Or is she right, and her parents *have* overblown everything?

> In the session, I pick up on the fact that Kiera is very observant and psychologically astute; furthermore, she is not uncomfortable with her ability to make the people around her feel uneasy and perplexed. If you were to try drumming up a conversation with a teenager like this by lobbing a few easy questions her way ("What kinds of things do you like to do with your friends?" or "Do you get along with your sister?"), she'd see an easy opportunity to make you feel as irrelevant as she makes her parents feel by responding with a sour, "I don't know." If you were to make a meta-comment such as, "You don't seem as concerned about these things that your parents were just talking about ..." she would see you as already siding with her parents, as well as feel patronized. Not a great start.

> So where else can you go here? In a case like this, I would turn to Kiera and ask the following, in a very collected and calm manner:

- *Is there anything that you've stopped caring about that you wish you still cared about?*

   And a kid like Kiera will pull her brows together and look a little annoyed and say, *What?* and I'd respond with, *Like, I don't know, maybe you used to care that your little sister looked up to you and now you don't, or maybe you used to care about all the animals that don't get adopted but you don't really think about that anymore .... Stuff like that.... What doesn't matter to you anymore?* And it really doesn't matter whether she comes up with an answer or just shrugs the question off because what you're really trying to do here is let her know (and her parents, if they're still in the room) that, without the need to challenge or confront, you've already picked up on her tendency to deny the significance of things that matter a great deal to the people who care about her. I might continue with,

- *Does anything scare you?*

   And then maybe,

- *In what ways do your parents misunderstand you?*

   And that would be enough, and if she didn't have much to say to any of the above I'd just smile softly to let her know that it was okay that she didn't have much to say, and redirect my attention toward the others in the room.

I'm not as interested in any content that could be generated by my questions as I am in making a couple of points, which would be:

- I'm discerning enough to pick up on Kiera's tendency to dismiss the importance of things that she probably should care more about (e.g., her relationships with her parents and sister; her risk-seeking behavior, her suspected heavy marijuana use, her plummeting grades, and her reluctance to let anyone identify her as a kid "in need").
- I'm not the type of therapist who's going to jump on her stuff when it comes up in session (her problems, anger, resistance, risky behavior, bad grades).
- I can maneuver well enough to stay out of her traps without engendering her frustration or defensiveness.
- She can come in and divert and obstruct as much as she feels a need to, and I will continue to be simultaneously patient and probing.

This is, in part, how we become credible to kids who come into therapy thinking, *"Yeah, I know what this shit is about and I'm not having it ..."* We say things or do things that intrigue or normalize or compel, or otherwise express that *this* therapy experience could be different, might just be worthwhile. It's also an example of the seamless integration of two parallel processes, that is, gathering information and intervening at the same time. You don't have to wait until you have it "all" to start the therapy, and you'll likely keep discovering new and telling things about your client(s) up through their very last session with you. I've found therapy to be a way more fluid process than the methodical and orderly one most of us first learned (e.g., developing a therapeutic relationship, followed by assessing the presenting problem, followed by identifying goals, followed by implementing interventions, followed by terminating the therapy). Thank god for that.

## Tailoring Your Approach to New Clients
## Based on Personality, In Addition to Diagnosis

By the time we leave graduate school, we're pretty well versed in the newest ICD or DSM codification. But that should really be just the beginning of our education about diagnoses and the process of diagnosing.

Here are examples of how standard diagnostic labels will tell you something about the person, but not much about the type of therapy or interaction style they'll need from you. Look at how different kids with the same diagnoses can show up at your office:

- **Oppositional defiant disordered kid #1** is withholding and non-communicative. He likes making the people around him uncomfortable and insidiously undermines the authority of adults in his presence.

- **Oppositional Defiant Disordered kid #2** is explosive and verbally over-re-active. He is overtly challenging of authority.

Even the therapist's initial approach to a new teen client can be a dealmaker/dealbreaker right there. Approaching Kid #1 with a lot of questions in order to engage him in a conversation says to him that you're missing the boat. You see he's not volunteering much information, yet you're continuing to interact with him as if he were about to. That exchange might look something like the following:

| | |
|---|---|
| THERAPIST: | So, what's happening with school these days? |
| CLIENT: | Nothing. |
| T: | What about at home? |
| C: | What do you mean? |
| T: | At home, like with your family, your parents … what's going on there? |
| C: | Not much. |
| T: | Well, why are you here then? (Always a bad question as it comes off as aggressive and challenging.) |
| C: | I really don't know. My dad dropped me off and said "Go in there and talk to the lady" so here I am. |
| T: | But you're not saying anything. (Of course he's not saying anything. That comment alone tells the boy that the therapist isn't reading him very well.) |
| C: | There's nothing I want to say. |

Or,

| | |
|---|---|
| THERAPIST: | So, how are you today? |
| CLIENT: | (Grunts.) |
| T: | What was that? Sorry, I didn't hear. |
| C: | Fine. |
| T: | Good. Did you have a good weekend? |
| C: | Sure. |
| T: | How are you and your dad getting along? |
| C: | Fine. How long is this session? |

In order to get anything organic going with Kid #1 you'd need to match your expression of interest to his so that it's neither overbearing nor wilting in the face of his disinterest and lack of responding. That's a tough needle to thread. Sitting with a kid like this and trying to generate some decent, legit conversation would leave many therapists feeling frustrated. But remember that this kid never asked to be sitting in your office answering your questions. The therapy is being *imposed* on him, and he probably has no way to voice his displeasure and re-luctance to join in other than by withholding. If you can, however, maintain an interest that *expresses curiosity rather than frustration*, then there are a number of possibilities through which the therapy could gain traction, albeit very slowly.

T: Good weekend?

C: Yeah, sure.

T: (picking up immediately on the, *Whatever you say, doc*, intonation here) Okay, I get it. That's not a conversation that's going to go anywhere. Maybe there's another …

C: Another what.

T: Oh, sorry, I meant another conversation that might go better.

C: Not really.

T: (smiling) Do you make every adult feel as if they don't know how to talk to you, or is it just me?

C: (very small chuckle)

T: I'll take that as – actually, I'm not going to take it as anything. That's how I got in trouble with you the first time.

C: What do you mean?

T: By assuming.

C: What did you assume?

T: That you had a good weekend. Or rather, that "weekends" would be an easy place to start talking. It wasn't.

C: (minuscule smile)

T: I don't know. What would be better?

C: Probably nothing.

T: As in, there's little chance that anything would be better, or as in, *nothing* itself would be better?

C: I don't know the difference.

T: I don't know either. It was kind of a weird question anyway, never mind (I'd then let the conversation rest a moment). Ever see the movie *Dead Poet's Society*?

C: What?

T: *Dead Poet's Society*. Ever see it?

C: Never heard of it.

T: So, there's this teacher in a crusty old private school for boys and on the very first day of class he marches his students over to the display case near the gym where all the sports trophies are. Next to the trophies are all these old team photographs from the early 1900s. The teacher tells his boys to gaze at each of the faces in the photographs, and they do. And then he says, "They're dead, boys. Carpe diem."

C: I don't know what you're talking about.

T:   I know. That's why I'm telling you this story. The teacher is talking about how you're doing things you think are so important and then, guess what, before you know it, you're dead and buried. I know, that sounds dark, but wait. He wants his students to appreciate that they're alive today. It sounds hokey but I have a point. This teacher gets these boys, who are all bored and think they don't care about anything anymore, to become *curious*. They haven't been curious about anything in years. It's like they're already dead. *Pause, and then:* **Rowan, what makes you curious?** And **Do you remember the last thing you were curious about?**

I'm not looking for a response here. It would actually be perfect if the session were to end right there so that my client wouldn't feel any pressure to actually respond and would know that that hadn't been my intent.

Continuing,

T:   Well, anyway, I was just thinking about that movie and whether anything ever got you curious anymore, like probably when you were younger, before being curious about things was no longer cool …. Hey, I gotta wrap up here, but maybe we'll talk again …?

I would have thought of this story for this kid because I'd have been sitting there thinking about how shut down he is, how unwilling to explore anything outside of his comfort zone – a zone in which such things as creativity, inspiration, artistry, innovation or any spirit of inquiry were absent. But I'm not going to say *that* to him. I'd have lost him in no time.

Rowan and I would probably never talk about the movie again. We wouldn't need to. The intervention here, in addition to having had a conversation of sorts rather than ten minutes of awkwardness, is in the *ever-so-slight prompting of a thought process* (hopefully) *evoked by my asking a question.* The slight shock and surprise elicited by my sudden switching from talking about the boys in the movie to the client himself – an old Milton H. Erickson technique[2] – has the benefit of disarming the teen momentarily and creating space for an alternative perspective. It also would make it harder for the boy to shake off the two questions when he leaves. Ideally, their brief resonance in his consciousness would lead to a curiosity about why I was even telling him about that movie in the first place, and a concomitant unconscious projection of himself into a story, expanding his consciousness, even if for a few moments.

Now let's look at engaging with Kid #2, the other kind of oppositional defiant kid. This teenager needs someone who would engage actively with him from the start, who would join and pace herself to his affect level, and respond authentically, casually, and legitimately to his challenges. The granular attentiveness to dialogue that would serve Kid #1 could very well come off to Kid #2 as too contemplative, too tentative. It would be boring and unappealing. The kid would be rolling his eyes within minutes, and the therapist would quickly be behind in the count.

## Not so good:

| | |
|---|---|
| KID #2: | What am I supposed to say here? |
| THERAPIST: | There's no supposed to. You can say whatever you want. That's what therapy is. |
| KID #2: | What if I don't want to say anything. |
| T: | Why wouldn't you want to talk about the things that aren't going so well for you? |
| KID #2: | Everything's fine. |

## Better:

| | |
|---|---|
| KID #2: | What am I supposed to say here? |
| T: | I don't know. What do you want to say? |
| KID #2: | Nothing, I have nothing to say. |
| T: | Okay, then just say that. |

Kid #2 looks over to you to see if you're kidding, but you're not. You're not trying any harder than he is to make something happen, but you're not trying to be clever either. You're just inviting him to join you in what might be the most honest dialogue with an adult he's had in a long time. For some kids, that's intriguing enough to show up again.

Continuing,

| | |
|---|---|
| T: | Seriously, that would be so much better than saying something you think I want to hear. |
| KID #2: | Why would I do that? |
| T: | *laughing* You're right, I have no idea why you would actually think about what I wanted to hear, and then say that. Forget I said that. I have no idea what we're gonna talk about …. |
| KID #2: | What's your dog's name? (*Now I know we're good.*) |

## Expanding Conventional Diagnoses into Descriptive Diagnoses

With a handful of exceptions, [3] a client's diagnosis or condition alone will never supply us with the information we need to formulate a viable plan or approach to their therapy.

My conversation in therapy with a client who is significantly compromised by her ADD and loss of motivation for schoolwork has as good a chance of sounding like the conversation I'm having with a depressed nonbinary kid who wants to know how best to come out to their grandparents as it does the conversation I'm having with a different kid with ADD. That's because I'm not talking about the diagnosis or condition with them – I'm talking about the way in which it impacts their respective personalities and thus their mood, judgment, self-concept, and relationships.

For instance, Aja self-harms as a means of communicating her disdain for her authoritarian, controlling stepmother. Layla neglects to hand in assignments because she believes she's making a point, the point being that no one can tell her what to do. These two girls have much more in common with each other than they do with either of my next two clients, one of whom self-harms to escape her feelings of inadequacy and loneliness, while the other is too busy scrolling and posting on social media to remember she has stuff due.

Diagnosis is important because it's shorthand; it gives us a quick picture of a client. But you can't "treat" self-harm of course any more than you can "treat" a person anxious about coming out to family members about their sexuality. However, with the information gleaned in your first couple of sessions, you can begin to expand a traditional diagnosis into something with more "color" to it, more "movement" to it, more utility to it. Here's an example of doing that with a boy I'll call Mason.

## Mason

Sixteen-year-old Mason was brought in for therapy by his parents. They described their son as angry, isolated, and depressed. He was an adequate student but had no interests or hobbies. He had one friend. This tells me something about *him*, but not too much about the *therapy* I might do with him.

Sitting with Mason, however, in the presence of his strikingly cold and aloof manner, told me a lot more. I've sat with many kids who hadn't wanted to come, or who had sworn they weren't going to speak during the entire session, but this boy was different. His stare was icy, daring me to try to get him to speak. I actually felt uncomfortable and challenged in a way that was not inviting but rather chilling. I even started to think, *Is this kid a sociopath?* His parents controlled so much about Mason's life but, ironically, walked on eggshells around him and were overly attentive, a style of parenting I found not only unattractive but unnerving as well.

One notable observation in this initial session was Mason's effort to make himself virtually untouchable. He remained unaffected by and largely unresponsive to anything that anyone had to say during the session. There was control and calculation in this dynamic, and I began to suspect that, in the wake of being raised by a set of very controlling but meek parents, Mason had decided to never again allow himself to be at the mercy of anyone or anything he couldn't control.

After this first visit, I modified Mason's diagnosis as follows: **"Mason is depressed" (parent's diagnosis) became "Mason is a boy whose need for control and intimidation muted his personality as well as his hunger for what life offers."**

Toward the end of their second appointment I dismissed Mason's parents from the room and thought about how I might generate some kind of conversation with this boy. I figured the last thing he'd want to talk about would be "his depression," but I couldn't think of anything *else* he might be willing to talk about. In fact, I was pretty sure he didn't want to talk at all. This being a kid with no time for subtlety or innuendo, anything I said needed to be bold and unexpected if I hoped to get his attention. It also needed to be about *him*, because that appeared to be the only thing in which he had any interest.

So, I said to Mason,

"I think you've sacrificed all your appetites for the sake of feeling you're in control."

Mason just looked at me, as if to say, *What the hell...?* I wanted him to be curious about how I'd gotten that impression of him, but would also have been happy to have him refute it.

"What are you talking about?" he replied sourly, brows furrowed.

"You're very stoic and measured. You don't let on about anything you want or need. I don't even know if *you* know what you want anymore." I am purposefully not phrasing anything in terms of a question that he'd either feel pressured to answer or use to withhold from me.

Mason didn't say anything in response. He just kept looking at me, but the ice was gone.

"It's all good,"[4] I continued. "I'd like to help out here but I don't know what that looks like yet. I don't even know if that's something you want. We know your parents want it, but they're only part of the equation. So, we'll see. But, in any event, Mason, [5] I have to wrap up. You okay leaving it here for now?

Mason had been watching me carefully, I noticed. Then he slowly nodded.

And that's how Mason and I began a dialogue that lasted over the course of several sessions, some of them slow going, with me talking more than Mason, and others more balanced. I can't say that any of them were "chatty," because that would have required a level of internal abandon that Mason couldn't have tolerated, but there were meaningful moments in them, reflecting themes of intimidation, control, and withholding, and pretty frank (on my part) and candid (on Mason's part) exchanges about his use of them in his relationships with his parents, with me, with teachers, and with classmates.

Years later, I ran into Mason's mother while out running errands. She and her husband were so grateful, she said, for the work I did with their son. Apparently, in its aftermath, Mason's remote, cold bearing had thawed out a bit, and he became a little more engaged at home. He made a couple of new friends at school, and even brought them over to the house, something he'd always been reluctant to do. Right before we parted, Mason's mom said, "Wait, I have to show you something!" and pulled out a recent photograph of Mason in his cap and gown at his high school graduation. He was smiling. I don't know whether that smile was genuine, or something he put on his face for the sake of the picture. But in a situation where he could have crushed his parents and left them dispirited or even shaken, Mason chose not to, and I liked that part of the update best of all.

## Scarlett

Scarlett's parents call and ask you to treat their daughter's anxiety, but once you meet with her you recognize that Scarlett's anxiety per se is not the problem. The real problem is her inability to tolerate even small degrees of anxiety in settings where there is no accommodation:

**"Scarlett has an anxiety disorder" becomes "Scarlett is a girl who made a personality out of her parents' chronic over-accommodation to her inflexibility and self-centeredness."**

Scarlett's parents have been over-accommodating their daughter's anxiety for years, that is, aggressively finding ways to shield her from the negative impact of her anxiety on her own general functioning and from its impact on her family. In the process, both parents have begun feeling very resentful of their daughter and, in their words, "… of her obliviousness to 'all the things [they] do to help her,' for which she is never appreciative enough."

Scarlett's parents also feel hostage to Scarlett's moods and volatility and proclaimed inability to meet age-appropriate responsibility and tasks. They work very hard to get their daughter to smile, to hide their own frustration when Scarlett's inflexibility causes them to have to cancel family plans, and to serve as the buffer between their daughter and the world at large.

Scarlett's parents may see their daughter's anxiety as the enemy, as the "thing to get rid of." A different lens on the problem suggests that Scarlett's parents can best help Scarlett not by protecting her from anxiety but by helping her experience it as something *manageable*. That's the parent piece here.

At the same time, working with Scarlett in private sessions could entail helping her to a) restore confidence in herself as one who can in fact deal with the normal stresses and frustrations in her life, b) cultivate a desire for independence, and c) help her see the liabilities of living a life where people feel they need to be "careful" around you and protect you from yourself.

***Everyone loses when over-accommodation is mistaken for compassion.***

## Lily

While sitting with fourteen-year-old Lily and her very busy parents, I had the impression that theirs was a family that easily recognized the most obvious of accomplishments – the ones that took place in the board room (for the adults) and the class room, baseball diamond, or recital halls (for the kids).

Lily didn't shine in any of those places though. She seemed to me the kindest of all three of their kids, and the most emotionally aware. She had several good friends, and kept them for years, which told me that she was a good friend herself. Lily read widely and thought about things deeply, and was a member of a few clubs at school that directed their attention to making others feel better, such as the Best Buddies program, for example, or volunteering for Special Olympic events. Lily was the kind of kid who shines in other people's hearts. Here's how I tweaked her incoming diagnosis after meeting with Lily and her parents for an initial session: ***"Lily is depressed and shy," became Lily is depressed because she feels invisible in her own home and has withdrawn from her family in order to "show" them how much this hurts her.***

With this as my hypothesis, I began mapping out a plan for therapy. In this case, and at this early point, I saw it as a matter of:

- Helping Lily to recognize that, contrary to what they tell aspiring writers, *telling* is a lot more effective than *showing*. However, in order to tell people what they need to understand about you, a person needs a voice. Therefore, I wanted to ...
- Help Lily to have a voice, as well as the language and confidence to use it effectively, meaning, in ways that will encourage her parents to listen to her and take her concerns seriously. Lots of kids have voices, but they don't use them in ways that invite adults to listen. Their voices are shrill or angry or disrespectful. They're sarcastic or they shut down as soon as the adult pushes back on it. As therapists of teenagers, it's important that we don't hastily authorize their voices and amplify their anger before teaching them the skills they'll need to hold an audience long enough to get their

respective messages across. They'll need to learn to regulate their affect and tone. They'll need to learn to stay chill while being dismissed or criticized so that they can respond with such composure the other party can't help but take them seriously.

- That meant I also needed to help Lily's parents to appreciate the way in which their relationship with Lily was leaving her feeling "unseen," and the importance of recognizing not only *what your kids do*, but *who they are.* I wanted them to understand their daughter's withdrawal as a function of her feeling invisible which had led to her being depressed, as well as an attempt to "show" them how "missable" she was.

## Lucas

Lucas, like Mason, was another boy to whom nothing seemed to matter. However, the origins, nature, and manifestations of his inner struggles were very different from those of Mason and, therefore, so was the therapy.

> Sixteen-year-old Lucas stopped letting things matter because it simply hurt too much. I'd seen him first as a thirteen-year-old, when he was being bullied for his slight build, un-athleticism, and painted fingernails. He returned three years later for more therapy of his own accord, describing himself as depressed. His manner was one of indifference now; he was flip and cavalier. It was not an attractive presentation. I was better able to work with "Lucas and his 'depression'" by expanding it and **understanding Lucas as "a kid whose escape into 'whatever' as a way of shielding himself from pain ended up shielding him from the very people who could and would have alleviated it."**
>
> Lucas knew that something in the way he was relating with the few friends he had wasn't working. They started referring to his humor as "too dark" and didn't like how sarcastic he'd become. Lucas suspected they were distancing themselves from him but had neither the self-awareness nor the relationship repair skills to correct his interpersonal trajectory, and so was simply stuck doing more of the same, over and over.
>
> I figured that the same things that were unappealing to me in how Lucas related were unappealing to these friends who were drifting away. But I didn't think that Lucas would have welcomed a conversation about his "indifferent attitude" and its effect on the people around him. He would have said something like, "My friends don't care about that ..." or "My friends think I'm funny, it's not an issue ..." Instead I waited for the right opportunity to come up in our conversation, meaning, some point where an exchange about his indifference would matter to *him*. And then I saw it.

Lucas is talking once again about the trouble he's having with his friends. He's pissing them off now and doesn't know why.

"I had a big fight with Elena last weekend," Lucas says, clearly saddened. "Am I really that bad at friends?" he asks, plaintively.

Lucas goes on to tell me about Elena and their argument, but shortly afterward summarily dismisses the entire weekend with a *whatever*. I'd been seeing this conversation as a potential window of intervention, but Lucas shut it down on me before I could do anything with it. So now I continue to wait for the next opportunity. This issue is so pervasive in Lucas's life that I am certain another will come.

It comes up again in the very next session when Lucas declares, "I'm tired of losing people."

"Do they know that?" I ask.

" No."

I pause to let that sink in – that he doesn't let even his own friends know they matter to him – and decide to hold off on doing more at this time. It's new for Lucas to offer such a candid expression of distress, and I don't want to spook him by pouncing on it. I want him to know that I will never entrap him in his vulnerability or candor, that he can drop it into our conversation, and then move away from it. All that makes it easier for either of us to come back to it later.

And it does, two sessions later. Lucas tells me about an incident at school in which he's going back and forth with a classmate on Twitter. He posts, #Killmelanie2013.

Melanie tweets back #Dontkillmelanie2013. Sitting in a class with yet no teacher having shown up, Lucas gets up and walks over to the front of the classroom, where he writes his entire Twitter post about Melanie on the white board. Teacher comes back. Lucas is sent to the principal's office.

Lucas is telling me about meeting with the principal but describes the encounter as if it were one between peers. He recounts how he told the principal that he didn't understand what the big deal was.

"Did you actually say that to him?" I ask, incredulous.

"Yeah … kind of." Lucas's delicate backtracking tells me he knows exactly where I'm going with this.

""Oh boy," is all I say. And then, looking Lucas straight in the eye, I add, "You know, most people would be sweating bullets in that situation, but your conversation with your principal sounds as if you guys could have been chatting about where you went on spring break." I continue. "My god, Lucas, so much of your mental energy is spent making sure people know they can't get to you. That you're untouchable in that way."

Lucas is quiet, motionless, listening. He's looking right back at me.

"This *"whatever"* thing you have going on," I say, "I know you think it protects you, but it really doesn't. It hurts you and hurts the people you care about. People need to know that they matter."

And that was the therapy, right there, or at least a big part of it. Someone like Lucas, reflective and trusting, who wants to feel better and understands he will need to do things differently in order for that to happen, doesn't need me to instruct him on how to let things matter or why that's important. He can take it forward from here.

*You don't always have to take them across the finish line in order to complete the therapy.*

But what if you do? I wonder sometimes if I count too much on the momentum of therapy to keep things moving forward past the point where a client and I have wrapped up. I am a minimalist in most areas of my life, e.g., decor certainly – and ... actually ... I'm not sure where else, so maybe not. But I am as a therapist, maybe because I'm reacting to all the overwrought and ornate case studies I read about that seem to make what could be a more fluent and straightforward process unnecessarily complicated and protracted. I don't always believe that all those points, lessons, and insights have to be driven home, and in fact believe that doing so often takes away from their integration. As a result, I err on the side of *under*-reacting, *under*-treating.

I remember a girl named Lily. I'd seen Lily on and off for nine years, ever since she was an anxious, shy second grader. Suddenly she was sixteen, navigating the things many high school sophomores start having to think about for real – drinking, smoking, sex, etc. A part of me felt like a parent (*Oh, my kid is growing up ...*) and another part – the therapist part – worried that, because of feeling a little bit like a parent, I'd do or say something to inhibit her from speaking candidly with me as she'd done for nine years. As a result, I hung back a bit as Lily shared with me her escapades, not asking, as I might have with another teen, how she was thinking about the choices she was making.

Until one day when, walking out the door after her session, Lily turned to me and said, "I can tell you're getting more and more concerned about me!"

And I'm thinking, *Am I? Was I?* I didn't think so. And then it occurred to me: Maybe this was her way of saying that I *should* be.

I didn't waste any time getting back to it at her very next appointment.

"Hey, Lily," I said, "remember last week you said something about me getting
more and more concerned about you?
"Uh *yeah ...*" she said, with an emphasis on the yeah.
"Was that your way of saying that maybe I should be?"
"Yes!"

Okay, so sometimes it takes me a little longer than it should. I became aware
of how easy it was for my thinking to be compromised in working with Lily, and
I carried that lesson forward: Maybe I *wasn't* always asking enough. Maybe a
good thing for me to start doing was to ask my teen clients, *Is there something
I'm not asking about that you've been hoping I would?*

I'd have laughed if someone told me before writing this book that I could
sometimes be conflict-averse in my therapy. Not anymore.

## Notes

1 *House* – season 1, episode 17. "Role Model" (2005).
2 Milton H. Erickson, *Collected papers of Milton H. Erickson on hypnosis*, 4 volumes
(1931–1977), edited by Ernest L. Rossi. New York: Irvington, 1980.
3 There are, for example, certain diagnoses for which there are recognized best practices and specific treatment protocols. I'm talking about all the other ones.
4 With a different teenager, I might have used his or her first name in this sentence
(e.g., "It's all good, Jimmy,") to make it warmer, more personal. But with Mason, I
thought it would be too much familiarity too soon, and he'd balk at it. So I left it out,
opting to wait until he would be more comfortable with informal expressions of engagement, casual though it would be.
5 In this instance, a short five sentences later, I did choose to use Mason's name while
talking to him. This was a better place to do so, a little distanced from the more
emotionally laden exchange about his stoicism and muted desires. Here he might
be better able to appreciate it as a low-key gesture of genuine interest on my part in
helping him and his family out.

# CHAPTER ELEVEN

# Revisiting Process and Content in Assessing Teenagers and Their Families

For all the yakking I've been doing about the need to modernize our thinking about adolescent therapy and our service models, I have to say there are some old standards whose utility has proven invaluable for decades. For our purposes here of assessing teenagers and families and coming up with tailored plans for therapy, process and content are two that I have in mind.

Content refers to the literal statements made in a conversation, meaning, the "story" that's being told and the issues addressed as a result. Process is the personal, emotional experience a person is having as they tell the story, or that others are having listening to or ignoring the story, or the dynamic unfolding between and among people (including and especially the therapist) in the room (for example, in an initial therapy session, a father is becoming angry as he shares his concerns to the therapist about his son, Elio, because Elio and his mother are making little "jokey" comments together while he speaks.) Irvin Yalom, existential psychiatrist, educator, and author, wrote extensively about content and process in two of his books, *The Gift of Therapy* and *Love's Executioner*.

A third lens through which to evaluate clients is that of looking for where the presenting problem or behavior results in any deviations from the norm of healthy, balanced family functioning. This is helpful whether meeting with individual teenage clients or with families. The degree of the deviation helps in determining the number and extent of accommodations the client's parents have made in response to their teenager's challenges. All three lenses, or tools, are discussed below.

DOI: 10.4324/9781003257080-11

## Departures, Process, and Content

## If you're meeting with a family, look for where the symptom results in deviation from healthy family functioning

### Neera: Helping a father see how his daughter's "typical teen behavior" is really her being rude

#### Is my teenager acting "like a teenager," in a bad mood, or simply being rude?

A father was describing the challenges of dealing with his irritable, moody daughter every morning in the hour before she leaves for school. He seemed to be very accommodating of her poor attitude and the way it was affecting everyone else in the household, so I asked him about that. He said, "I oblige Neera's bad behavior in the morning because I want her day to get off to as good a start as possible. It's just who she is. Besides, don't all teenagers act that way in the morning?" Insert emoji with big bulging eyes.

Here's the problem: It had become all about Neera. She was learning nothing about the need to regulate her moods in the company of others, or at least their expression, something which likely was impacting relationships with not only her father and siblings, but relatives and teachers and friends too. She was learning nothing about being part of a community (in this case, her family), where other people's wishes matter, and where everyone is expected to contribute to its welfare. She is learning nothing about being empathic, or generous, or patient – all qualities essential for the self-awareness, emotional intelligence, and respect for others needed to build and sustain healthy relationships in one's life. Moreover, one other unfortunate take-away for Neera is that if you are difficult enough, people will go out of their way to make accommodations for you.

We can help parents like Neera's father (and by proxy, Neera) by pointing out that while nobody blames the girl for feeling as she does – her moods are inarguable – she can be held more responsible for how she allows them to impact the people around her. Snapping at people, slamming cabinets, and yelling at someone when they are trying to help you get out the door are not natural phases of adolescence. They are things teenagers do because their parents, believing them to be a natural part of adolescence, let them. All of Neera's behaviors are things she could control, even if her bad moods make it harder for her to control them than someone who wakes up feeling good.

I suggested to the father that he view his Neera's behaviors and attitudes through a lens of "choice," meaning, that these are things she is choosing to do, or allowing herself to do. If he looks at them that way, does he feel any differently about her behavior? Is he willing to impose consequences should his daughter refuse to change her ways? Does he have a good response for when she yells, "That will just make things worse!?" If not, could he and I spend some time together coming up with some?

Some readers may wonder why I'm not talking more about the emotional issues underlying the poor behavior. They are always a part of my thinking and a part of the conversation; I can't imagine discussing a teenager's behavior without addressing their emotional and mental status. However, I don't think it's useful to make them the primary focus in the therapy as long as the acting out behavior is continuing. These two conversations can take place at the same time, but exploring the depressed, anxious, angry, or otherwise troubled nature of an acting out teen without simultaneously making an effort to hold her accountable for that behavior is rarely productive. With the teen's feelings being discharged through the behavior, and the parents growing increasingly reactive and/or resentful, it's hard to lead a kid to that place of authenticity and vulnerability where honest conversation about how they feel can manifest.

## Often enough, though, process trumps content

Watch closely for reactions your client has to what a parent or stepparent is saying. Are there nonverbal behaviors that dispute the family narrative being presented? What's missing in the family – humor? gravitas? animation? empathy? Is anyone surprised by what somebody just said. Go there, right away.

### Hugo: Helping a father and his son better understand the connection between their relationship and the boy's depressed mood

I'm sitting in an initial session with fourteen-year-old Hugo and Hugo's father, both of whom had mentioned Hugo having been depressed for the past year. I am tracking Hugo's response to his father as he talks about him in a very positive light. I notice that every time Hugo's father proudly mentions Hugo's ability to remain calm when frustrated, or to appreciate other perspectives even though he may not agree with them, Hugo turns and looks at him as if he's surprised his dad spends any time at all thinking about him, let alone thinking well of him. So I decide to say something about that.

> "You look surprised to hear your dad talking about you that way."
> "Uh, yeah. I never knew that," Hugo replies, softly.

Now I'm looking at Hugo's depression through the lens of his relationship with his father, specifically the discrepancy between how Hugo believes his father thinks about him, and how his father actually does think about him (or appears to). It may not explain everything about why Hugo is depressed, but it's a valid starting point.

> "Guys, here's what I'm wondering," I begin. "Hugo, you say you never knew your dad thought these things about you – that you remain calm, that you take on other perspectives easily. Is it because this is the first time he's said anything like that in front of you," and looking over at the father now and then back at Hugo, I add, "or, because your dad has said these things before but it's hard for you to believe him or remember them?"

> Hugo's dad jumps right in here, saying, "I tell him this stuff *all the time*, and he never believes me. My son can never take a compliment, and it upsets me because he's such a great kid, and everyone loves him, but he doesn't see it."

That was a lot of information right there, and it gave me a starting place for the therapy I did with Hugo from that point forward. Most of it was individual work, a focus of which was to unpack the discrepancy between how Hugo saw himself, and how others saw him.

But let's say that the conversation in that first session had gone in a different direction. Let's say that Hugo, in response to my question about whether his dad had ever said these things before, pointed out that his dad never says anything positive about him or his siblings, that he was in fact rather critical, and that this was the first time he ever heard his dad say anything nice about him. And let's say Hugo's dad looked both a little annoyed and sheepish, and muttered something about not wanting his kids to get "big heads."

I might have responded with, "I understand … (I am choosing here to normalize the dad's concern about his kids getting big heads in order to ward off any resistance). Some parents worry that if their kids hear them speaking positively about them that they'll use that as a way to, I don't know, get out of stuff like, *Well if I'm so good at taking care of grandma when you need me to then why do you get on my case if I don't want to do the dishes?* Or they worry that, like you said, they'll get big heads and be impossible to deal with." I would turn to Hugo with a smile and ask, "So would you get a big head?" And from here, depending on Hugo's response, you could go anywhere …

### Emily: Helping a young, impulsive teen open up some emotional channels for adult input and support

Thirteen-year-old Emily is a whirlwind of a kid who spun my head with her rat-a-tat story-telling and animated expressions.

> "At school I'm like 'Look at me! I'm EMO, I'm a scene girl, I'm a candy girl!' And I like kissing boys! I kiss lots of boys in the mall. I play the jelly

bracelet game. I make out with boys in the mall and at school! I hate all my teachers except one."

"Oh –"

"I don't do anything around the house but I will if I get permission to get piercings! My teachers say I'm not at school to socialize but I tell them, 'Yes I am.' I won't get help from teachers because I'm mad at them ...."

I realized that if I wanted to get into this conversation, I'd need to make my own room. It reminded me of trying to play double Dutch jump rope as a kid, watching two girls spin jump ropes in opposite directions wondering how I was going to insert myself into the game.

Finally, Emily pauses. I jump in.

"Wait, what does being mad at your teachers have to do with getting help?"

I am not expecting any sort of real response from Emily to my question. I would expect, if anything, just a "Huh? I don't know," and then a hop, skip, and a jump away. But I would be making a point, understated and a little off-center. I'm letting her know that I am totally engaged in her soliloquy, and yet dispassionate enough to be able to discern the appearance of a statement of hers that, at least to me, is qualitatively different than the others. It's one where I can join in on the "conversation" by raising a question, an opportunity her other statements don't afford. And the point I'm making, of course, is that not everyone equates being angry at someone with not being able to go to them for help. I call this a "drive-by" intervention: fleeting, under the radar, just a pinch of an idea.

"I don't need anyone!" is how Emily replies.

For her next session, Emily comes in with her mother. At some point in the conversation, Emily's mother mentions how Emily had stayed home from school with bad period cramps earlier in the week.

Looking over at Emily and smiling gently, I ask her mother if Emily lets her help her when she's not feeling well. I ask this because I want a way to track back to Emily's remark at her prior session about not needing anyone.

"Usually, but only on her terms," the mom replies. "If it's something *I* think would be helpful, like using a heating pad or drinking some hot tea, she's, like, 'No thanks.' But if she's up in her room and decides that a meal from Chick-Fil-A would help her feel better, well, then she has no problem asking for that!"

Emily looks over at me and smiles. She's happy with her mother's assessment.

"But I'm a softie," Emily's mom adds. "And Emily is very good at taking advantage of that."

My idea for how to help Emily is beginning to take shape. So far, there are *three issues we could address*. One is the way she **filibusters conversations** in which she's anxious, or wants to be in control, or maybe is simply showing off. An example of how I might begin addressing this with Emily would be to say, one day when she's doing another filibuster, "Oh my god you have so many things to say and so many feelings about them sometimes I feel as though there's no room for mine!" I'd do this with a smile and a sparkle in my eye and no expectation that Emily would or should make room for me as she speaks; the purpose of my comment would be only to make her *aware* of what she's doing, and maybe a little self-conscious about it – not in a shameful way at all, more in a self-reflective way.

The second issue is Emily's **pseudo-independence,** an early and premature assumption of autonomy that renders her resistant to the input and advice of those who have only her best interests in mind.

And the third is Emily's **exploitation of her mother's generous and conflict-averse nature**. There are other themes to add into the therapy as well – aren't there always? – for example, the quality of her judgment and the seeming discrepancy between how she portrays herself when with others and who she is when not in the public eye.

Emily comes by herself to her next session. "Me and Nick were about to do it and he said he'd just pull out, but I said no."

"Good for you."

"Yeah, I didn't want to. I made out with Jordan but he's a prude. Some friends smoke weed but I don't like the smell. I don't do it."

There was a little more space in this conversation and I took advantage of it to comment.

"You're not nearly as reckless as you seem, you know," I say to Emily. "You pull that off well."

Emily smiles. She is happy with my assessment too.

Below are several in-session, **private process observations** that I've drawn from sitting in an initial session with a teenager, or a teenager and his parent. They weren't necessarily going to determine what the whole therapy would wind up being about, but they were instrumental in helping me to discern some of the operative dynamics that were driving the problematic behavior or keeping it in place and, in the process, refine whatever working diagnosis I had at the time:

> ... This teenager relates to his parents as if they were all peers or room-mates; there is no recognition of any hierarchical boundary between him-self and his parents.

> ... This mother is quick to protect her teenage daughter from recognizing the ways in which her behaviors are offensive to others.

> ... This teenager seems so different from the one her grandmother/guard-ian described over the phone to me – more congenial, more self-aware, more empathic.

> ... These parents have been avoiding therapy for their daughter for years and now I see why: They are all about image and 'what other people think,' and their daughter being depressed, let alone in therapy, doesn't fit.

> ... This dad is saying all the right things in here but looks like he's just one wrong comment away from blowing his fuse.

> ... This teenager uses her learned helplessness as a way to get her parents to "cease and desist" from calling her out.

> ... This teenager looks like he wants to connect with his father but doesn't have the emotional courage or skill to let him know.

## But sometimes, content is king

### Ivy: Helping a teenager's parents to shed their blind spots and acknowledge their daughter's perceptiveness while also helping the teen to trust her voice and deal constructively with family frustrations

Sixteen-year-old Ivy comes for therapy to deal with long-standing depression and low self-esteem. Along the way, she's shared with me some legitimate concerns about the way her parents manage her brother's aggressive and in-appropriate behavior at home. Ivy's brother, Ian, was diagnosed years ago as being on the autism spectrum. He's pretty functional when at school or at some of his after-school activities, but when he's home he regresses, screaming for periods of time when he doesn't get his way and occasionally running around the house naked, which deters Ivy from bringing friends over. Moreover, every time the family goes out to dinner, Ivy's parents defer to her brother, who de-mands to go to either of the two restaurants he is comfortable going to. Never does Ivy get to choose.

Ivy complains that despite her mother's frequent vocal grievances about "how much [she] has to do around the house for everyone," she continues to get up every morning to pack Ian's lunch for school. Ian is fourteen years old. Ivy's concerns have to do only partly with these frustrations and the way that her parents' management of Ian affects her life negatively. They also have to do with her concerns for Ian, in terms of a gross lack of accountability regarding his behaviors and responsibilities that he will have to face when no longer living at home. And every time Ivy raises these concerns, her parents shut her down. Sometimes it's by dismissing them as "no big deal" or as things Ivy says because she's "jealous of the attention he gets" (huh?) or as things he can't help. The last one makes Ivy see red.

Why is addressing Ivy's concerns about her brother important in a therapy that is otherwise focused on her depression and low self-esteem? Because maybe part of her symptoms have to do with not feeling as if she has a voice in her family, or a voice that's taken seriously. Maybe it has to do with her feeling patronized, in the wake of comments like, *Wait until you're a parent, and then maybe you'll have a different point of view.* Maybe it's because she feels as though her feelings, her impressions, her insights will never matter to her parents, especially as long as they don't align with their myopic views about mental disabilities and the dangers of expecting less than someone is capable of being or doing.

The interventions I made with Ivy and her parents included the following:

- Meeting with Ivy's parents alone in order to discuss their taking Ivy's impressions and reactions more seriously and being open to the likelihood that she has some good points.
- Also, helping them to see how their over-accommodations of Ian could be a disservice to him in both the short and long run.
- Validate and normalize Ivy's feelings about her parents' treatment of her brother (*"I hear this a lot from kids who have a sibling with some kind of disability and see their parents treating them in ways that keep them very dependent on them or feeling entitled or just plain annoying!"*)
- Working with Ivy to better manage her frustration if her parents don't change.
- And, secondary to that, helping her to separate her relationship with her brother from her parents' relationship with her brother so that her resentment toward them doesn't infect how she feels about Ian, whom she truly loves and cares about.
- Better understanding Ivy's world outside of the home and finding out whether she feels differently when there and, if not, what other factors in her life contribute to the sustained inner experience of depression and low self-esteem.

## Be ready, however, to pivot from one focus point (e.g., content) to a more significant one

### Amanda: "Cutting" is not a diagnosis

The presenting problem is "cutting." All that tells you is what the kid does when she's unhappy or stressed or angry or trying to make a point. It doesn't tell you what your job is. You may think, *Well, I have to get her to stop cutting*, but you don't. In fact, you don't have to make anything happen. Therapists get in trouble when they believe that it is their responsibility to make the bad thing stop. You may have to put safety measures in place to protect the child or teenager, but you don't have to make the cutting stop.

Amanda cuts when mom says mean things to her. She says that her mother's remarks make her mad, and then the cutting makes her feel better. That was it. A pat answer to a complex matter, and one that leaves no apparent opening for a larger conversation.

In situations like this, I sometimes start to think about "antidotes," as in *what could be an antidote to this behavior sequence of Amanda's?* Her behavior, and her thought process about it, struck me as very passive: *My mom hurts my feelings, so I hurt myself and then feel better. That's all there is to it.* The antidote to passivity is *activity*, so I begin to think about Amanda becoming *a more active agent* in her life, where she feels the greater power of agency than that of victimhood.

> I ask Amanda, "Do you ever *say anything* (activity) to your mom when she says something hurtful?"
>
> "No, she wouldn't listen." (passivity)
>
> "She might not. But some things are important to say even if no one listens. It's just important that you say them" (action).

I don't want Amanda learning to take action based on how she thinks the other person will respond to her – it makes it too contingent, which undermines the sense of agency and power it's supposed to generate. This is an important part of the therapy because from here, Amanda and I began talking about the different ways in which she thinks of and presents herself as being at the mercy of other people.

As a result, the diagnosis of **teen with self-harming tendencies** evolves into a more descriptive one of a **teen who defaults to passivity when threatened, then identifies as a victim, and then defends herself through passive-aggressive acts toward her mother**. The therapy is shaped around the idea of self-advocacy and shredding the notion that getting back at another, especially at great expense to yourself, could ever bring true emotional gratification and health. This part of the therapy – teaching Amanda that the position of *I am a victim* will never be as powerful or gratifying as one in which she is saying, *I am present and will hold you accountable for hurting me* – isn't all the therapy, but it is critical.

**Symptoms don't determine the course of therapy.**
**The *person* of your client does.**

# CHAPTER TWELVE

# The Macro

## The Therapy is in the Conversation: Moving Therapy Forward One Step at a Time

An intern of mine once asked me a terrific question about how one transitions from a general conversation with a teen in session to making an intervention. Giselle had said, "As soon as I say something that sounds even remotely like an intervention, the conversation just dies off. What can I do to keep a lively interaction going while still being able to address the issues that come up?"[1]

We can see, though, embedded in Giselle's question the reason why she and so many others struggle to have an impact on their young clients without making them spook: Giselle had asked *how one transitions from conversation to intervention* as if they were separate things. In my approach, the conversation becomes the *vehicle* of the therapy, the therapy (or intervention) being embedded within the conversation, not as a gimmick, nor a pre-planned strategy, but as an organic exchange between therapist and client, simply because the therapeutic opportunity becomes available and the therapist sees it. Here's an example:

> Sixteen-year-old Liam is talking with me during his therapy session the way he usually does – while walking around the office, playing tug-of-war with my dog, and complaining about his mother, his teachers, and his boss. Our conversations are a playful mix of banter, baseball talk, curiosity about me, exasperation with everyone else, some stuff about Liam, and snacking. I assume a more informal sitting position with Liam, because it seems to relax him, so my boots are on the table or my legs are looped over the side arm of my chair. I follow him around the office with my eyes and voice.
>
> Liam is a bully — at home mainly — but he projects a bully's demeanor by the way he walks and the ever-present scowl on his face. He doesn't think of himself that way, of course, and wonders why anyone would be

 DOI: 10.4324/9781003257080-12

hesitant to approach him. One day he's telling me about what he plans to do on Halloween. Too old to go trick or treating, Liam has decided to put up skeletons, skulls, oversized spiders and other props on his front lawn, and jump out at the little kids when they come for candy.

"Oh my God," I say, without looking at him, sipping my soda. "That is so mean."

"No it's not." he responds, making a face. "What are you talking about? Besides, it's Halloween – you're supposed to do that stuff."

"No," I say, calmly. I take another sip of my soda. "You're supposed to give them candy, not a heart attack."

"Well, I did it last year and no one complained." Liam says, as if that settles the matter.

I turn around in my chair and look at him. Now I'm the one making a face. "No one complained …?"

"Nope. Nobody."

"Of course no one complained. Every kid on your block is scared to even talk to you. Which one of them is going to complain?"

Liam stands there and looks at me.

I smile, and say warmly, "You're still surprised every time I mention people being intimidated by you. It's as if you have no idea …"

Liam shakes his head and goes back to throwing a pinkie ball against my wall.

As soon as Liam mentioned scaring the kids at Halloween, I was pretty sure I'd be able to find a way to make use of it somehow, to bridge it to something about him that was relevant to why we were meeting. Liam is a bully at home, too, and uses his physical size, volatile temperament, and oppositional nature to intimidate his mother, although he sees it differently. It is in that way I'm always "scouting" for some story or expression or comment to use as a springboard to a bigger conversation, a therapeutic conversation, by which I mean only that it is something that has meaning for the client. My client may or may not like what I said, but he remembers it.

Ideally, the conversation and the interventions (in this case, putting a light on Liam's need to relate through intimidation, as well as his denial of it) can't be easily teased apart; they're not something so distinct from each other that the client feels, *Oh, my therapist and I were having this funny conversation and then she had to get all serious on me* …. Rather, the two are part of a fluid therapeutic process, *a succession of words and moments that reach a tipping point*, minute or grand, resulting in or contributing to some intra-psychic or interpersonal shift. Good therapeutic conversations facilitate engagement, and it's through the engagement that something therapeutic happens.

**At its best, therapy is unscripted and serendipitous, but not un-orchestrated.**

## The conversation is the therapy

When a teenager's choices don't make obvious sense, remember that people never do things without a rationale – even if they don't know what that rationale is. Even crazy-seeming behaviors, such as self-destructive acts, have a purpose and are driven more by an emotional logic than any kind of rational logic, which actually has very little currency when we talk with kids about their "irrational behavior." Under the shade of your curiosity, however, and your respect for your client's behavior – even when not understood – sometime come stories out of which you and your client begin to make sense of choices that were previously indecipherable.

## Helping Markus to do the smart thing rather than striving to avoid feeling like a loser

Contrast these two responses in the context of working with school avoidance. I was the therapist assigned to seventeen-year-old Markus, who was living at the residential treatment center where I worked early in my career. Complaining vigorously about what he saw as blatant deficiencies in the teaching staff, Markus decided he was going to stop attending school.

Three or four days go by before Markus starts feeling the pain of having made a bad decision. He's lost his privileges of going off campus, of playing basketball in the gym after dinner, of hanging out casually with friends.

"What?" I asked him in session, seeing him agitated.

"I'm bored," he answered.

"I can see. I think you had a different outcome in mind."

"I don't know what I thought …"

"I think you were trying to make a point only to find out that no one is really listening. It doesn't feel good, I know."

"Maybe."

"Let's go there then, because right now it seems like you feel you'd be giving in if you went back to school. It doesn't have to mean that, it probably only means that to you, in your own head, no one else's. But I get it – if that's what you think *other* people are going to think, then you're not going to want to go back. Except – you do. Look, at worst, you made a miscalculation. No, actually, what would be worse is if you don't go back, even though it's what you want to do, because of worrying that if you did others will think you gave in and, in your words, are a loser."

That's what I did say, but I could have said this:

"You know, you say you want to graduate, and if want to meet your goals, you're going to have to figure out a way to do things you don't want to do in order to have freedom to do things you want to do," which is nothing more than a lecture disguised as a motivational speech.

**Kids who default to maladaptive behaviors in order to preserve their sense of pride often need encouragement to step outside that zone. Sometimes that means talking about and getting them to tolerate the uncomfortable but anticipated thought or emotion.**

Teenagers can get stuck when cornered with problems that pit their pride against their better judgment. We may not be teenagers anymore, but we're also not strangers to the feelings we had back then, and maybe still do:

- It's hard to change while everyone waits to see whether you do.
- It's hard to change if it's an adult's idea because now it's contaminated, even if you really liked it before.
- If someone else helps you with a problem, then it doesn't really count.
- Sometimes, being right is more important than doing the smart thing.

If you're working with a teenager who is making what appears to be irrational decisions, see if one of the sentiments/beliefs listed above might be the obstacle. You can be as direct as simply asking her, for instance, "Hey, I know that for some kids – and some adults, too – letting someone help them with a problem is worse than having the problem itself, and they won't do it. What about you? I wondered that when I heard you say earlier, 'I'll just figure it out myself ....'"

Or maybe your client has repelled any idea – good or otherwise – originating from an adult, and you see them handicapped by their rigidity because of their refusal to accept the one viable solution to a problem, the solution to which happens to have come from his stepfather.

"Are you really ...?" I might start out.

"Really what?"

"Really gonna pass on your stepdad's idea?"

"I'll figure something out."

"Henry, he's already figured it out for you. This problem can disappear."

Silence.

"What?" I'd ask.

"Nothing. I just don't want to … do that."

"Because it's his idea and not yours?"

"Because it's … I just don't think it's a good idea."

"This is the first time I've ever not believed what you've said. I think you'd rather go down with the ship than ever let your stepdad think that he was able to contribute something positive toward your life. How long are you going to hold his feet to the coals for having had the nerve to marry your mom?"

Henry looks up at me in a way that says, *I don't know … I don't want to feel that way anymore, but I can't stop.*

In this way, the conversation about Henry's reluctance to accept his stepfather's idea led to a larger conversation about his feelings regarding his parents' divorce, his mother's remarriage, his stepfather's "intrusion" into the family, and most consequential, perhaps, Henry's inability to shed a deep-rooted resentment toward his stepfather that he himself recognized as having long passed its expiration date.

## Helping Sylvie use her voice to speak up even if she's the only one who will hear it

I have known Sylvie since she was twelve years old and she's now a sophomore at a small liberal arts college in the northeast. Sylvie is personable, funny, insightful and loves therapy. She continues, however, to default to a victim type of role in her relationships with her parents and some friends, and regarding events in her life in which she feels she's been anything less than perfect. In this session, Sylvie is complaining that her father doesn't reach out to her to see how she's doing or to arrange a time to visit her on campus.

"Have you asked him about it?" I asked Sylvie, not as a challenge, but with curiosity. I knew her dad and thought it odd that he would have suddenly become so remote.

"No. He'd just yell at me and I'd end of feeling worse about myself."

There are a couple of different ways to go here with Sylvie. One is to respond very literally to what she just said – that were she to inquire about her father's seeming lack of interest, he would somehow lash out in response, making her feel bad about herself. But I'd gone there before several times, in an attempt to dislodge her from her victimhood in which she often saw aggression or persecution where there was none. It was an old go round, and I wanted to approach the issue from a different angle this time, one which circumvented the whole *What did he actually say that made you feel so bad (and was it really that bad)?* I responded by making the point that sometimes it's less important how someone responds to what you say than it is that you say it.

"Sylvie, you speaking up and asking your father why he hasn't reached out recently is really about *you*, not about what he'll say in response. The challenge and the growth for you here are *in speaking up for yourself without knowing how the conversation will go.*"

"What if he gets mad?"

"Then he gets mad. I think you can handle him being mad better than you can the resentment *you'll* feel from whatever reason you come up with to account for his lack of contact. Besides, your dad being mad at you *used* to crush you. I don't know that it has to anymore," I said, hinting at the maturation Sylvie exhibited over the past year that she had yet to recognize.

Sylvie did speak with her father and, to her surprise, found he didn't get mad and instead shared that he'd been wondering too why there was so little contact between them now. "I thought you were looking for some more privacy or space or something, now that you were in college," Sylvie told me he said to her, before adding, "I'm sorry, Sylvie, I was trying to be respectful, not distant." The two then wasted no time in setting up a lunch date for later that week and promised each other they'd speak up if something felt off instead of stewing on it silently.

When I asked Sylvie what she made of her father's reasoned and warm response, given her expectation that he'd yell at her, she just smiled and said, "Well maybe he didn't yell at me this time, but there's no saying about the next ...."

"Oh my god," I said, "what it takes to get you to shake off something you so want to believe is true ..." and Sylvie smiles at me. "But, seriously," I added, "another thing to think about here is whether there was something in the way you brought this issue up with your dad that made it easier for him to come forward with that more congenial response?"

"What's congenial mean?"

"You know, nice, agreeable."

"Oh, maybe. I don't think I had an attitude when I asked him. I just kind of asked him."

"There you go, then. You might not like hearing that you sometimes play a role in how your dad responds to you, but the good news about it is that you then have some measure of control over it, as well."

"I know, I know," Sylvie says. "My mom tells me that all the time."

I laugh. "Smart mom," I say.

### Helping Camila learn to speak to people, even if they're "assholes"

For the second time this month, seventeen-year-old Camila's father is an ass-hole and she's not talking to him.

"You need a second gear, Camila," I say.

"What do you mean?" she snipes.

"You need a gear for talking with people who you think are assholes. Cause sometimes you need to deal with them, like your dad."

"It won't do me any good to talk to that asshole."

"Look, you say you want to go to Cornell and that 'he took it away from you' by canceling plans to go up to the Open House. What if you said, 'Dad, this is important to me, and I know I blew the trip to Pitt (because she got high and missed her ride). But maybe you and I will be in a different place six months from now when I have to commit. Would you at least let me continue with the application and reschedule the tour?'"

"He's not going to change his mind," she says.

"*It's not only about him changing his mind*," I reply. "It's not even about *him*. It's about you being able to talk with people you're angry with in order to pursue something you need from them."

"I don't want to hear his point of view because he's wrong!!"

"Maybe he is, I don't know. The point isn't for either one of you to change the other person's mind. You want to see if he can leave open the possibility for seeing things differently in the future. Not to mention trying to stay connected to the guy – your dad – even though you think he is, as you say, an asshole."

Camila smiles when I say asshole.

## Helping Parker recognize that caring for relationships can be more important than being "right"

Sixteen-year-old Parker is an angry girl, negative and unpleasant in her attitude and hard for peers to like. Nothing satisfies her, and she's always mad at someone. Parker has withdrawn from her friends because she believes "they don't care" (that she's so depressed). "I mean, c'mon," she says, bitterly, "they don't even bother to ask me how I am anymore."

Well, when you think about it, "they don't care" can mean anything:

- It could mean that Parker's friends *have* asked her, but she doesn't remember because it doesn't suit the narrative she's created for herself.
- It could mean she expects more than is reasonable in her friendships; for instance, maybe in her friend group *no one* really asks anyone how they are unless it's obvious that something is wrong.
- It could also mean that she's become so negative and angry that her friends are hesitant to ask her how she is because they think she's going to get mad or lash out at them.
- Or it could mean exactly what she said, that her friends have stopped caring or never did from the start.

I ask Parker to tell me more about this and she relays an exchange she had with one of her friends in which her friend said that she never asks *anyone* how they are anymore because it's too much for her to deal with and she finds it overwhelming. "Basically, she's saying that she doesn't care and that I'm just one more person who's a burden to her. That's how it sounded to me."

*"That's how it sounded to me"* — this is a gift. It's a gift to a therapist because it gives me a platform from which I can, together with Parker, make a distinction between *how something sounds* and *what was actually said*. Parker saying *that's how it sounded to her* leaves open the possibility that it could have sounded different to someone else. I didn't have to insert that possibility myself (as in, *Do you think it just sounded that way to you?* which is sure to offend). Is she going to be interested in the difference between truth and perception? I don't know, but it's a potential starting place.

"Oh wow," I said, "that's interesting, because what I heard your friend say was something a little different ...." And then I wait to see what Parker's response is.

### If she says ...

*Well, I don't really care anymore.*

I respond with, *Wait, what changed? You're bailing on me. Is it because I said I heard something different from what you heard from your friend?*

*No. I'm just tired of talking about this …*

*Okay, but I'm still left feeling like you were hoping I'd just agree with you …. And what fun is that? (I'd add that only if I had a relationship with the girl that was playful, a little tongue-in-cheek.)*

**If she says …**

*Like what? What do you mean different?*

I'd say, *Like, I didn't hear her say that you and your problems specifically were a burden to her. What I heard her say was that she feels overwhelmed* anytime *one of her friends is struggling, so she just doesn't ask anyone anymore.*

**If she says …**

*No, I know she doesn't really care and that's fine ….*

I'd say, *Oh my god, Parker, don't go there. That's what a person says when they don't want something or someone to matter anymore but they still do have feelings about them. I know these people matter to you, and I think you just want to know that you still matter to them.*

## Helping Elena to scale back her judgmental, critical manner of relating

Elena loves to study serial killers. One day she is talking to me about one who lived in the last century. She says his name, and I look at her rather blankly. She says his name again, louder. I shrug and say, "Still doesn't ring a bell." "Are you kidding me!" she exclaims, practically yelling. Staring at me, she presses on: *"Do you really not know who he is?!!"* And so, looking at her disdain-ridden face while breaking into a gentle smile, I say, "You're looking at me like I'm a total loser …." Elena breaks into a big smile and laughs at herself for a moment. (Or maybe it was at me.)

This works as an intervention precisely *because* I'm not telling her to change anything about how she reacts to people who don't know things she thinks they should know. I'm not asking her why she felt a need to respond to me that way, and I'm not telling her that I thought she was being condescending — I don't have to; Elena gets it by my response, and because I'm not pushing back on her, she can join me in the bizarre humor of the moment – that is, her talking to me as if I'm an idiot – and reflect on herself just a bit. I'm sure I wasn't the first person to have said something to Elena about how judgmental she was, but I might have been the first person whose head she didn't bite off in response.

So, it's a year later and I'm sitting with Elena and she's telling me about a movie producer of high acclaim. I don't recognize the name, and say so. She looks at me and says, "Oh, you know, he's the one who did …." And I stare blankly, and she says, "He's done a bunch of other movies, too. Have you seen …? I slowly shake my head no. "Oh, okay," Elena says, "well, whatever, the point is I love his work." And I smile and say, "Oh my god, Elena, that was so easy. Remember what you said to me last year when I didn't know who your serial killer was?"

"Yeah, I've gotten better," Elena says, smiling, not skipping a beat.

## Using joining and indirect feedback and capitalizing on the phenomenon of identification to prompt Sidney's unconscious process of self-transformation

Here's another girl, a few years younger than Elena, who also was in the market for better self-awareness about the aggressive and un-inviting manner in which she came off to others. Everything about the tone and tempo of our conversations, however, was different from the more measured conversations Elena and I shared. The other big difference was that Elena thrived on the direct feedback she got from me in her therapy, whereas Sidney, who related almost exclusively through arguments and tantrums, needed a more finessed delivery of feedback around which she wouldn't be able to organize a defensive stance.

Sidney, thirteen and astonishingly bright, was truly one of the most entertaining kids I can ever remember working with. She was funny and insightful, but also impulsive and highly excitable. Years before I started seeing her, Sidney had been diagnosed as being on the autism spectrum. She was highly attention-seeking and didn't read social cues well. She also had a lot of difficulty respecting other people's personal space and boundaries. As a result, Sidney had trouble making and keeping friends, something about which she'd grown very dismissive ("I don't need friends!").

My conversations with Sidney were always a lively mix of banter, storytelling, fantasy, play acting, and offhanded discussions about any number of things going on in her life. She was startlingly candid about her problems with the kids at school, as well as about being the black sheep in a family that vacationed only in places where they could go off the grid and hike for hours at a time. Sidney, you see, hated any kind of physical activity and considered herself "addicted" to electronics. Sidney would also mock her older sister for her willingness to oblige family rules and household responsibilities, and generally spent her time complaining.

I was reviewing this case with a psychology intern who was learning to work with teenagers and showed her a video clip of a session which included this exchange between Sidney and myself:

ME:     "You love to keep people guessing!" I said to Sidney.
S:       "Of course I do! I want to be in charge!"
ME:     "What do you like about being in charge?"
S:       "Don't you like being in charge?"
ME:     "It depends. I don't know, I don't think so. I don't like feeling as if I'm in charge of *other people*. But I do think that you like it!"
S:       "Of course!" Sidney says. "Then I can manipulate them! That's how I get what I want!"

"Would you say anything to Sidney afterward," my intern asks, "about how she comes off to other people. Like how aggressive she is, and how others aren't going to like it? I mean it seems she could use some insight on her behavior ..."

The short answer to this is, *No*. I shared with my intern that I would not have followed this exchange up with anything regarding how aggressively Sidney comes off to people. For one thing, I said, she had just unabashedly (rather proudly even) told me about how she liked to be in charge of other people so that she can manipulate them. I'd worry that speaking up critically so soon after hearing this would make Sidney regret having told me (Well, if *that's* what you're going to do with the things I tell you about, forget it!). I'd have felt as if I had betrayed her, inviting me to tell me about herself only to return the volley with condemnation. Moreover, I'd have hijacked the conversation in order to "educate" my client or make a point, and that's one of the ways in which we lose kids. It's important to not turn everything into a lesson.

This doesn't mean I gave Sidney the impression that what she was doing was okay, or that I liked the way she interacted with others. But rather than lecturing her about being aggressive, I would just express my own, unadorned reaction to her stories about dealing with teachers, classmates, siblings, her parents, saying things like:

- "You did *what?*"
- "No way."
- "You're kidding, right?"
- "You said that to your teacher?"
- "Wait, what's weird about your sister wanting to do the dishes?

In addition, there was no reason for me to believe that Sidney was interested in hearing any kind of direct feedback about her interpersonal style which, if true, meant she wouldn't have been *ready* to hear it, which means she probably would have become very defensive with me, a dynamic we had yet to encounter in our relationship. Sidney loved our conversations, and I thought if I could use them to foster a *better emotional awareness in general*, as well as a pleasure in having conversations in which there was no manipulation or need for either one of us to be "in charge," then Sidney might be able to expand her repertoire of interpersonal behaviors to include some new, healthier ones.

Another way that I intervened with Sidney with an eye toward helping her become less reactive and more pro-social was to appreciate as fertile soil for emotional skills other parts of her personality that few ever saw and even fewer recognized. In my office and in our conversations, Sidney could be herself, all of it, not just the parts she showed to the kids at school or her family members. I got to see her clever wit, her spot-on assessments of other people, her discerning judgment regarding what people didn't like about her, and her utter transparency – the latter always an appealing quality in a person. I even got to see the ways in which she could be thoughtful, empathic, even kind, and I let her know just how lovely that was.

I never needed to tell Sidney to be nicer to people or to stop mocking her sister. Had I done that, I would have become just one more in a herd of adults telling her to stop doing behaviors which, at the time, aligned with how she was choosing to show up in the world. Sidney stopped on her own, part of it having to do with wanting my approval but a bigger part was her own wish to temper the more impulsive parts of herself in order to align with her refurbished self-concept in relation to how she wanted to show up in her life now.

What I think happened was that therapy showed Sidney another, less aggressive, less domineering way to be in the world and to relate with others. More important was that it showed her she was capable of doing it and capable of enjoying it as well. Our therapeutic relationship served as a bridge to the larger world: *You can do this and have this in here with me, so therefore you can do this and have this out there with others.*

Sidney gradually stopped whining for attention and pulled back hard on the meltdowns, opting for a few cross words and retirement to her bedroom. She began expressing some warmth toward her family of hikers, her humor having changed from a biting sarcasm to an exaggerated and humorously woeful resignation to her fate. She felt less anxious around people, making her less reactive in their company, although she still struggled with her peers. I think it's always difficult to get others in your immediate social environment to accept that you've changed, especially for middle school children who lock in pretty hard to stereotypes and reputations. My hope was that she'd be better able to capitalize on her more evolved self once she got to high school, with its larger and more mature crowd of kids.

## Talk with your teenage client about the empathy she doesn't feel for others.

Thirteen-year-old Danielle exploits her mother's wish for the two of them to get along and mocks her mother's tentativeness whenever she tries talking to her.

ME:      "My god, Danielle, you punish your mom because in your opinion she doesn't answer your texts quickly enough. But you don't see that she's afraid to say anything without running through it in her mind several times for fear that she'll say the wrong thing and make everything worse."

D:      "I can't believe you think she's afraid of me!"

ME:      "She's afraid of saying the wrong thing and ruining the little bit of connection you two still have. But, I think you like that she's afraid."

D:      (Sneering) "Why would I like it?"

ME:      "Because it allows you to control the relationship. Or at least to feel as if you do."

Danielle stares at me.

ME:      "I can't think of a relationship you've ever told me about where you feel like the other person is your equal."

Danielle again sneers at me.

ME:      "I don't know …. What feels so powerful to you just sounds so lonely to me."

I wouldn't have expected Danielle to respond to my last comment; it was only something I wanted her to hear. I believe that when kids feel that we're waiting for them to respond to an emotionally poignant remark, they distance themselves from it and the remark loses its power. Here, I simply held out my hands and raised my shoulders in a very slight shrug and, after waiting a few moments, gently moved off to a different topic.

It would be the first of many exchanges about empathy, or Danielle's lack thereof, that Danielle and I would have over the course of therapy. She left abruptly, however (see Danielle in Chapter 15, Avoiding Power Struggles…), so I don't know what impact these brief conversations about empathy might have had, especially in a character so intent on subduing others with her aggressiveness. Had I had more time with Danielle, I would have expanded the conversation about empathy to include times where its absence on her part might have affected her negatively in some way that she wouldn't have been able to avoid recognizing. I also would have brought the issue front and center, in its most powerful form, which would be the places it does and doesn't show up in the therapeutic relationship, on both our parts.

## Making a point, plain and simple

Sometimes, making a point to my client is exactly want I *want* to do. And only that.

In this case, my point to fifteen-year-old Shay was that what she so casually dismissed in her life was, in fact, worthy of attention. Shay started coming for therapy at the behest of her mom and school guidance counselor. In addition to having problems keeping up with her in-school as well as homework assignments, Shay was having trouble maintaining friendships. Shay also spoke rudely to teachers and admin, offering only blank stares when asked what was bothering her. Her worst behavior, though, Shay saved for her mother, cursing at her directly and refusing to accommodate any of her requests for help around the house, toning down her attitude, avoiding picking fights, and cleaning up after herself.

I'd seen Shay already for a couple of weeks before this brief exchange came up in a session. She was telling me just how rude she'd been toward her mother the night before.

"I know it doesn't bother you," I said. "It should, but I understand that it doesn't. You're never going to come in here and say, *'Janet, I need to do something about how I talk to my mom.'*

Shay laughed.

"So," I added, when she's thought I was all done, "who *should* I be talking to about that?"

Shay looked up at me suddenly and, unsure of how to respond, said only, "I don't know …"

"Me neither," I replied, smiling, moving off the topic of her disrespect before she got defensive. The thing is, I'm not really expecting Shay to tell me who else I should discuss this problem with. What I'm doing is making the point that her manner of speaking to her mom is *worthy of a larger conversation*, and hinting at the fact that, at some point, if she and I couldn't get a handle on it, I probably *would* have to include others (namely, her parents) in my work with her in order to get her to curtail her impulsive aggressiveness toward adults and boost her capacity (and desire for) emotional self-regulation.

## When your own feelings get in the way …

A lovely fifteen-year-old girl who I came to adore sits in front of me in session telling how her dad calls her a "fat ass," among other ridiculously insulting names.

> Before I could respond, Jillian says to me, "It's okay, he just doesn't want me to be fat like he was as a kid …. You know, my parents didn't get a book about raising kids when they had me (clearly mimicking words they've said), so he's just doing the best he can."
>
> "He could do better," I insist.
>
> "Maybe," says Jillian, "but it's okay. My mom tells him to shut up, if she's around, but he usually doesn't say it in front of her."
>
> "Wow, Jillian" I said, "for real you are so kind and forgiving, and you're a delight to sit and talk with. I hope you dad knows what a gem of a kid he has in you …."

It can be tempting to appropriate and voice the outrage you think a client of yours should have toward someone who mistreats or disrespects them. But it's not helpful to take up someone else's umbrage; after all, it's *theirs*. If your client wants a louder voice, then you can move forward by helping her to develop one. And if she doesn't, then therapy is the inquiry into whether that's because of conflict avoidance or complacency or feeling deserving of the insults.

Or maybe, in this case with Jillian, *I'm* the one who's too sensitive. Maybe my beliefs about how family members should communicate is so skewed, and I've yet to learn that this is another way for families to relate – yes, through sarcastic banter and snide remarks and nasty jibes – and that while I may not like it, it's not my battle to pursue.

I also imagine that my fondness for Jillian fueled a countertransference, maybe an unconscious rescue fantasy. You see, her father, though not psychotic, was seriously paranoid and severely restricted his daughter's contact with the world outside of the home. It was amazing he let her go to therapy at all; in fact, my first (and only) meeting with him felt like a job interview for the Secret Service. I found the man quite likable despite all this, but I knew he spent hours every day trying to indoctrinate his daughter with conspiracy theories and Apocalypticism which, for the most part, Jillian resisted. Thus, my urge, I suppose to be her *cavalry*.

Jillian and I never got to finish working together, however. Her parents decided to move to another, less suburban community where the cost of living was lower. Jillian was devastated, her needs once again unaccounted for.

## Letting your teen clients learn by watching you.

Sometimes as a therapist you can worry so much about what you're doing and saying that you forget how much you can influence your clients just by your presence and the way you show up in the therapeutic relationship. Our young clients especially watch us, and seeing us demonstrate patience, acceptance, flexibility, humility, candor, and an easy and kind humor can be extraordinarily therapeutic. I find opportunities to share with my clients how I have negotiated situations of conflict, embarrassment, self-consciousness, tension, and criticism. I might tell them how I handled bad news or when I found it hard to extend an apology but did it anyway.

Doing group therapy with a co-therapist offers opportunities for clients to witness our interpersonal skills (and deficits) in action, for example, when we might respectfully disagree with our co-therapist, or move in deftly to bail her out of an awkward moment. Several years ago, I worked closely alongside a colleague, Kristen de Marco[2], doing equine-assisted therapy with a group of girls from a residential center for foster kids. Some of the moments I remember most vividly were of those girls transfixed by Kristen's ability to have easy conversations about hard things, to be inexpressibly kind, to demonstrate profound degrees of empathy and compassion, and to be playful and find small moments of joy in otherwise dire circumstances. It was a masterclass in the role of modeling and creating reference experiences in the therapeutic relationships we form with kids.

## Notes

1  This material first appeared in the article, Speak easy: Keeping it real with your teen clients, *Psychotherapy Networker*, March/April 2017.
2  Founding and Executive Director of Gateway HorseWorks, a non-profit organization that incorporates horses in the mental health treatment of all individuals and particularly those in our more marginalized and vulnerable communities. Kristen is also an EAGALA® Certified Equine Specialist.

# CHAPTER THIRTEEN

# The Micro

## Timing

In therapy as in comedy, timing is everything. In much the same way that a stand-up comedian reads her audience in order to tailor the delivery to the mood and "personality" of the audience as a whole, so does a therapist need to read her client in order to time and sequence interventions to be as effective as possible.

But being the inexact science and the art form that it is, the practice of psychotherapy continues to be compromised by the gap between what we understand about its process and our ability to distill that understanding into the words and actions that will most effectively and efficiently move it forward. Reducing theory into the right words, expressions, interventions, and actions has no formula and no template, and then there's the whole timing thing. A lot of us came out of graduate school well versed in theories about the human change process but short on the actual skill set to make them happen.

This chapter describes some of the more nuanced clinical sensibilities related to timing, many of which can serve to elevate a therapist's game. For instance, with some teenagers you want to strike while the iron's hot: An issue comes up, and you hop on it or it's gone. With others, it's too much too soon: You hop on it, and *they're* gone. What follows are examples of the different responses from clients, interaction styles, defenses, affect states, and needs you can glean from the session that will guide you in terms of timing, as well as how best to incorporate those insights into the therapy.

DOI: 10.4324/9781003257080-13

# Timing and bridging conversations

## Ian and his poor approach to conflict resolution

Ian is a sixteen-year-old boy with bright red hair and a temper to match. He is trying very hard to be a young thug, but his sensibilities sometimes get in the way. He's one of those kids you think is never going to show up, but there he is, week after week. If I were to have asked him what he wanted out of therapy, he'd look at me like I was crazy to even think that he comes to therapy for any purpose of his own. *Don't I understand that he's here only because his mom makes him come?* Ian's face would say. So I never asked him. But he kept coming. Once, I inadvertently wrapped up the session a little early. "There are still two minutes left!" he alerted me.

With Ian, therapy takes place in short bursts – an exchange of words here, a look there. They are moments when I can ever so briefly hold out a mirror of his humanity to his face, or its ugly opposite, and he is forced to recognize his compassion, his lack of it, and his inner conflict between the two.

One week, Ian texts me shortly before his session to tell me he's not coming. He gives no reason. He comes for the following session but walks in without saying hello – unusual for him. He's making a point, but I don't know what the point is that he wants me to get. "Hey, what's up?" I ask, casually. "Last week you bailed on me and this week no hello." In response, Ian just laughs and starts playing with my dog.

I don't address it again – this time. I don't because I want Ian to know that it's okay to acknowledge or respond to something I say about the therapy or about our relationship without him then becoming trapped in a long or deep conversation about it. I also know that had I asked him *Why*, as in why he'd canceled or why he came in without saying hello, he'd have just said, "I don't know" and dismissed it as one of those stupid therapy inquiries about something unimportant. I'll have wasted an opportunity that could be more productive later.

We go on with the session as it is and I wait for a "bridge" (to this topic) to come up again, later, another time, another day, when he'll be less defensive. There will be more distance from it, and he'll remember that I didn't pounce on it the first time it came up.

Any one of the following are potential bridges:

Ian tells me that he was supposed to go to his grandparents' house for dinner but decided to stay home at the last minute.

"Hey, that's kind of what you did here! What's up with that?"

Ian describes going back home after an argument with his mother and deciding to give her the silent treatment.

ME: "Oh, maybe that's what you were doing that day you came in and didn't say hello or anything …. But you didn't seem mad so I guess I missed the point."

I: "No, I wasn't giving you the silent treatment. I was just thinking about other things …"

ME: "Wait, have you ever given me the silent treatment here, and I didn't pick up on it?"

I: "No."

ME: "Okay, what about other things I haven't picked up on? Tell me, what do I miss?"

Ian just smiles and shakes his head.

This entire exchange has a playful lilt to it. Ian can tell that I don't really think he ever gave me the silent treatment, but it gives us an opportunity to talk about any number of things: missed cues, making points through action, etc.

Now I get a little more serious and a little softer in my voice. I ask Ian,

ME: "What about that day you didn't come? What happened there?"

I: "I got in a fight with my mom and was pissed off and didn't want to come, that's all."

ME: "Who were you punishing – me or her?"

Ian looked up at me and held my eye contact for a long moment. "I don't know. Nobody?" he says.

I smile ever so slightly and leave it there. That's about as long a conversation about something serious Ian can handle; any longer and he gets self-conscious about talking with me in a way that suggests that there is therapy taking place. And it was enough anyway. The point isn't so much what happened then – as in, the day he argued with his mother – but in his embryonic awareness of the dynamics taking place between him and the people he interacts with.

## Timing and patience

### Max and his displaced anger

Let's say you want to address a client's anger at his mother, which seems displaced and out of proportion to what you now know about their relationship. Asking about this directly often leads to unsatisfactory exchanges that only highlight your client's defensiveness and your misfire. I think a better way to address this is by waiting patiently for a conversation you and your client are having down the road some, for example, one in which you notice your client being particularly forgiving of someone – a friend, relative, maybe his father. It doesn't have to be a big "noble" gesture, just a hint of where he gives someone some slack. You're looking only for a way to connect the current conversation with the one from a few weeks ago where he lambasted his mom.

"That's nice what you said to your dad," I say to Max. "You were very patient. It seems different with your mom, though ..." leaving the implicit question unspoken. Asking why sometimes shuts down a thought process that would otherwise carry on for a few moments. In this case, Max might be wondering to himself why. He doesn't have to say anything to me about it for it to be an important moment. He could be having that moment by himself.

Carrying this forward, maybe in a next session you pick up on another remark he makes about his mom. Let's say, for instance, he says something about how she never apologizes, or how she never thinks she's wrong. There's your second bridge.

"Well, that could be why it's harder to be patient with her ..." I remark. You give an empathic interpretation. In other words, you're saying that you understand why he does it that way; you might have done the same.

## What *not* to say here:

*"Do you think that's why you get so mad at your mother or have a hard time being patient with her?"*

Why not? Because it's obvious that *you* think that's why he gets so mad at her, so it would feel to Max like some kind of contrived question to which you already know the answer, or think you know. Kids hate answering questions posed in this way. It's patronizing.

The idea here with Max is to eventually pick up all these little threads and weave them into a conversation where *he* would be the first of the two of you to mention his impatient manner of speaking to his mother. It might be something like this, "I don't know, sometimes I just get so mad at her .... I know I shouldn't, but it just ... she just gets to me." And an understated, "Tell me more," from you at that moment can be enough to advance this issue forward, where you're both looking at it from the same side of the fence.

## Sasha's dismissal of Mother's Day as a proxy for her mom

Thirteen-year-old Sasha took every opportunity to let her mother know how angry she was with her. Some of it seemed warranted, but a lot of it seemed overly righteous, as in Sasha wanting only to make a point that her mother was failing at her most important job.

As a client Sasha was very defensive, pushing back on anything suggesting she was other than justified in her behaviors or attitudes. I'm looking for something in our conversation that would allow me to address her righteousness and antipathy toward her mom without her feeling attacked, and I find it in a discussion about Mother's Day.

> "Ugh," said Sasha. "On Mother's Day my mom set up this stupid scavenger's hunt for us (Sasha and her two siblings) where we all had to run around finding things."
>
> "What was the matter with the hunt?" I asked.
>
> "It was just excessive," Sasha replied.
>
> "As in, too big a deal?"
>
> "Yes, totally. And too long. I mean, it's not *that* big a holiday ..." she added, with an edge in her voice.

Mother's Day. Perfect. But I wasn't going to hop on it yet, given the edge in Sasha's voice and her intent on pitching the holiday as not *that* important. I figured that had I challenged her then with such questions as, *You don't think Mother's Day is important?* or *What do you mean, not that big a holiday?* Sasha would have been all too ready to push back. We'd never have returned successfully to the topic again.

Instead, I wait for another time, maybe a week later, maybe three. The important thing to bear in mind is that *when a kid is making a point to diminish the importance of something you think she knows is important, it might be better to be patient and wait.*

Two weeks later I hear Sasha scoff at the idea of going trick or treating.

> "It's so stupid," she says, dismissively. "Sure, let me dress up in a costume and go ask for candy ..." There we go, I'm thinking – that's it right there.
>
> "You don't like too many of these holidays, do you?" I say. "It's kind of like that whole Mother's Day thing ..." And so, the topic is back in the conversation but unobtrusively, and hopefully in a way that Sasha might be able to tell me what it is about Mother's Day that makes her so dismissive about it. "Talk to me more about what bothered you that day, and why Mother's Day didn't deserve to be *that* big a holiday. I always wondered about that ...."

With a different teenager, one with whom I enjoyed a friendly and unguarded relationship, I might have handled it entirely differently. I might have gone into the Mother's Day thing right away, after Sasha had first mentioned it not being *that big* a holiday. "What? Mother's Day not important?" I'd have said, smiling. "Do you know that Mother's Day ranks number one for the most phone calls made in a day, for the entire year!"

## Timing and scouting for opportunities to carry forward a conversation thread

"How come you're always correcting your mom?" I ask fourteen-year-old Sammie, who is sitting next to her mother. "It's like you walk around with a red pen all the time. You call her out on these little things that don't matter but make it seem that you want to make a point."

"I guess ..." Sammie replies.

"Do you do it with anyone else"

"No," she replies, like, that was a stupid question.

"Good," I say. "You definitely don't want to be *that girl*."

The three of us laugh at this – me, Sammie, and Sammie's mom.

Again, "I guess ..." says Sammie.

"No. You *really* don't want to be her!"

That's just the first of a series of interventions that brings this teenager's attention over to her tendency to criticize or judge others. I leave it there for now and wait, scouting for a next opportunity. I'd be looking for some reference to a situation where a person, or even group of people, passes judgment on another. It could be in a Netflix episode, or something that happened at lunch in school, or something Sammie witnesses at the show barn where she rides horses. It might come a session or two or more later, and I'd see if there was a way to use it to revisit our earlier conversation about her and her red pen and keep it "alive."

One day Sammie starts telling me about some of the older girls at the barn and how they talk behind other girls' backs. "I'm sure they talk about me too."

"What kinds of things do they say?" I ask.

"They all have opinions about whose horse isn't going well and why, and what that rider should do differently, and why she isn't winning as much as they are .... It's really annoying."

"Oh god it's like they all have red pens!" I say. Sammie looks up at me and laughs. "*They're* those girls!" I add.

151

I let Sammie finish telling me about her story and decide to leave things there for now. I wasn't getting the sense that Sammie was uncomfortable with or even very aware of her own tendency to be judgmental, so using this exchange to address the issue would have been premature. I'd come back to it, and now with it having come up twice in two different contexts, it would even be easier to spot opportunities to do so or open up one of my own.

Two weeks later, Sammie is telling me about an incident at her barn where some of the girls started bragging about how little they ate.

"Yeah, they actually managed to 'drop' the size of the britches they just bought for the horse show next month," Sammie says.

"Wow, this stuff doesn't change," I reply. "The kids in my barn were doing the same thing fifty years ago."

"Ever since I've been at that barn I've gotten really judge-y myself. I always feel like I'm not good enough."

"For whom? For what?" I ask.

"I don't know … myself?" Sammie answers. "I don't know. But I know I feel better when I can go home and then get on my sister's case about something …"

"Or your mom's?"

"Yeah, or my mom's."

"You don't have to carry that red pen home, Sammie," I tell her. "It probably does make you feel better in the moment, when you're telling your sister or your mom about something they did wrong. But you've shared with me enough about yourself that I don't think it feels good to you afterward. Leave it behind and let me help you find a different way to deal with the drama at the barn. Believe me, I'm only too familiar with it."

Does this have anything to do with Sammie's presenting problem, her depression? I couldn't imagine that it doesn't. People who feel good in general feel good about themselves, and if they are feeling good about themselves, they're not walking around with red pens. They're more inclined to help the people around them feel better, not worse. We help kids leave depression behind, or anxiety or insecurity, not by talking about depression but by talking about their lives in the broadest sense, finding the threads that support the symptoms, and deconstructing them right there, in the micro, in the stories about barns and dance studios and school lunch tables.

## Don't Overstay Your Welcome

Many parents get in the habit of "staying too long at the party," so to speak, trying to get every drop of conversation out of a moment where their teen happened to be chatty. It's like they're worried they won't see that again for a while, so they grab it and hang on. Sometimes hanging on means staying silent but expectant when the teen pauses, introducing an awkward moment in what had been a pretty good back and forth. Game over.

Therapists sometimes will do the same, for the same reason. We fare much better though when we're mindful about *moving off a topic as soon as we notice that we have lost our client's interest in it.* It never helps to try to extend it, or get in a few more words, or reinforce a point. When teens are done with a conversation, they're done, and they look done as well, so trying to prolong it tells them you're not doing a good job of reading the room and respecting their experience. There are also kids who will feel relieved to learn that their therapist won't drag out a conversation they don't want to have — that way, they won't always have to worry about finding an "exit strategy" out of them and, as a result, are freer to listen to what you're saying to them.

It's different though with kids who always scoot off topics as soon as it sounds as though you're trying to bring a more meaningful conversation forward. In such cases, it's usually more productive to say something about that, without making it sound as if you're telling them that they *can't* scoot away anymore. Laying down a rule like that – essentially a prohibition against their natural, defensive behavior – is too controlling, and will result in power battles and miserable interactions. Instead, you can point out what you observe – empathically, non-challengingly – and see if that, along with the heightened self-consciousness it will bring about in the teen, moves the dial. Here are good and not-so-good examples of how to comment:

**Not-so-good:**

**Therapist**: "I think you're trying to avoid talking about your feelings regarding going away to school in the fall. Every time it comes up, you change the subject. Don't you think you should be talking about it though? You leave in just four months."

**Better:**

**Therapist**: "Hey, what's with the change of topic whenever college comes up? Something we should talk about?

Figuring out what to say in therapy and when to say it is hard enough with teenagers who want to be sitting with you and talking about their mental health. It becomes appreciably harder when you're sitting with a teenager who doesn't. Let's go there next.

CHAPTER FOURTEEN

# Avoiding Power Battles with Teenagers in Therapy

*Once you give up control, you gain the power to influence.*

Adolescent therapy is a fertile soil for power battles between therapists and their young clients, but not for a moment do I believe that it's because teens are irrepressibly defiant or controlling. Many factors contribute to this, from the dynamic of *You can't make me*, in cases where therapy is foisted upon an unwilling teen, to the sensitive nature of therapy itself where clients and therapists both feel a range of strong emotions, to manifestation of transferences and counter-transferences or reactions that can result in either party feeling too vulnerable or self-conscious or manipulated. It also doesn't help that, for many teens, therapists are stand-ins for authority figures, an envoy of their parents or some other agent of control. Wrestling matches to control the direction of therapy, its relative importance to the teen, and the narrative, as well as therapy's other dimensions show up among even the most eager and healthy of teen clients and their therapists, as the dance of sway and influence, reserve, and circumspection unfurls.

Some of the worst battles take place when therapists have a goal in mind for a client and a plan for therapy, but don't feel as though the client values what they are offering. Sometimes these goals are shaped out of the therapist's anxiety, and not the client's interest in changing. An example would be a therapist who is unnerved by her client's high-risk behaviors and yields to her own felt need to get the client to stop them. The anxiety might be enough to make it hard for that therapist to shift her approach from one of frustration to one of curiosity, where she might ask her client, "You know, the more I offer, the less useful I feel. How am I missing the mark here?" That one shift, however, can make all the difference in the world, because instead of saying what amounts to a twist on that old parent line, *I know you better than you know yourself*, it says, *Tell me what I need to understand in order to work with you in ways you'll find helpful.*

Fortunately, with all the attention on youth mental health and the broader dialogue it has enabled among children, teenagers, and young adults, kids from all these demographics are more actively seeking out mental health services than ever before. Young people who would never have wanted to set foot in a therapist's office are more comfortable coming forward to address their depression, anxiety, challenges with friends or their insecurities, and fewer are the ones who put up a fight at the door. Nonetheless, therapists still find themselves in tricky clinical situations that feel like land mines, a three card Monty game, or middle school all over again. Here are several examples of side-stepping and otherwise navigating clinical hazards.

## Gamey Teens

### Lena: The girl who weaponized "confidentiality"

I am sitting with fourteen-year-old Lena and her two mothers. Lena is the queen of opposition and makes life extremely difficult for her moms. I'm working with the family unit while a different therapist is working with Lena individually – not my preferred way but that's how the case came to me. Lena has been trying hard all session to disparage me and prevent me from having any influence on her parents.

I ask Lena what she and her therapist are doing in their individual work.

"Therapist–client confidentiality," is all she replies, smug and resolute.

"What are you talking about?" I ask. It sounds like I'm playing dumb here, but I'm really just pushing back on her idea that therapist–confidentiality is a good enough reason for her to keep me in the dark.

"Whatever my therapist and I talk about is confidential," Lena replies, tilting her head up, as if she's won something.

**Unproductive response #1:**

"Well, technically you "own" the privilege, so you can tell me anything you want."

This is somewhat legalistic and formal and forces Lena to come up with another "legitimate" reason, undoubtedly pissing her off in the process. She's not ready to just say "I don't want to because I'm being difficult and playing with you," so you're forcing her hand – never a good move. Likely she'll just retort with, "What if I don't want to tell you anything?"

**Unproductive response #2:**

"Well, that's true. Okay."

Having taken Lena's comment at face value, you now have no way to challenge Lena's noncompliance.

**What I said:**

"I'd rather you just say you don't want to tell me, instead of talking about all that confidentiality stuff."

"I don't want to tell you," Lena replies.

I smile now and say, "I like that better."

"I do too," she says, with the smallest of smiles. And I simply smiled back, a small one, before looking away.

What you *don't* want to do here is tack onto the end of this exchange something like, "Good" or "Okay, now we're on the same page" or "So what did you guys work on/talk about?" All this will do is force Lena to recant in the wake of her brief acquiescence.

Besides, you've made your point, and that's the important thing. *What Lena and her therapist talk about isn't important.* What *is* important is your effort to secure, in a brief exchange like that, something authentic from which the therapeutic relationship can gain traction.

In the following session, Lena's biological mom describes how Lena had bitten her the night before and gave her a black eye. Lena plays with her phone as this is happening.

I turn to Lena. "I cannot believe you still have your phone."

"Why do you say that?" she asks.

"Because it's beyond me that you could clobber your mom like that and still have phone privileges. I don't even know who I should be talking to – you or your mom."

"You're supposed to be my advocate," Lena challenges.

"I'm on everybody's side here," I respond.

"You're supposed to be unbiased." Lena tries again to unseat me.

"Yes and my unbiased opinion is this: you biting your mom is just not cool."

I turn toward the two mothers sitting in the room with us and say, "My god your daughter makes you work very hard." It's my way of referencing the unrelenting push back and other challenges Lena fills her relationships with. In response, Lena belches.

## Payton: The girl who refused to speak

Payton's mother told me that therapy would be a hard sell, and I told her not to worry, to just get her daughter to the session and I'd take it from there. If Payton were to swear up and down that she wasn't going to speak, I encouraged her mom to tell her, "That's fine, take it up with Janet."

Payton did get to the scheduled appointment, along with both parents and her younger sister *and* her grandmother, to whom she was figuratively and literally attached. She had her armed wrapped around grandma's neck as if she were being rescued from the shoals of a storm-tossed beach. When her parents said, "Okay, Payton, we need to get started. Let go of grandma and she'll wait outside," Payton was a no-go. She didn't even say anything. She just closed her eyes and held onto her grandmother even more tightly. Payton is fourteen.

"It's okay, there's no problem," I said finally. "Let's *all* go sit down." I figured I could make that work more easily than I could get Payton to separate from her grandmother. Besides, why shouldn't her grandmother be there, if she were this important to Payton? But before anyone was even seated, Payton's grandmother had disentangled herself from Payton and, in a far sterner voice than the parents had used, said, "Payton, that's enough. You're not eight years old. I'm leaving with Heidi (Payton's younger sister) and will see you afterward."

Payton watched the beginning part of the session with a simulated bored face. It was clear she wasn't speaking so I never tried to engage her. I didn't even direct any questions her way. Occasionally, though, while talking with her parents, I would ask her a quick yes or no side bar question, such as, "What your mom said, was that on target?" I'd wait three or four seconds and, if there was no response from Payton, I'd go right back to whomever I had been talking with. No big deal.

Sometimes Payton would answer with a word or a nod, but most times she wouldn't, choosing instead to stare back at me blankly. I saw this as Payton's invitation to play her version of the principle of least interest: *Who, between the two of us, wants Payton to speak more than the other?*

In cases like these, where the teenager doesn't speak, there is always the question of whether it's because of a skill deficit, severe family conflict wherein the teen is afraid of using her voice, a longstanding depression that has led to apathy and hopelessness, or something else. Martha Straus[1] points out that kids who don't talk in therapy often have had a significant disruption in normal development and feel un-empowered and disconnected from others. But with Payton, it was a "something else"; this girl was playing with us, evident in her puckish smile, impish eyes, and imperial manner.

Of course, the more I heard from Payton's parents about her refusal to join in family activities, her physical altercations with her younger sister, and her dismissive regard for all adults, the stronger became Payton's wish to comment. I made a couple of easy "on ramps" into the conversation for her to do so, for example, turning briefly to Payton so that she might clarify something simple her mother had said (e.g., "Is that the same friend you mentioned before?") or to answer an easy question ("Wait, Payton, is your mom talking about last year?"). This way Payton's terse comments could be gradually incorporated into the conversation without it looking as if she suddenly "changed her mind." And because her entry was graduated and subtle, it also reduced the chances that her parents would make a remark about it (e.g., "So you finally decided to join us!" or "Nice of you to show up!") which, in turn, would cause her to retreat.

By the time this first session was over, we'd covered a lot of ground, and I could see how Payton was using her silence at home as a way of controlling her parents and sister. Her willingness to participate in anything was currency, and she doled it out sparingly. This part of her personality alternated with a very regressed, child-like part in which she would deflect, perseverate, deny, and lay blame.

Payton now comes every other week for therapy, albeit with her grandmother in tow. It was a deal she cut with her parents. "Fine with me," I told them. "Esther could be terrifically helpful. I'll be glad to have her there."

And I *was* glad to have Esther there in the sessions with Payton and me. It was through her that I found out Payton's parents were feeling too battered by the unrelenting defiance and recalcitrant attitude of both their two daughters to put up much resistance, until it became too much to bear.

"Does the situation where the two girls are pummeling each other count as one of those situations?" I asked Esther. Payton laughed out loud at this.

Esther then told me how Payton had lied to her mother about the dates for swim team try outs at her school. "Why did you tell your mother the wrong dates?" Esther inquired.

Payton stared at her silently. She wasn't answering.

"Here's where I'd put my money," I interjected. Looking over at Payton, I said, "That's what someone does when they want to miss try outs. Are you worried about not making the team?"

"Yeah," Payton said, surprising her grandmother with her swift and honest response.

"I'm guessing that's something you didn't want to share with your mom ...." I am speaking to Payton as if she and I have conversations like this all the time.

"I don't know," Payton said. "She never listens to me."

"Yeah, well, that'll make it hard to bring stuff up," I said. "I hope it gets easier for you to do that."

Payton nodded at this.

"I also hope that soon you'll feel okay going to try outs even though you're not sure you'll make the team."

Payton nodded at this too, keeping the eye contact.

About two weeks later, I met with Payton's parents. During this session, Payton's mother mentioned that after Payton's last session, she had gone to her mom that evening and told her that she was really anxious about the swim try outs and that was why she'd told her the wrong date.

"Can I just not do swim this year?" she asked as well. Her mother had said, *Of course, no problem.* Perfect. It's exactly what Payton needed to hear in order to gain some measure of faith that her silence was not the only way to effect the changes in her life she wanted to make.

## Winnie: The girl who capitalized on her personal power to shut people out

Fifteen-year-old Winnie had recently been discharged from the hospital where she'd been admitted because of severe depression and suicidal thoughts. She was emotionally remote, aloof, and private. Not the *Hey thanks but I like to keep my business to myself* kind of private but the *Get the f#@% out of my face* kind of private. Winnie's parents spent the initial session with me contorting themselves into what they hoped was the right amount of ingratiation in order to get something, anything, out of their daughter, who sat there impenetrable. It was difficult to watch. Winnie had grown accustomed to using her personal power to intimidate others and shutting down was her way of executing a cease-and-desist order.

I met with Winnie privately for the second session. She sat there, looking away from me. Her affect was stone cold.

I begin with, "Your parents get nervous when they try to get you to talk with them, don't they?"

Winnie turns to look at me. "What do you mean?" she asks, begrudgingly.

"Like they're hoping to get something out of you before you lose your patience and shut them down."

159

"What makes you think that?"

"Because I see you hold back what they need in order to know you're okay, so they ask again, more tentatively, and the next thing they know you're furious with them for being in your business."

"Well, I don't think therapy works so I don't have anything to say to them anyway." (A nonsequitor but I'll roll with it.)

"What makes you think therapy doesn't work?" I ask Winnie.

"Cause I'm a pessimist."

"Oh," I reply lightly. "Well, I don't think you necessarily have to be an optimist in order to become less depressed." My strategy here was to get Winnie to "decouple" pessimism and depression. I knew I wasn't going to be able to bump her out of her pessimism. Winnie rather liked her identity as a pessimist, so in that moment therapy became a matter of finding a way that she couldn't hide behind her pessimism as a way of dismissing the possibility of feeling better.

"You don't?" Winnie asks.

"No. I think a person can be a pessimist and feel less depressed. They'd just have to make sure that if something changed for the better, they'd let themself see it."

Winnie turns away from me and stares into the wall.

I continue talking. "Winnie, it's obvious to me that you understand the power behind letting certain things matter more to other people than to you. You also know that it gives you a lot of control in your relationships. The thing is, no one sees this happening because there is nothing to see – you're not actually "doing" anything. I think that's why adults don't understand why they feel so nervous around you."

"What are you thinking now?" I ask Winnie, after a period of silence.

"I'm thinking about if what you said might be true."

It would have been easy for me to have found myself trying to draw Winnie into a conversation of sorts while she sat there resisting all my efforts. But clearly, she didn't want one. The messaging was loud and clear. This was how Winnie handled situations where she had to interact with people not of her own choosing. She gave them nothing and watched them squirm. It's easy to dislike someone like Winnie, because she makes you feel so uncomfortable and inept in her presence. And in the ambiguity of her silent, stoic bearing – in that way, she reminded me of Chief Bromden, in *One Flew Over the Cuckoo's Nest* – you could wind up relating to the frightening and indifferent Winnie of your mental projection rather than what must have been a very sad and lonely girl with little sense of herself or her future.

I didn't work very long with Winnie, and I don't remember the reason why. But I do remember that exchange we had in the very beginning of the second session and an abrupt lifting of the heaviness oppressing us both as soon as she said she was thinking if what I said might be true. It was, on her part, quite an admission, and I appreciated what it must have taken for a girl like her to have said it. I'm left to wonder what other things Winnie might have been willing to say in a place where she, and the mechanics of her relationships with others, were laid bare without judgment nor any attempt to disencumber her of them.

## Acting Out Teens

It's no surprise that many of our teen clients, especially ones newer to the process of therapy, feel uncomfortable with the setting, the relationship, or the dialogue of therapy. The ones who are eager for relief, or who relate easily with a supportive adult figure, or who easily rise above their discomfort and engage, settle in nicely after a little while.

But others do not, and they make it their crusade to thrust upon you the feelings of anxiety or vulnerability or ineptitude they wish to avoid. Therapists working with clients in residential treatment centers, blighted urban areas, or the juvenile justice system, where you find clusters of conduct-disordered kids, can find a lot of their clients trying to act like bullies in session, evading contact and pushing back on efforts to get them talking about themselves. I've found the same thing in a suburban private practice (partly because behavior problems are hardly limited to those institutions, and partly because I tend to get referred kids who've not done well in therapy elsewhere!).

So here are two boys, both sixteen, whose initial moves are to try making me feel more uncomfortable than they feel and exert some kind of control over the relationship and/or conversation.

### Leon: The provocateur

"I don't even know *what* to say to that," I tell Leon, after he asks me "what kind of bullshit therapy" I do with kids. Leon is sixteen, court mandated for therapy in the wake of his parents' vicious divorce and his escalating acting out.

"You mean you don't even know?" Leon says. "Aren't you supposed to know what you do with all the kids you see here? Can't you be sued for not knowing?"

I hold still for a moment before saying anything, tilting my head at Leon. "Let's just say I call it 'Janet' therapy." Leon laughs at this and I add, "Now can we dispense with the face-off and have a real conversation?"

Leon's face flattens and he stares at me. I raise my eyebrows and open my hands and ever so slightly nod my head one time, as if to say, *So, okay?* to which Leon unclenches his jaw and responds with a small nod of his own. He relaxes back in his chair.

### *I think we're good now, I say to myself.*

What I tried to do with Leon is engage him in a way that wouldn't take us down some rabbit hole of defensive banter. I responded to him in a way I thought he could respect, which was insightful but very frank, suggesting he might get more out of the genuine contact with me than from its evasion. Had I challenged him directly, or in some way tried to match his aggressive style, it would have been as good as saying, "Game on, bro."

## Cal: The boy in need of the thrill

Cal was a sixteen-year-old boy who had nothing but contempt for the adults who were trying to teach him, counsel him, and raise him. He was a restless and bored kid, irritable and contrarian.

Cal's parents sought out therapy for their son after he was expelled from the private school he'd attended since kindergarten. Apparently, he'd acquired a colorful set of legal charges that included breaking and entering, burglary, and property destruction, among others, and the school said enough.

After talking for a while in the initial session with his parents present, I asked Cal about the charges. He skipped over that and went right to his expulsion from school. "It doesn't matter, I was getting sick of that place anyway. All my friends already graduated last year." Cal was glib about the charges, his expulsion, and his parents' concerns for him. He lay stretched out on the couch in my office, enjoying his parents' ginger treatment of him. After the first session, Cal told his parents that I "irked" him.

Cal came by himself to the next session, which I had invited him to do. I asked what he'd been up to since the last time we'd spoken.

"Been going out with friends but even that's starting to get boring," Cal says.

"Yeah, you already seemed bored with it even before this mess," I said.

Cal looks at me with the slightest wrinkle of a smile in the corners of his eyes. I think he liked that I would say that.

"What are you going to do?" I ask.

"What do you mean?"

"If it just keeps getting more boring?"

"Do more drugs I guess," he says.

"What a miserable solution."

He looks up at me and smiles.

"I did a bunch of speed a few weeks ago and ever since then I've felt really spacey. I think I messed myself up."

"How much speed?" I ask.

"Too much. I don't know, I've just been feeling out of it."

"I'm sure you looked it up online. What did you find out?"

"Not too much – except that it happens. I mean, other people have done the same thing and felt that way too."

"Did that make you feel better?"

"Kinda."

Next session. We are talking about summer jobs and Cal says something about wanting to pay back his parents for the attorney fees. "And also the fines," he adds.

"How much," I ask.

"Ten thousand dollars," he answers.

"So tell me what a 10K spree looks like." Being able to have *unguarded conversations with clients about the behavior in question* is one way to avoid dead end dialogues and expand the setting for therapy.

Cal tells me about his spree. He was with a couple of buddies. They started by painting graffiti on some commuter trains. Then they smashed down the door of an abandoned home and threw rocks at its windows. They got drunk. They got arrested. All in a day's play.

I didn't know if Cal was looking to lure me into a little dogfight about his wanton destruction of public and private property or impress upon me what a bad ass he was. He might have, in response to my question, simply been sharing with me an escapade he had found (and still found) thrilling. What I did know, however, was that I wanted to keep the conversation going, but without asking questions that Cal would find too therapy-like, such as, *What made you decide to do those things in the first place?* or *Were you feeling angry at the time?* or

*How did you feel when it was over?* And part of that involved making sure I didn't change the "temperature" of our dialogue by introducing expressions of alarm or gratuitous curiosity that might be mistaken for an attempt to "analyze" him.

> "Okay," I say, "I never like to destroy things so I can't tap into the appeal of it. But I *want* to get it. So tell me." (Here I'm acknowledging right out of the gate that I know nothing about what it feels like to want to destroy things, as opposed to trying to convince Cal that I understood his desire to do so. At the same time, I express curiosity, not from the point of rapport building or joining [the gratuitous curiosity I referred to earlier], which to me would seem conniving. I asked because I wanted to know. *My question was about me, not Cal,* and felt authentic. I think that's why Cal answered it so easily.)
>
> "It's taboo," Cal responds. "It's just something you don't do. You don't smash down a door, you don't throw rocks at windows … Nothing deep-seated about it …"
>
> "No, I know, I get that," I say. (This was my way of saying to Cal, in so many words, that he was safe from my making some "psychological meaning" of his behavior.)
>
> "It's not like I'm 'getting my anger out' or anything stupid like that …"
>
> "I figured," I assure him. "That's more like when someone picks up a laptop and smashes it on the ground." (I added that to let Cal know I understood how destruction for the sake of boredom or pleasure is in a different box than destruction because you're really angry.)
>
> "Yeah, that would be, like, being pissed off."
>
> "I wonder if it's more of a guy thing, because you just don't hear a lot about girls going out to smash and destroy. They may do other transgressive acts, but not that—"[2] (Here I'm simply trying to broaden the conversation by making it more dimensional, discovering other tangents we might explore.)
>
> "—No, no girl is going to do that, smash windows, doors," Cal interrupts.
>
> "Well, I'm thinking now that, if that's the level of thrill you really like then no wonder why everything else is so boring to you, especially school."
>
> "Yeah," Cal says, with some animation in his voice. "And the legal ways are too expensive!" he adds, referring to the ATVs he loves riding on the rare occasions he gets to do so.

This little exchange could easily be taken as just chatter between therapist and client. And in a way, it was. It was light and spontaneous and easy to keep going.

It didn't have an overarching agenda of its own and didn't cause the client to become defensive. But it *was* intentional, on my part, that is, there was forethought and purpose in everything I was saying, even if I was coming up with it in the microseconds before speaking.

In retrospect, I realize that what I was doing, *or moving Cal towards* I'd prefer to say, was Cal's gradual awareness of and interest in his own actions and emotional needs. His doing the actual psychological work to make sense of those things at that point in time would have been a more challenging and less plausible outcome – though not impossible, were Cal to have been willing to use his intelligence and forethought to temper his impulsivity. But even a little movement along that developmental line of emotional self-awareness can make a difference for someone, in Cal's case showing up perhaps as greater self-restraint or perspective-taking or transparency. And then, should he want, Cal would have the rest of his life to take it forward.

## Excitable, Reactive Teens

### Amara: The girl who used her temper to back everyone off

Seventeen-year-old Amara comes into my office furious at her custodial aunt and announces that she's dropping out of high school and finding a ride to Florida where another of her aunts lives (noncustodial). "She said I could come down and live with her, as long as I get a job. And she said my boyfriend can come too." Amara adds, resolute and angry. "Dori (Amara's custodial aunt) hates my boyfriend and won't even let him drive me to the beach this weekend. I don't care, I'm going anyway!"

Hardly surprising, Amara has a long history of being impulsive and using poor judgment, especially when it involves boys who like her, or say that they do. Amara and I have a good relationship; we've worked together intermittently for about two years through a series of episodes of high-risk acting out. She has a 3.9 GPA, which she protects –except when boys enter the scene.

Here's where a therapist, feeling a sense of urgency to make sure Amara doesn't act on her plan to leave the state, could respond very literally to Amara's threat to go to Florida.

"Right, live with your aunt? In Florida?"

"Do you really think it's a good idea to not finish high school?"

"Your GED? Then what? And you, with a 3.9 GPA?!"

"And your aunt down in Florida actually spoke with Dori about this plan?"

But I just waited, calmly, thinking about where I wanted to go with this. I didn't want to respond to Amara's plan too literally, as in, asking her questions about it because that sort of "enlivens" the plan, giving it credibility, as if it's something to be taken seriously in this moment. I also don't want to dismiss it and make Amara think that I don't take her seriously or doubt she would go through with it, because with a kid like her, that's just the prompt she needs to say, *You don't think I'd do it? Watch me!*

I instead decide to ask Amara to tell me about her new boyfriend, which would let her know I'm interested in this story and her anger and her wish to leave, but without elevating the affect around it. Asking her to tell me about her boyfriend would be a way to have a conversation parallel to the one at hand, that is, a related one, but with less heat.

Before I could get to that, however, Amara mentions something that had happened at school earlier in the day.

"I was so mad at my aunt that I left school early today. And I cannot believe this girl in school – we're friends! – she and I were supposed to present this project today that we've been working on, but I told her I couldn't do the presentation because I was leaving and she got really mad at me! She didn't care that I was upset, she was worried only about her grade!"

"Wait, what?" I say, astonished at Amara's egocentrism and lack of perspective.

"She only cared about herself!"

"Wait, what *should* she have done?" I ask.

"She should have been more interested in how I was doing than the stupid presentation."

"That's a pretty big ask," I say. "And that's even for a very good friend," I said.

Amara gets quiet.

"I don't know, Amara … I know you're angry and didn't feel you could do school, but I'm thinking too about this other kid (modeling being empathic for two different people at odds with each other). Maybe she *needed* to get that project in, maybe she was counting on it to bring her grade up. Maybe making sure the presentation got done today was as important to her as your feelings were to you," I said.

"Well, she should have just told me then," Amara replies.

"Like you're so easy to tell things to …"

"Yeah I know …." Amara says, aware of how she intimidates.

"If she's a friend of yours then I'm sure she knows, too." Amara smiles at this. She likes being seen as the hot head to whom you better watch out what you say.

"What's the girl supposed to say?" I ask Amara. "She probably felt totally at your mercy, like she had no control over a situation. She might have had a lot riding on it."

"Well, I just couldn't get up in front of the class and talk about climate change."

"I understand that. And she might have been able to also. But feeling that she had no say in the matter probably made it difficult for her to appreciate how bad you were feeling."

"Well, she's supposed to be a friend," Amara says, defensively.

"Well, that's the other thing about it, Amara. It probably felt to her like a test, like, if you're really my friend, you'll understand. And if you don't, then the hell with you. You do this with Dori all the time."

"I guess," Amara says, looking around my office.

"I really want to help you get a handle on this. You'll lose good people who really care about you but who can't or won't want to give you what you're demanding.

"I know. Do you have anything to eat?"

"Oh my god, when you're done with something, you're so done. Yeah, I do," I reply, smiling. I pull out some sodas and a tub of snacks. A minute later Amara is sitting on the couch with her legs folded and her affect bright. She's chatty now, and says, "I like having you as my therapist because you always have stuff to eat!"

That whole exchange about what happened at school could have ended in an impasse but didn't. Amara's the type of kid (a little like Danielle in Chapter 12) with whom you're best off being very direct. That, coupled with a familiarity, warmth, and reasoned points, was the kind of approach Amara could deal with and the kind of relationship she could join; her range wasn't very broad, but we managed to hit the right spot and ran with it.

Stuffing my own face with animal crackers, I say to Amara, "You know, I once ran away from home."

"No way!"

"Yeah, but not like you're talking about. It was kiddie stuff, but still. I was around seven or eight, but I remember it to this day. I was mad about something and left my house and hid on a neighbor's porch. I wasn't sure what to do after that, so when my mom called out the front door for me, I went home. I don't even know if she'd realized I'd 'run away.'"

I tell Amara this story because it's an example of that unexceptional human experience of believing you're ready to act on something before you really are, underscoring the fact that our wishes to be autonomous and on our own can make us assume responsibilities we're not ready to shoulder. I wanted to put Amara's attention on the *ambivalence* inherent in making big decisions like the one she was contemplating and invite her to explore it with me.

I wasn't telling Amara that she shouldn't go to Florida – I didn't have to. I just directed her attention to another part of the decision-making process, that is, what you feel *after* you've acted, where you can get hit with the elation of having been right, or the despair of recognizing you made a mistake. By doing so, I'm encouraging her to flesh out her thinking more broadly than its current focus on simply picking up and leaving, an impulsive and daring move which delivers, in fantasy but not necessarily in real life, gobs of gratification. Therapists often think of interventions as big, recognizable moves, but many good therapies are made up of understated prompts and compelling invitations for clients to examine things from an alternative perspective.

"I don't know if I'm going to go to Florida," Amara says after a bit. "It's so hot down there and there are so many bugs."

"Way too many bugs," I commented.

And about closing out this conversation or topic? It wasn't necessary and could even have been detrimental. Sometimes putting too fine a light on something makes it wither away. Amara understood the point I was making. I thought that asking her to comment on it or reflect on it further would be forcing the issue, potentially taking something away from her experience in session that had led her to a change of heart about moving to Florida. I wanted instead to conduct the end of the session in a manner which would demonstrate my faith in Amara's ability to extract what she needed from it, digest it constructively on her own time, and employ it in service of her own well-being.

The next chapter continues with this theme of avoiding power struggles with teen clients who present in challenging ways, some intentional and some not. It's a comparison case study of three different girls, two of whom look like the same kid on paper, but all three of which required a very different approach from one another. It highlights how clients' personalities, as well as their interpersonal and defensive styles, can inform your conversational slant and your decisions about how to conduct the therapy, including how best to confront when necessary.

## Notes

1 Straus, M.B. *No-talk therapy for children and adolescents*, Norton, 1999.
2 In her book, *Adolescence: The Farewell to Childhood* (Jason Aronson, London, 1986), author Louise Kaplan speaks about this difference between boys and girls in reference to the kinds of acting out they do. Males, she cites, take risks in the world at large, acting out their personal dilemmas on the larger social environment. They act in groups, which provides the peer approval and narcissistic enhancement they seek. Typical behaviors include vandalism, joyriding, theft, shop-lifting, assault, and the like. Girls, on the other hand, express their personal dilemmas within their personal relationships. Less likely to act out on larger social environments, they more often commit "secret" crimes: gossiping, concocting romantic alliances, lying, and bingeing.

# CHAPTER FIFTEEN

# Three Contrarian Girls. Three Different Therapies

Here are three very different girls who I saw in therapy over a span of a couple of years. On paper, two of them almost looked like the same kid. They each carried the same diagnosis, and they each thrived on conflict. They were very good at getting their parents, teachers, and counselors to engage with them in all kinds of power struggles.

But there the similarities end. With Danielle, you avoid power struggles by *owning* what you believe and think and say. Blink with this kid and you're blown off in an instant. With Elise, you avoid power struggles *by refraining from challenging or pushing back, by allowing.* Anything that threatens her self-concept as a victim, or her bleak and pessimistic view of the world at large, will trigger a rush of hostility and opposition. And then there's the third girl, Rachel, with whom you avoid power struggles by *waiting* … very patiently, without jumping on her remarks that pull for therapists to respond. The answer is in **not** reacting with alarm.

The first two girls, Danielle and Elise, are both emotionally volatile, immature, and highly attention seeking. There is a high level of mother–daughter conflict in each case. Both girls' fathers live apart and are abusive. Remember that with Elise, confronting or challenging the status quo will be problematic. However, confronting or challenging is absolutely necessary in order for therapy to work at all with Danielle.[1]

## Danielle

Thirteen-year-old Danielle loved to scare people off with her in-your-face manner and outrageous comments. She arrived in my office – courtesy of her

DOI: 10.4324/9781003257080-15

mom – and was stinking mad about it. She didn't agree with anything her mom had to say: that Danielle had become more and more angry over the past few months, that she didn't seem to care about school anymore, that she was rude and disrespectful at home. All that was wrong in Danielle's world, according to Danielle, was that her mother wouldn't let her live with her dad.

That Danielle was going to be a challenging client was obvious. She was dodgy (totally ignoring questions or comments), gamey, and provocative. Early in the therapy she commented, "In school the other day, my friend and I yelled down the hallways, 'Babies in blenders! Babies in blenders!' It was so funny!" She wore the chainsaw earrings her father had given her for Christmas, as well as a perpetually insolent expression on her face. She'd have eaten a newbie therapist alive.

This was a kid who motored through (and over) her family, her friends, her day. She had attitude in spades, but self-reflection or empathy? Not so much. With a kid as volatile as Danielle, I assumed that any session might be her last. Instead of thinking about the evolution of her therapy, I scouted for little windows of opportunity to present unfamiliar but potentially intriguing perspectives – not asking her to talk about them or consider them or even focus on them – just getting them on her screen for a moment.

On paper, treatment was about tapering down her defiance, getting her invested in school, and reducing her idealization of dad. But in the office, it was about getting her to stop shadowboxing long enough to hear what she needed to hear but which nobody dared to say – which was, that a) intimidating everybody around you is a hollow victory in the end, b) finding entertainment in another's pain is never an attractive quality, and c) beneath the tough-girl persona, she probably was someone worth getting to know.

Remember, this was a young teen who steamrolled over everyone and was exceedingly reactive – exactly the kind of kid who makes therapists anxious about saying the wrong thing. Will she mock me for asking this question? Is she going to roll her eyes if I respond with something kind? The type of kid with whom you feel you're just one wrong word away from losing her.

But had I become too careful with Danielle, too tentative, I think she would have read this as a sign that, just like the other adults in her life, I was hoping to connect with her by steering clear of any tension or conflict. That would have been a mistake on my part, *because it was through conflict that Danielle connected*; it's the only way she knows how.

The other problem with being too careful was that it would become apparent to Danielle that I was willing to sacrifice the authenticity in the room and in the relationship for the sake of keeping what would have amounted to a false peace. This was a dynamic that Danielle played very artfully: she would keep raising the ante on her outrageous behavior while her mom or teachers or prior therapists tried to find ways to ignore it or pretend not to be appalled by it.

Let me share with you this dialogue from one of her sessions:

"I can't stand my mom's boyfriend," Danielle spits. "He's such a pussy. He actually gets nervous when tries to talk to me. And he's, like, what, fifty years old or something? He keeps buying my brother and me all these things just so we'll like him but it's such bullshit." She laughs an unkind laugh, expecting me to appease her with a grin of my own.

But instead, I say, "I feel sorry for the guy." Danielle looks up at me, hard.

What? I ask her with my face.

"You *would* feel sorry for him," she says, with disgust. "Forget it." She reaches into her backpack and takes out some homework to do for, presumably, the remainder of the session.

"How come I always have to have the answer you want me to have in order to keep the conversation going?" I ask Danielle.

Danielle looks up at me and through her questioning sneer and slight shake of the head manages to communicate, *You are such a loser.*

I keep on. "You're right, I *would* feel sorry for the guy. I feel sorry for *any-one* who wants to get to know you because you make them feel like an idiot for trying. And I feel sorry for your mom, too, because she seems to really like this guy but also wants your approval so that she can feel she's doing the right thing. But you see them struggling with all this, and yet you don't help them out. Instead, you laugh."

"Why would I want to help them?" Danielle looks genuinely puzzled.

"Wow," is all I manage to say, suddenly very still. Danielle looks up, disarmed, and unsettled by my response. She stares at me for a moment, and then turns away.

And right there was the therapy – in that brief collision of our two different phenomenological worlds. In Danielle's world, being cavalier and mean was okay and even cool, but in my world it wasn't. For a few moments, Danielle felt what it was like to be in my world where the rules are different, and it made her uncomfortable. I don't think she'd ever realized how dependent she was on being around people who would accommodate her (by avoiding conflict and feigning approval) in order to make her lifestyle work.

If I had tried to connect with Danielle simply by being understanding or "neutral," the conversation might have gone something like this: When Danielle said, "I can't stand my mom's boyfriend. He keeps buying my brother and me all these things just so we'll like him, but it's such bullshit," I would have responded with, "What would you rather him do?" But, by following Danielle's lead in this way, I would merely be condoning her dismissive position. By saying "I feel sorry for the guy," I was getting across the point that her statement wasn't as incontestable as she thought it was, but without directly challenging her. If I'd suggested that she "cut him some slack," I'd basically have been telling her to "be different," which is exactly what all the other adults in her life have done, unsuccessfully. But by saying that *I* would feel sorry for her mother's boyfriend and have cut him some slack, I was sending a similar message, *but in a way she couldn't really fight*, since I was stating my own position.

In my way of approaching this case, I would never have told Danielle to cut him some slack or think about how her mother felt or anything like that. It would only have given her something to fight with me about. All I was doing was describing *my* reaction to what she'd been saying and to how she thought about relationships, as well as to the absence of accountability revealed in her behavior.

So, what was the therapy exactly in that brief collision of worlds? Danielle is like the emperor whose lack of clothing nobody dares to point out. In this exchange, without telling her she should change anything about the way she conducts her life, I was able to put into the room the things I thought she needed to hear about herself, in a way she wouldn't be able to repel:

- I don't agree with you, even if it makes you uncomfortable.
- I am going to feel sorry for your mother's boyfriend, even if you don't.
- Not everyone associates compassion with being a loser.
- You try to control conversations by punishing people for responding in ways you don't like.
- You try to control relationships too, and your mom tolerates it because you mean so much to her and she's afraid of losing you.
- None of this is particularly nice.

Danielle and I kept at it week after week. She never missed an appointment. Sessions were a lively mix of storytelling, debate, humor, confrontation, rages on her part, and the two of us visually appraising each other. Sometimes I met with Danielle's mom and tried to get her to be less ingratiating and stand her ground more often, even if it meant being "punished" over the next few days by Danielle's snarky comments and defiance.

But two months into the therapy, we ran into a situation we couldn't get past. Apparently, Danielle's dad had been kicked out of his apartment for non-payment of rent. It wasn't the first time. Danielle wanted her mom to pay his deposit on a new apartment, and she wanted me to join her in pressing her mom to do so. I said,

> "Danielle, I can't. Your mom would be crazy to do that …." By the look on her face, I knew we were done. "I'm not coming back," she said.

> "Hey," I said, softly, "how come my not backing you on this means we don't meet anymore?" Danielle looked at me and said nothing. Since I knew she had already disconnected from me, I quickly changed tack from *trying to process the end of therapy together* to *thinking about what I wanted her to take away from it* which, among other things, was a reference experience of having genuinely, if briefly and despite herself, connected with someone whose values were antithetical to her own.

> "It's okay, Danielle," I said. "I understand. I'm hoping that one day you'll make more room in your world for people who don't always agree with you. That'd be cool." Danielle turned her face away from mine and began to cry. I never saw her again.

This was not an ideal end to therapy. That would have been a chastened, more insightful Danielle who saw the error of her ways and became a kinder, gentler, more compassionate young person, one maybe who started getting better grades in school and made friends with kids who'd blanch at the idea of babies in blenders. But most therapy cases don't end with a complete resolution of problems, and they don't have to. I don't think we necessarily need to carry our clients across the finish line in order for our work with them to matter. That's all it really has to do – *matter* – and our clients get to be the judges of that.

### Elise

Sixteen-year-old Elise was having a difficult day at school. Depressed, picked on by classmates, and not getting the attention or sympathy she wanted, Elise decided to head down to guidance and talk to her counselor. Early in that conversation, Elise said, emphatically, "I hate everybody."

Elise's counselor (who later asked to consult retrospectively with me on this case) responded with, "No, you don't hate everybody. You don't hate me, you don't hate your mom, you don't hate your therapist (me)." And that was the end of that. Elise got up and walked back to class. After all, what's the point in expressing how you felt if someone was going to tell you that you had it all wrong?

I asked the counselor what she didn't like about Elise's statement that she hated everybody. "It's just so negative," she replied. "I wanted her to realize that there were all these people trying to help her and that she didn't really hate them."

But maybe Elise *did* hate them, or she hated them that day or for that hour. Maybe she needed everyone *else* to believe that she hated everybody. It doesn't matter. Elise is "allowed" to hate them.

Nothing productive would ever have come out of challenging this girl's negativity. How are you going to convince a salty, contrarian kid like this that she doesn't really mean what she says? And why even try? It would just make for a big power battle over whose perception was correct. Moreover, the paradigm is limiting: In order to get better, Elise would have to stop being so negative. Good luck with that one.

The way I saw it, Elise *didn't* have to stop being so negative. *She could hate everybody, and still get better.* The strategy here is to "decouple" two things erroneously viewed as inseparable that are hobbling progress. Kids will let go when they want to let go. I believe that the work of therapy is not getting them to do it but helping them *want* to. More important, though, is the idea that clients don't have to let go of their way of doing things or of their symptoms in order for them to take the therapy forward. **Elise could hate everybody and have a big blind spot for the liabilities of being a lone wolf, yet still be attracted to the idea that letting others align with her could in fact help her to feel better.** That's forward movement.

I suggested to Elise's school counselor that instead of trying to do therapy right out of the gate, she try to give her students more room to make the comments they wanted to make. In the case of Elise, I offered that she might have responded with something like, "Yeah, I think I have days when I hate everybody, too" or "What was your day like that you ended up feeling like you hate everybody?" or "How long do you think you'll feel this way?" all said or asked sincerely, not somberly as if trying to ferret out an underlying pathology. These questions would have assisted the counselor in joining Elise by normalizing what she felt instead of turning it into something "bad" or abnormal. Moreover, such responses would likely have prevented the conversation shutdown by communicating, "Yes, I understand how you can feel that you hate everyone in the world, and today seems to be one of those days for sure. But nothing about that needs to keep us from figuring out ways to help you make it through the school day."

Elise's counselor had tried for too much too soon. I also didn't think that, in general, it was the right approach for Elise, whose aloof demeanor and critical manner made it hard for anyone to make much of an impression on her. Without the traction of a relationship in which the counselor or therapist mattered to her, Elise would have no interest in hearing about anything other than what she wanted to hear at that moment, which would have been any remark that could be morphed into something validating Elise's jaded outlook.

What was the difference between Elise's counselor's efforts to champion an alternative perspective and my similar efforts with Danielle? It was the girls' personalities and interpersonal relationship styles. Elise was impenetrable and remote. She considered little of what others said or did. By contrast, Danielle took in everything around her, and would then spit it out on the floor in front of you. But for all her pugnaciousness, Danielle *engaged* with the people in her world, and each moment of engagement held open the possibility for these people – a therapist, teacher, parent, coach – to leave something of themselves behind.

## Rachel

Rachel, fifteen, was referred by her family physician when her mother discovered she'd been cutting herself. She offered no resistance to therapy and came to her sessions eagerly. Dressed in gray and black, and often wearing a hoodie pulled down low to cover much of her face, Rachel was funny, warm, kindhearted, likable – and brimming with self-contempt. Sophisticated and circumspect while in my office, she was, I learned, quite different when among her friends. With boys, Rachel flaunted her sexuality – wearing tight clothes and a good deal of makeup, flirting strenuously – to make up for what she believed to be her subpar looks and personality. Partly because she was by nature empathetic to other people's pain (being only too aware of her own) and partly to compensate for her own feelings of inferiority, Rachel had become the go-to person for all her friends who wanted to discuss their problems. She was content to absorb their pain in exchange for feeling valued and tended to say yes and agree to do things even when she really didn't want to. At the same time, she had a reputation for being someone you wouldn't want to cross, sometimes lashing out when frustrated or when she became aware of some injustice suffered by a third party. Over all of this lay an unmovable mass of depression and anxiety, a heavy cloud she'd been under for years.

Rachel was also very reckless and self-destructive in a willful, intentional kind of way. In the beginning, she told me the kind of things she did – something guaranteed to raise any therapist's anxiety level. She burned her arms at night with a heated safety pin or cut herself with a knife in order to focus her thoughts away from her problems so that she could fall asleep. Though she'd never engaged in sexual intercourse, she mused out loud about when and with whom and with how many boys she should start having sex. She frequently drank too much and had experimented with drugs.

Historically, so many of the adults in Rachel's life had reacted with such urgency to her self-harming and high-risk behavior that Rachel had never had the chance to stop and consider whether she actually wanted to continue with any of it. I often felt tested when she'd report to me in session her more dicey escapades: *Would I respond as every other adult had or would I be able to provide a holding environment that could keep both her, and her privacy, safe?* I began to understand that one key to working effectively with Rachel was in *not* reacting with obvious alarm, even though everything about the situation and her clear anguish seemed to clamor for it. It felt right, albeit counterintuitive, to wait and not react.

Here were other interventions I mulled over, looking for the right place to introduce them. For example, I wanted to affirm Rachel's essentially benevolent nature and generosity, but I had to do it in a way she wouldn't find patronizing or gratuitous. She'd always made it hard for others to compliment her, mainly because she was uncomfortable when evaluated more favorably than the self-image she held onto – a kind of unattractive loser who you shouldn't mess with – and consciously projected. Praise made Rachel uneasy; I think it made her feel beholden to a standard of being that she then felt pressured to keep up. In other words, while her low self-image maintained her depression, it felt safer than risking the failure and disappointment of not being able to live up to the good opinion and high expectations of others. Once, she told me that she didn't mind the low points of her depressive cycles because she knew that from there, it could only get better.

So instead of frankly pointing out to Rachel what I regarded as her instinctive kindness, I just said during one session that I'd been moved by the stories she'd told me about caring tenderly for her two younger brothers when her mother was away. I liked, too, her bold and successful effort to get two girls to stop teasing a third online. "You keep these two facets of your personality – your caring nature and high sense of justice – under such wraps though; nobody sees these parts of you." I said this simply as an observation and opinion – not advice, not necessarily Truth. There was nothing about my comment suggesting she needed to respond. But she did, with a shrug. "It's no big deal," she said.

One day, Rachel comes in and tells me that her boyfriend had just dumped her for another girl in her grade. "She's much prettier than I am anyway," Rachel says by way of explaining. "So I really can't blame him." This is exactly the kind of statement that makes many therapists want to give Rachel a pat little speech: Being pretty isn't everything; or If that's how your ex-boyfriend appraises girlfriends then maybe he's not such good boyfriend material after all; or You're pretty, too. But had I done that I would have made this exchange all about what *I* wanted or needed her to believe. Instead, I wanted to provide Rachel with a place where her thoughts about boyfriends and being pretty could stand uncontested – not because they were ideals to stand behind, but because there needed to be a place in her life where what she believed could be part of a larger conversation, rather than being dismantled on sight.

On the heels of her remark about her ex-boyfriend, I asked Rachel, "Are there differences between boys who pick their girlfriends based on how pretty they are and those who base their decisions on a whole bunch of different things?" And we talked together about that, each of us musing out loud. A little later I look at her directly and asked, "Hey how come when you tell me about the boys in your school, it always sounds like they're in the driver's seat?" and we talked about that for a while. My goal here was to present ideas in the form of questions, which she might answer or not – the answer wasn't important, only the question was. Because it was these questions, with their gentle counterpoints to Rachel's pliant manner around boys, that would nibble at the edges of her way of thinking about boys, girls, and the relationships they create with one another. They helped keep the conversation open and move it forward, little by little. The therapy at this particular juncture was embedded within this conversation, in the form of my seeding the idea that Rachel could ask for more, that she deserved more.

My challenge to Rachel was decidedly understated. It's a tough place to come on full force because the beliefs being challenged were her feelings, not mine. There's a limit to how strong you can make a point about something that's neither yours nor under your control.

I think a better place to come on strong with adolescents, and only if the therapy calls for it, is when it involves something the *therapist* feels strongly about. But – and here's the hitch – it must be expressed without signaling to the teen that he or she, as a result of how *you* feel, is expected to do anything differently. It's a way of saying, *I'm not going to pretend that I think what you're doing is a good idea*, **without** adding something along the lines of, *so therefore I think you should …* It's what those kids at the treatment center taught me – that the less pressure I exerted on them to change, the franker I could be in my opinions about what they were doing or thinking, and the less defensive they became about entertaining them.

> Rachel responded to my question about boys always being in the driver's seat by saying, "I don't know," followed by a description of all the kids she sat with at lunch: They're all boys. They're all druggies. They're all failing classes.
>
> I asked, casually, "Why not others?"
>
> "Because I don't care," she replied. She then added, "Actually, I think I just really hate myself."

It would have been tempting to ask, in deeply concerned tones, "But why? You have no reason to hate yourself. You're such a lovely, kind, good person." But responding like that – essentially dismissing Rachel's feelings – would have only caused her to clam up. I chose to say nothing and nodded ever so slightly as my way of letting Rachel know that I heard her, respected how she felt, and had no need for her to dress it up. We sat together quietly and easily for the remaining few minutes of the session.

Soon after this session where Rachel said she thought she just hated herself, I started noticing changes in her demeanor and in the stories she brought to therapy. She looked more carefree and said one day that she was aware of "smiling a lot." She told me she'd been writing poems about "conscience" and "putting down the knife." Rachel shared a story about her mother suggesting she'd been cutting herself because of a boy. She was very offended by this. "These are *my* scars!" Rachel cried out to me in session. "I don't do this because of a boy. That would be kind of pathetic, don't you think?" At some point in the conversation, I found the right opportunity to say to Rachel, "I like that you have a *No* in you now." She nodded.

Shortly thereafter, Rachel's mother called me to say that Rachel had indicated she wanted to come in to therapy less frequently since she didn't have all that much to talk about anymore. "Absolutely fine," I said. "Happy to hear she thinks she's doing better. I do too."

It was interesting to me that Rachel didn't raise this with me directly. I suspect she was worried about hurting my feelings or maybe she just couldn't say to my face that she was ready to move on. In any event, I chose not to pursue it.

I'd probably handle it differently today. I saw Rachel close to twenty years ago, and I think I didn't have the confidence then to address this particular termination with this particular client in a way that wouldn't have become awkward or clumsy. That has countertransference written all over it. It seems now that I didn't want to "mess" the therapy up in the last lap, perhaps an anxiety about Rachel becoming disillusioned with me in the eleventh hour. How ironic that I would have evaded the traps of becoming too careful in the beginning of her therapy only to succumb to the temptation at its end.

In her last few weeks of therapy, Rachel reported a new interest: serial killers. With insight and compassion, she talked about how they were often dehumanized by the media and even by the people who were studying them. Interestingly, she added, "If you dehumanize them, then you can't understand them or catch them. It turns them into monsters, but they're human, too." I understand how some people might have been a little spooked by Rachel's interest in serial killers, but I took it as a reflection of how she had managed to re-humanize *herself* in her own eyes, an important first step in allowing others to see her that way as well.

I think Rachel needed to know that I could sit with her in her darkest of places and not get scared off, and that she and I ourselves could keep her safe. Years later, I went to the movie theater in town with two of my sons, and there Rachel was, selling the tickets. She ran out from behind the sales booth and gave me a huge hug. Before heading back into the booth, Rachel turned to my boys and said, "Your mother saved my life." That's something you don't ever forget.

## Note

1 A version of this appeared in Why teens hate therapy, mistakes therapists should avoid, *Psychotherapy Networker*, September/October 2012.

# CHAPTER SIXTEEN

# Being On Everyone's Side at Once

## Working with Teenagers and Their Parents Together and/or Separately

Well, she doesn't ever do anything around the house anymore unless my parents nag her fifty million times, and she's always in a bad mood," Paige's thirteen-year-old brother says.

"Paige's a great girl," defends her father. "She has so much potential. But she's just making bad choices."

"What's happened that you and her mom expect so little of her now?" I ask.

"We feel bad for Paige because she seems so unhappy. We don't want to add to her stress."

I tell Paige's parents that I understand their reasoning, and that it would appear the kind thing to do. "But I actually think you should be asking Paige for more, not less."

Abruptly, Paige picks her head up to look at me. Uneasy perhaps about where this conversation is going, she decides to join in. I acknowledge her joining by turning toward her and addressing her directly. "You make your dad work very hard," I say, referring to her miserly responses so far in session whenever he asks her a question in an effort to better understand what she's going through.

"Are you sure you want to talk about this with Paige in the room?" Paige's mother hurries to ask.

"I wouldn't think of saying it without her here," I replied, looking over at Paige.

This is Paige, the same girl from Chapter 9, who asked why she should be worried about the rest of her family when she was the one with all the problems .... This

DOI: 10.4324/9781003257080-16

passage is an example of keeping *what should remain a family conversation* from becoming fractioned off into separate parts that then become family secrets.

## Establishing simultaneous, flexible, resilient, non-exclusive alliances with everyone in the room

Many of the problems that prove unresolvable when we meet alone with our teenage clients can be more easily sorted out when we have the client's family (or parent(s)/caregiver) in the room with us. The vista broadens, perspectives multiply, and you have more potential agents of change to work with. In addition, having family members or other caregivers present in the sessions also keeps a teenager's lack of participation from stopping the therapy, and offers them an opportunity to see what therapy with you could be like without having to buy into anything up front.

But of course not all kids come with a family, and some have families whose members aren't going to be helpful because of their own problems, limitations, biases. Whereas prior chapters discussed clinical situations that took place in both individual and family therapies, this chapter focuses on the latter and the relationships you establish with different members of a family, and how they can all work toward a common goal. The one thing that most everyone can agree on in a family in turmoil is that no one is really having a good time. Everyone wants the situation to change, even if they don't agree on what that change should be.

All that said, many therapists were discouraged in their training programs from seeing both a teenager and his or her parents, with exceptions made for occasional joint family meetings. Getting together with parents without the teen present was thought to compromise the therapeutic relationship between the therapist and teenager either by introducing a measure of doubt regarding the therapist's true alliance, or because of the risk (inadvertent or otherwise) of lapses in confidentiality.

But in all my years of practice, I've personally not found this to be the case. My goal when working with families is to establish simultaneous, non-exclusive alliances with everyone involved, even when it's understood that going forward, I will primarily be working with the teenager individually. It's what I call being on everyone's side at the same time – creating flexible, dynamic partnerships with each person involved that allow me to support one without bailing on the others, and challenge different members without them feeling as if I'm taking up sides against them.

This position permits me to move or rotate fluidly, constructively, and comfortably among all those who are present in a family session, as well as between individual, family, and parent sessions with the same family, alternately challenging, supporting, clarifying, and mediating. Mixing these different therapeutic configurations allows me to maximize possibilities for sustainable change, while still maintaining the integrity of my alliance with the teenager. It also gives me the opportunity to discover and address issues that would otherwise never come into play when only one perspective is represented in the room. What I am always trying to do is present myself as a potential resource for the entire family.

## How useful is unbending confidentiality for today's teenagers and their families?

For a long time now, the industry of adolescent mental health has used its promise of safe places and confidentiality to attract clients. Parents use this all the time as a means of cajoling their teen into agreeing to see a therapist. "Just remember," I hear parents tell their teenagers, "Janet isn't allowed to tell me anything you tell her!"

But building therapies around those principles of privacy shortchanges us. We end up mirroring the fragmentation and secrecy in families that already exists and, silenced by these promises, leaving parents in the dark. In some extreme cases, adhering inflexibly to these principles leads therapists to form alliances with their teen clients that seem more like activist coalitions serving only to fuel the teenager's rage and sense of righteousness toward the parents. It is next to impossible to address issues of accountability and personal responsibility once those forces are unleashed.

Moreover, a lot of what teenagers struggle with these days has less to do with things they need us to keep confidential and more to do with things they need our help in sharing with their parents in facilitated conversations – such as when kids feel invisible to them or grossly misunderstood, or when parents don't recognize how their arguing or their criticism or dismissive attitudes are hurtful and distancing to their kids, or when kids feel alone in what may be a sea of emotionally detached family members or feel overwhelmed by pressures to excel in academics, athletics, extracurriculars.

## What do you say when parents challenge your ability to help them or their teen because of your age or level of experience?

"I'm a lot younger than some of my clients' parents, and get defensive when it seems like they think I'm too young or inexperienced to be effective or offer good advice. How do I prove to them that I'm capable of helping their kid?"

This is something many recent graduates experience as they start working with clients without the "protective" title of intern. Even more seasoned clinicians get a wary look from parents who interpret a cautiousness or tentativeness or youthful appearance as inexperience or a lack of authority to get the job done.

In either case, the result is that the therapist feels as though he or she needs to prove themselves to be up for the task.

Therapists typically respond to this pressure by citing their credentials – degrees, clinical placements, years in practice, etc. in an effort to verify competency. But answering the call to prove yourself by "proving yourself" is probably the worst thing you could do, as it puts you on the defensive, and emboldens the parents' skepticism.

Maybe you *are* new to the field. Maybe you *don't* have much experience with the types of problems with which this family presents. It's okay. That's what supervisors and colleagues and consultants are for, and what you really want is for these parents to understand that if you were to start thinking that you were in over your head, you'd get the guidance you needed. You want them to understand too that your relative youth or newness to the field doesn't necessarily mean you can't handle things. Native talent and emotional intelligence and great training transcend a lot of traditional markers of competency, and in few places is this more apparent than in the practice of psychotherapy.

Allow families or parents to entertain their doubts and give them room to make a change. Here's the sort of thing I would say in that circumstance:

> "I don't know how to make you feel more comfortable with me working with your teenager and it would be a mistake for me to try. All I can say is, I have ideas about how to help him which I've shared with you, and we can go forward with them if you'd like. If they help, we do more, and if you feel I'm not the right person, you'll move on and it's fine." Any attempt to defend your competency will come off as junior and defensive. Own it (your lack of experience, your childlessness), and let them decide.

If you're asked whether you have children or teenagers of your own, I recommend simply answering honestly. *Yes, I do, and they're 8 and 11 and 13.* Or *No, I don't*, followed by, *Does that make you wonder about whether I can be helpful?* I'd take the initiative to bring that question forward, front and center, so that the parents won't have to feel sheepish about asking it, and we'll all know what everyone's thinking. If a parent were to say, *Oh, no, actually I was just curious. I'm not worried about that at all*, I'd say, *That's terrific, let's get started then.* No big deal.

## Managing first sessions with families

I never like meeting with teenage clients by themselves for a first visit.[1] I'd learn only part of the story and have nothing against which to evaluate their narratives. Meeting with parents first is even worse – me privy to the parents' story about their son while he has to wonder in his first session with me what I do and don't know. Besides, the optics are bad. I always ask that at least one (prefer-ably both) of the parents or caregivers join the teenager in their initial session.

So, there you are in front of a cluster of related people who are unhappy with one another or having trouble getting along. The parents look at you and maybe the adolescent doesn't. They are all waiting for you to speak. I like to start by asking the parents what they shared with their teen about our initial phone call, or how they described to her what we were meeting about. That way, I get an idea about how open the parents are with their teen, how honest they are with them, and what the teen knows. I'll also ask the teen if he or she was onboard to come. This is all done very informally[2] everyone situated with something to drink or snack on if they want. My office is a big space with multiple couches and huge windows and a wall to wall red (!) carpet, so there's plenty to look at, allowing for this beginning conversation to be interspersed with incidental, casual comments that put everyone at relative ease. My dog (a darling pit bull) provides comic relief.

Parents will often use my opening question as an opportunity to launch into their concerns about their teenager. After a few minutes, though, I tell them we'll circle back to all that, and ask them to tell me instead about them and about their family – what they're like, who does what with whom, how do they spend their weekends, do they vacation and where and are things usually better then or worse? I see who speaks. I see who doesn't let anyone else speak. I find out if there is a voice of reason in the room or if members just want to come off as having been right. I look for what's missing: boundaries, respect, compassion, clarity, assertiveness, self-respect, hu-mor, affection, genuineness, directness of communication? Can I move the parents toward more compassion or humor or benevolence if I see it in short supply, or toward more firmness if that's what's needed? Do they know how to communicate their concerns without becoming overbearing, patronizing or overly reactive?

And the teenager? I try to figure out whether he'll need support in the ses-sion to say his piece or if he's confident enough by himself. I'll ask if he shares any of the concerns that his parents spoke about. Does he have any of his own? How well do the parents tolerate their teen pushing back on some of what they say in session? What would the teenager like to get out of the session and would he like to come back to meet with me privately? I'm listing many ques-tions here, but most of them are for my own contemplation. Some I may ask, but never too many; I want a conversation, not an interview.

## What if the Adolescent Doesn't Talk?

Parents (and sometimes therapists, too) worry when kids don't talk in family sessions, believing it to be a necessary part of a successful therapy. It doesn't have to be. There can be times when a teenager's involvement is minimal, and the therapy still moves forward, and sometimes it makes sense to work with just the parents. I never try too hard to "get" a teenager to become involved;

instead, I think about how I can make the conversation interesting enough so that he wants to join in. If he doesn't, he doesn't, and we move on.

Some teenagers might be reserved or reticent to speak in the beginning of a family session and, if that's the case, I like to give them time to settle in before asking too much of them. The advantages of giving kids some time before making anything of their reticence include the following:

- It reduces pressure on the adolescent to talk, which has the secondary effect of making it easier for them to do so should they wish.
- It disorients the adolescent because he very possibly was expecting to be peppered with questions by the therapist; it's another way of communicating that your therapy will be different.
- It assesses the flexibility and maneuverability of the parents. Will they be able to follow your leads about communication and the dynamics surrounding power and not feel compelled to solicit their teen's involvement? Or do they keep plying her with questions trying still to make something happen?
- It takes the wind out of the sails of a defiant teen who might have been expecting to use his silence to thwart the process.
- It also offers the teenager an opportunity to hear what the adults' concerns are and change on his own (flight into health[3]) before doing it in response to their requests or injunctions.

Typically, after the initial session with teenagers and their parents, I'll invite the teen back to meet with me privately a couple of times, with the idea of circling back to the parents in a follow up session afterward. I let everyone know that there will be parts of my conversation with the teenager that will stay confidential, but that there may be other parts helpful for the parents to know about that wouldn't compromise the teenager's privacy. I don't think it's very fair of us to take someone's child under our care and say, *Sorry, can't tell you a thing about what we're doing or about how she's doing. Confidentiality, you know....*

Whenever shaping those parameters of confidentiality with my clients, I like using the request developed by adolescent and family therapist Ron Taffel: "If there's anything you don't want me to tell your parents, let me know."[4] Taffel distinguishes his request from the more common and hackneyed statement that kids in therapy are uniformly told: *"Anything you tell me is between us. But if I feel there is an immediate danger to yourself or anyone else, I'll have to share that information ..."* Rather than simply promising confidentiality in all but extreme situations, Taffel's question hints at the possibilities for family reform that can result from therapists' liberation from binding confidentiality and the judicious use of material in order to inform/update/edify parents in service of the teenager and/or family.

I ask my teenage clients directly whether there are things they wish their parents understood better about them or their life outside the home. I ask if they're able to have conversations with them about harder topics without them deteriorating into arguments. I ask if they'd like me to try clearing up some of those misunderstandings or help move some of the recurring conversations forward. Most say yes, but none ever want to be there for it. *Have at it*, they tell me, *and good luck!*

Most of the time I'm content to meet with the parent or parents by themselves and often prefer it, especially if I need to address their parenting approach or discuss sensitive matters with them that they'd be uncomfortable talking about in front of their teenager (for example, marital conflict or personal mental health issues). But sometimes I want the teenager there with me when I meet with the parents, either because it's a conversation I hope they all will revisit at home by themselves, or because I want to create a space in the family for that teen's voice and model for him or her how to use it effectively. Many teenagers are apprehensive about voicing their concerns to parents, fearing retribution or more arguing. Others don't have the skill set to address difficult topics in a way their parents will appreciate before becoming defensive and shutting the whole thing down. Others have simply given up.

## Confrontation in a first session

Sometimes in these first family sessions, issues arise quickly, calling upon the therapist to make decisions about whether to stay on track or pivot to the process unfolding in the room.

Here, I'm trying to get an angry, blustery father to realize the limits of control in his relationship with his daughter and the price he is paying for doubling down on it. Whereas some therapists might have felt anxious challenging the father this early and without much of a therapeutic relationship at all, I trusted the dialogue to draw him in. It was up front, no nonsense, bold and (I believed) spot on. This father especially could respect that type of exchange more than he could one that's cautious and evasive.

> Seventeen-year-old Vanessa sits stiffly in my office across the coffee table from her father and stepmother. She says very little in this initial session, partly because she wasn't speaking to her father, and partly because he leaves little room for her *to* speak.
>
> Twenty minutes in I find out what's really brewing under all this tension. Vanessa is refusing to tell her father whether she is in fact seeing this boy who used to be her boyfriend some months ago. The father didn't like him then, and doesn't like him now, for reasons he's never explained.
>
> "Look, I just don't like the guy, okay?" the father replies testily when I ask what he doesn't like about the boy.
>
> "Okay but keeping everyone in the dark isn't helping the stand-off with your daughter," I tell him.

187

"What? I have to say I like him to get her to talk to me?" (This I saw as the father's attempt to deflect the focus away from his taciturn presentation and instead make it seem as though I'd just told him his daughter's cooperation was contingent upon his liking the boy. If I were to have fallen for this, I imagine the conversation would have gone as follows: I'd have responded with, *"No, not at all! You don't have to like him –"* and the father would cut me off (before I could say anything to suggest he was intentionally "missing" my point) with something like, *"Well that's what it sounded like!"*, reinforcing *his* point that he heard me say he'd need to like the boy in order to get his daughter to talk with him rather than what I *did* say, which had to do with him being more open about his very strong opinion.)

"It has nothing to do with whether or not you like the kid, Byron," I replied. And then, reiterating my original point, I said, "It has to do with your belief that saying you don't like him should be a good enough reason to shut this whole thing down. It's like saying, *Because I said so* to a kid."

"He says that all the time," contributed Vanessa. I smile at her, as if to say, *I figured.*

Again, missing my point, Byron asked, "She's my daughter. Shouldn't I be able to ask her whether she's got some thing going with this guy?"

"Of course you can ask her, Byron, and it's a fair question. But the way you talk with Vanessa and the way you ask her … it's just not particularly inviting –"

Byron cuts me off. "What, Vanessa? Do I have to send you a formal invitation to get you to speak with me?!"

"Byron, stop," I whispered. Byron stopped and sank back into the sofa. He looked defeated. "Don't go there," I said. "Can I help you start over again?"

"Yeah, okay."

Byron finally saw that he was just digging himself a deeper hole with his bombastic manner, and that if he wanted to change things in his relationship with his daughter, here was an opportunity to do so. Going forward, I'd meet with him privately one time and his daughter once privately before doing a session with both together. For the purposes of demonstrating what *being on everyone's side* looks like in a case such as this, I'll draw up a scenario where, during this joint session, I notice that Vanessa, despite her father's expressed wish to reach out differently, cuts him no slack and maintains her withholding stance.

"What's the matter, Vanessa?" I'd ask. "You dad's here on good faith but you're still holding his feet to the fire."

"Just because he's all willing to come here now and pretend to be this great father doesn't mean I should automatically not be angry anymore," she replies.

"No, it doesn't. You can remain angry and still it doesn't. You can remain angry and still have something positive happen here."

"I don't see how that's possible."

"Okay, here's one way. You're mad because your dad's parenting style often leaves you feeling belittled and angry. He learned in that first family session we had that if he kept it up, he was going to lose you, and it scared him. That's why he's here. No one expects you to dump years of resentment out the window and suddenly feel like everything's okay. You just have to dump *enough* to see that he's showing up, and showing up differently, and give him a chance to change."

After a few moments, Vanessa replies with, "Okay."

"Cool!" Byron calls out. "So does that mean you'll tell me whether you're seeing that boy or not?" My head swivels and I give Byron the stink eye. "Only kidding, guys!" he says. "V, I don't even care about that right now." He smiles softly, to which Vanessa responds with a small smile of her own.

That's what being on everyone's side looks like. By closely following the process in session, you can discern who needs support, who needs to be challenged, and who needs a little of both and you go there. Because you're able to be the therapist each person in the room needs you to be in any given moment, you can move forward more assertively earlier in the therapy than you might otherwise believe is possible.

Here's another case where I felt it necessary to challenge a parent right out of the gate, in both the first and second sessions. This is seventeen-year-old Grayson, whose parents were using humiliation and shame as tools of discipline, much to the emotional collapse of their son.

Grayson was a quiet, introverted boy with two legal charges pending against him, one for driving under the influence and another for disorderly conduct. He wasn't a bad kid at all; this was the first time he'd ever been in any kind of trouble, let alone with the law, and he was very depressed about the situation he'd put himself and his parents in. The problem was that his parents didn't think he was remorseful "enough." Grayson's understated emotional expressiveness did him no favors here, where it made him seem glib and cavalier about the ordeal. In fact, he was anything but.

In this first family session, Grayson's father declared that he was going to show Grayson the $2400 attorney bill. "That might make him take this more seriously."

189

"What makes you think he doesn't take it seriously already?" I asked.

"Parent's instinct, I don't know. I've just lost faith in him. I don't believe him anymore."

"What's happened that you don't find your son credible any longer?"

"February 17 and June 6," the father replied, listing the dates of the legal charges.

"Your son is a lot more than those two incidents" I replied. "People express remorse in many ways, some more apparent than others. I don't know your son real well yet, Bruce, but I imagine it's important for him not to feel as though he has to grovel for your forgiveness."

"Well, maybe he'll have to..."

I looked up at Bruce and said softly, "I don't know what you expect your son to do with that comment...."

Grayson comes to the next appointment with his mother. Outside of the harshly critical eye of his father, Grayson began talking about the two incidents where he was charged. It was the first time he'd ever done so.

"This is the first time I can talk about this," Grayson said, "where I can say how bad I feel. It was dumb, I know."

And his mother, not hearing or appreciating the concession in her son's candid remark, and the opportunity it affords for healing and moving forward, chose to say, "Well that's what I don't understand. If you knew it was such a bad idea, why the hell did you do it again?"

"Barb," I jumped in, "you've been waiting months for your son to start talking to you again. He's trying to. Don't make him regret opening up about what happened or he'll return home and go right back down to the basement, all depressed and mute again."

"Well, what am I supposed to say then?"

"I don't know, maybe you don't say anything but you touch his shoulder to let him know you appreciate his honesty. Maybe you say, 'Thank you for saying that; I thought you didn't care ...' Or you ask him what made it easier for him to talk about this today."

"I know what made it easier," Barb said. "His father isn't here."

"I wondered about that. Grayson, is that true? That it's easier for you to talk about this without your dad here?"

"It's easier to talk about anything when my dad isn't around," he said.

And that's how we began a conversation about something other than re-hashing the legal charges and whether Grayson was sufficiently remorseful.

Here's another example of challenging a client early in therapy, the reason being that the incident in question was rather brazen and too big to ignore. Moreover, it happened in front of me in the session. This is also a first appointment with a new family, one in which the mother and her seventeen-year-old son, Kyle, are not getting along. Kyle was the one to ask for therapy, and both parents accompanied him to the session.

It didn't take long at all to identify Kyle's contrarian nature, and I said something to that effect.

"Contrarian? That's exactly what I am!" Kyle stated. "That's exactly the term I would use to describe myself."

I asked if there were any times that were easy between Kyle and his mom, where they actually enjoyed each other's company.

Kyle's mother started telling me about their recent trip to NYC to visit colleges. "It was a pretty cool weekend actually," she said. "We toured two schools and walked around the city. I liked it. I think Kyle liked it...."

"No, I didn't like it," Kyle retorted. "I was miserable almost the whole time." Ouch.

"Well, I thought we had a good time ... I'm sorry you didn't," Kyle's mom said, deflated.

Looking at Kyle and his mother, I said, "Well that was either an honest misread or some revisionist history going on ..."

Kyle wasted no time. "I'm telling you, I did not enjoy that trip," he reiterated, looking over at his mom.

"Wow, Kyle," I said, "now it just looks like you're trying to make a point more than you're trying to figure out what's going on between you and your mom. That's not contrarian any longer; it's just mean."

Kyle looked down at his feet and replied weakly, "I was just sayin' ..."

Turning to Kyle's mother, I asked, "Are you often left a little stung by some of the things Kyle says to you, like what just happened here?"

Kyle's mother nods her head. I think if she'd spoken, she'd have cried.

"Kyle," I said softening my manner with him now, "does this (pointing back and forth between him and his mom) have anything to do with why you asked to meet with a therapist?"

Kyle just shrugged still looking down at his feet.

"Guys let's do this," I said, "let me spend some time with Kyle by himself. I think this is a good time to switch things up a bit. Kyle, you okay with that?"

"Yup," he replied.

Meeting with Kyle by himself that day, and in subsequent sessions, I learned that the way he showed up in that first session was the way he showed up everywhere in his life. He related with the few friends he had only through competitive debate, got in physical fights with his boarding school roommate, didn't care for tennis people, theater people or teachers, and wanted to climb the ladder into the upper echelons of finance – the only career he deemed worthy of pursuing. Being that critical, angry, and judgmental, no wonder the kid was depressed and tired and alone. I did find him much easier to work with when he was by himself – less defensive, more open, and a little better able to address all the conflict he was experiencing between himself and everyone else in his orbit.

My approach here with families is built on the same principles I talked about when working with clients individually – remaining credible, respecting the autonomy of clients, relating authentically, and holding clients accountable for their choices – but adds the element of including parents in the therapy in service of helping their kids. Sometimes, the parent is the only one invested enough to make the difficult calls and put into effect the necessary changes at home or in the parent~teen relationship. Sometimes, however, it's the parent who needs therapy more than the teen.

## Notes

1 I do, however, make exceptions for older teens such as high school juniors or seniors, especially if they sought out the therapy themselves or their issues relate to them personally and don't involve the family. In such cases, I'll see the teenager by herself first, and maybe find that I don't need to meet with any parents or guardians at all; it's just me and them.
2 No notepad – ever. You can't be present if you're jotting down notes, and clients don't like it. However, after each session I do write down anything I'll want to remember, including dialogue if I think it's demonstrative of some teaching point.
3 ... an abrupt "recuperation" by a prospective client after or during intake interviews and before entry into therapy proper or, more commonly, by a client in ongoing therapy in order to avoid further confrontation with cognitive, emotional, or behavioral problems. *American Psychological Association Dictionary of Psychology,* https://dictionary.apa.org/flight-into-health.
4 *Breaking through to teens: Psychotherapy for the new adolescence,* The Guilford Press, 2010.

# CHAPTER SEVENTEEN

# Bolstering the Resolve of Parents Who Struggle to Hold Their Teens Accountable

For many parents, the task of balancing their expressions of compassion and support for their teenagers with the need to hold them to account for the choices they're making is a struggle. Our current narrative about adolescence, the challenging times in which we are raising our kids, the communal pressures under which they are learning, socializing, and competing, and the deteriorated mental health of teens due to the Covid-19 pandemic, social media, and anxiety about their futures draws such sympathy from parents that they feel conflicted over imposing the standards necessary for healthy emotional and social growth and development. As a result, the bars for everything from social courtesies to work ethic to frustration tolerance have lowered, and the results aren't pretty.

Let's look at some of the reasons why kids are getting the bye.

## Why some parents struggle to hold their teens accountable for their choices and behaviors

- They feel guilty about the role of their past decisions on their teenager's mental health (e.g., divorce, moving multiple times) or their unavailability (e.g., working long hours as a single parent) and this causes them to let their kids get away with things.
- They are very easily manipulated or put on the defensive by their teenager whose comments or retorts get the parents to cease and desist with their efforts to hold the teen accountable.
- They have trouble establishing boundaries or following through with consequences that matter.

DOI: 10.4324/9781003257080-17

- They worry about overburdening or overly stressing their teen with responsibilities and end up enabling their teenager's resistance to accept new challenges or tasks.
- They excuse poor behavior as a function of puberty, hormones, or teens' "immature" brains.
- They dismiss their teenager's moodiness as "typical teen angst."
- They are exhausted by the push back from their teen, and want only some semblance of peace in their home.
- Their innate temperament, family-of-origin issues, or a recent history of high conflict in the home renders them so conflict-averse that they simply accommodate the teen's behavior/attitude in order to avoid any trouble.
- They are anxious about doing or saying something that will escalate the conflict or otherwise "make things worse."
- They are worried about coming off as unsympathetic or out-of-touch. They also might be worried about losing out to the more indulgent parent, especially if the parents live separately.
- They are trying to shield other family members who are at the mercy of their acting out sibling who may not think twice about causing a scene in restaurants, at holiday dinners, and family celebrations.

People feel bad for kids who feel bad, and this creates blind spots. These blind spots allow children and teenagers to show up as less than their best selves, and then that becomes the new normal. "Well, what can you expect," says a sixteen-year-old client of mine by the name of Naomi, describing one of her good friends from school. "He's a fifteen-year-old boy, and he's had a tough summer with his parents separating and all …," using those as reasons to excuse his coarse, insensitive, immature, and misogynistic behavior. Along those same lines, I very frequently see parents accept an astounding degree of disrespect from their kids, even very young ones. That behavior, too, appears to have been normalized, crammed into the overstuffed drawer of unbecoming conduct that is too often attributed to "typical teenage behavior."

Let's look at some of these reasons up close and explore ways to help parents push past the obstacles, be they internal or external, so they can be the parents their kids need them to be:

## Parents whose anxiety about over-stressing their teen causes them to enable their teenager's resistance toward new challenges or responsibilities

Some parents have difficulty balancing their natural inclination to protect their teenager with their teenager's need to learn how to handle frustration, failure, criticism, anxiety, and the recognition that they are not necessarily the best nor the smartest one in the bunch.

The therapy here consists of helping parents to distinguish between *helping* their teenagers and *enabling* them – not always an easy distinction in the best of circumstances, and even harder when you're a worried parent trying to give an assist to your troubled or disabled child. Many parents worry that insisting on certain standards of civil behavior in the home will add more stress on their already stressed-out teen. We can remind them though that there is a difference between making demands on your kids, and having expectations of them.

What makes this whole balancing thing even more challenging are all the extenuating circumstances that can come into play. Can I shift the line toward more accommodation if my kid is struggling with depression? What if he has low self-esteem? Learning difficulties? What does helping look like in this case? What about enabling? It's hard to watch your kid struggle and not intervene.

Parents help when they …

- … provide the support their teen needs in order to do the task to an age-appropriate level (anything from remembering assignments to writing thank you notes to making sure there's printer paper at home for an upcoming project).
- … demonstrate faith in the teen's ability to manage the anxiety or frustration engendered by the task, while also offering support/ideas/strategies to make it less taxing.
- … remain warm and emotionally accessible while also holding the teen accountable for how she chooses to handle herself while trying to meet the expectations (e.g., acting sulky or blaming others is not okay).

Parents enable when they …

- … do something for their teen that the teen says she can't do for herself but needs to begin learning how (e.g., **Me**: Why are you making all these phone calls for your nineteen year old daughter and setting up these appointments for her? **Parent**: Because if I don't do it, then she won't call. **Me**: How about if you hold off making appointments for things that matters more to her than to you, like that job she wants, and just do the ones you need to make sure happen, like that dentist follow up?)
- … lower standards so that their teen "makes the grade" (Jo is responsible for feeding the rabbits and cleaning out their cage but she does a terrible job, her mother says. "You don't send her back to do a better job?" I asked. "Ugh, we'd be at it all day," her mother replied, "with Jo saying it's fine and me saying it's not. So I just go back later and finish cleaning the cage. At least she's doing *something*….")
- … tell their teen she doesn't need to do it (chores, remembering appointments, being polite) because of her disability or depression or anxiety, at which point you can say, *It's not helpful to your daughter for her to learn that*

*having problems or not feeling your best is a good enough reason to bow out of your responsibilities, unless of course it's for a short period of time or the situation is more urgent. You can try helping her on her really bad days, but as her world expands into high school and jobs and college, there will be fewer and fewer people who are going to want to pick up the slack for her. She's better off getting some batting practice now at doing things she doesn't feel like doing while she's surrounded by people who at least will be nice about it*

- … protect their teens from the consequences of their choices (Maia rages every morning and, once she's missed her bus, demands to be driven to school. This makes whichever parent driving her late for work. The conversation with the parent may sound like … *Let's talk about that because it's not a healthy situation for your daughter or for the family …. Maia's not even trying to regulate her moods or their expression. You feel at her mercy and get resentful because you know you're going to have to drive her to school most mornings. She's angry at you for yelling at her to hurry up so she yells back …. Her two brothers have to be miserable as well…. Let's structure the situation so that the impact of Maia's choices in the morning – meaning, her casual disregard of time – fall on her at least as much as they do on you. For instance, it could be that you and her dad refuse to drive her if she misses the bus and she doesn't get to school that day (only suitable for a kid who absolutely does not want to miss school). Or that Maia has to make restitution to you guys by donating an hour of her time on the weekend to one of your favorite charities for each day she's driven. Let's also find out why mornings are so hard for her – is it a habit or skill deficit or part of her disability?*)

## Helping Shivani's parents to stop enabling her anxiety avoidance

A mother brought in her thirteen-year-old daughter, Shivani, saying she'd grown concerned about the increasing amount of anxiety her daughter has been experiencing. Shivani is trying very hard to get through middle school with all As. She is in her third quarter of her 8th grade year.

Shivani's anxiety was showing up in the following ways:

- Shivani cannot leave an answer blank on a homework assignment. She feels she needs to complete everything, even if it's not being graded.
- Shivani checks her homework sheets at least a dozen times every evening - and this is after she's completed it. She can't resist the impulse to check them over again and make sure there are no blank spaces.
- Shivani insists that her parents help her prep for exams and has them test her repeatedly with flashcards, etc., way past the point where she knows the material sufficiently. If they are tired, busy, or tell Shivani that they don't

think she needs more prep, Shivani's anxiety rises until she has a full-blown anxiety attack, during which she screams, cries, and yells at her parents that they are going to make her fail.

- In order to avoid these tantrums, and to keep Shivani from having levels of anxiety that are overwhelming, Shivani's parents oblige most of her requests, even when they know they shouldn't. Even when her parents have gone to bed, Shivani will pound on their door and insist that they wake up and test her again with the cards.

Shivani's parents aren't helping her to manage what are clearly overwhelming degrees of anxiety, and their approach has only reinforced the problem. By agreeing to Shivani's demands to be tested over and over again, they are enabling her anxiety to basically rule everyone's lives. My helping Shivani in this instance consisted of helping her mom to set appropriate limits around test prep, for instance, she would help her for one hour max any day she asked, and only for major tests. Once her parents went to bed, or if they said they were busy or tired, Shivani needed to stop. Less accessibility to her parents, though, meant they needed to help Shivani know how to get help for herself through other means, such as textbooks, websites, and the teachers' web pages.

If Shivani didn't respect these new boundaries, the parents were to impose some consequences. For example, each time she ignored her parent's redirection and persisted, Shivani's phone would be shut off for fifteen minutes. Her parents had tried for years to get Shivani to stop by telling her *No*, but Shivani would carry on crying and yelling for hours, while pounding on their bedroom door. When *no* is not enough, parents need to bring in something else that matters enough to the teen that they consider stopping.

All the conversations above took place with Shivani and her mom together in the first couple of sessions, with me continually checking in with Shivani and keeping her included in the conversation. I wanted to make sure she understood what I was telling her mom and why I thought it was important. After hanging back for a while, Shivani came to accept what she already knew to be true: that her current way of handling anxiety was causing a great deal of stress in her relationships with her parents, which made her even more anxious. She understood too that she wasn't developing the skills she'd need to manage high school come fall.

There was another important element to the therapy, and that was helping Shivani to develop an appreciation of the impact of her anxiety management on the people around her. These conversations I held privately with just Shivani. She was such a considerate girl in other contexts – in school, with friends, at her dance studio – and I didn't want her getting locked into the habit of indulging her own needs at home at the expense of her parents and sister, which would create/prolong an ugly dynamic. And, finally, Shivani and I spent time talking about anxiety management skills and grades and perfectionism and all those things that seem like good ideas but leave people feeling tied up in knots.

### Parents whose guilt makes them look the other way, and say yes when they want to say no

Some parents whose life choices have made their kids' lives harder feel a need to even up life's balance sheet. That means they are probably going to be a little too ready to overlook problematic behavior, bail their kid out of situations, make excuses for them when they act poorly, or tolerate disrespectful treatment because they feel bad about their role in some of the challenges their teen has had to face. Parents whose teenagers have had it extra tough (trauma, ugly divorce, loss) often have the hardest time with this. That's how parents end up allowing their kid to drive to a concert with questionable friends ("He's missed out on so much already....") or pretend they didn't see him taking that six pack from the garage.

Other reasons why parents wrestling with guilt may rationalize their leniency:

- "I feel bad for my son because of how his dad treats him so I try to make things easier for him when he's with me."
- "She's already been through enough with the divorce and moving and all.... I don't want to be another source of stress in her life."
- "I'm hardly home in the evenings during the week as it is now that I'm the sole provider, and I don't want to spend that time arguing, so I just let a lot of things go…"

One way to help guilty parents is to get them to **separate the two things that often get conflated:**

1) how bad parents feel for their teenagers, and
2) the expectations they have for them.

Here's what I will say to a parent in this situation:

"If you're feeling this kind of pressure to make up for lost time or a bad experience, the solution rests in separating out the two things that are getting stuck together in an unproductive way – one, your sorrow (or guilt, if feeling personally responsible) about the past situation, and, two, your desire for your teenager to have a better, easier, or happier time.

"What will help you to disentangle the two is for you to deal very directly with your teenager about both issues, but to see them and discuss them as separate matters. You speak to your sorrow, you speak to your desire for your daughter to have it better now, and you speak to how parents sometimes fall into the trap of trying to make up for tough times by being a softie and letting their kids do too many of the things that keep them happy. Then you tell her that while you'll always be mindful of the impact of your past and present decisions on her, you'll no longer use it as your excuse to let her get away with things.

"Speak with your daughter as candidly and warmly as you can about these things. It's okay to say, if you haven't already, that you've always felt bad that your drinking, or the problems between you and your ex, or your pre-occupation with keeping the family business afloat, affected her. It's not important to justify or rationalize what happened, so avoid saying things like,

- I did the best I could!
- Hey, lots of kids have it worse, you know....
- You should be kind of grateful because that's how we were able to send you to private school.

Here are other examples of how you can help parents explain to their kids, in a very emotionally honest statement, why their behavior might look different now than in the past:

"I've felt so bad about how many times we've moved and how many friends you've lost that I let you manipulate me into allowing you to do as you please in terms of your social life, and it's not good, it's not even safe anymore. I still feel bad about the moves, and probably always will, but it's not a good reason for me to give you a free pass to do whatever and go wherever you want."

"You know, I love you like crazy, and would do anything for you. I know too that you've paid a price for my decisions and that's made it hard for me to set limits with you that I should, but it's a disservice to us both. I'll help you with XYZ but it's not okay to take your anger out on me, or to use our past as an excuse to bug out of responsibilities or be rude."

There are many teens who recognize their parents' guilt in the accommo-dations they are making for them, and they go on to exploit it. A parent might have to say something that touches upon their teenager's exploitation in order to disempower it, such as:

"I can't tell whether you're using the divorce as an excuse to act poorly or if you're really struggling with this more than we've realized. I want to help, but also don't want to feel taken advantage of."

Or you might coach them to say,

*"Look, I really am sorry that I couldn't give you something better than this, but you can either hold my feet to the coals for the next several years, or join me in trying to do something about it."* Talk with them about finding other ways of expressing their regrets so that they are free emotionally to

199

make the parenting choices they want to be making, not the ones they hope will make their teenager "feel" better.

## Parents who see their teenager's behaviors as things they "can't help" rather than as choices being made

A boy's diagnosis of ADHD can mask a boatload of bad behavior. Getting the boy's behavior under control may be less important than getting his parents to see their son's behavior *as a function of the choices he's making*, not things he can't help doing. This can be a game-changer for the family, because once parents decide to define behaviors as choices being made a lot can change. Like the parents noted above who need to separate their guilty feelings from the expectations they have of their kids, these parents will do well to separate ...

1) the expectations they have of their child, in this case, that their son with ADHD *can* control his temper, put away the groceries when he sees you come home from the store, refrain from cursing at you, find a way to be on time, and find strategies to remember his skates for hockey practice, ***from***
2) how hard it will be for their son to do those things.

It will always be harder for kids or teens with ADHD to sit still in class, focus on assignments, remember to walk the dog. *But that doesn't mean they shouldn't be expected to do those things.* When parents give their kids the bye for no reason other than it will be hard for them to do something, or that it will be hard for the parent to enforce, they lose the opportunity to communicate to them that the larger world will expect them to be able to handle age appropriate tasks and responsibilities, that the people in it won't care whether you have ADD or OCD or ODD – they just want the job or assignment done. Friends, partners, employers, roommates, and even family members will run out of patience if a young adult tries to hide behind a diagnosis in an attempt to escape responsibilities.

### *Braelin*

Braelin is a fourteen-year-old girl attending a private school for learning-disabled kids. While personable and kind, she is also immature for her age, socially insecure, and highly attention-seeking. All that leads her to say things that cause a lot of drama between her and her eighth-grade classmates and, ultimately, drives them to turn on her with a pack mentality out of which they say such remarks as, "You should just kill yourself."

I'd been seeing Braelin in individual sessions, and occasionally speaking with her mother via Zoom or a brief phone call. There were frequent incidents at home in which Braelin would have an outright melt down when denied something she felt entitled to, or when she perceived rejection from her peers. "They told me I looked like a disgusting rat!" Braelin said to her mom, from her school bathroom fifteen minutes into her seventh-grade prom. "You have to come get me now!" she demanded. These incidents almost always ended in a flurry of tears, threats to cut herself, and expressions of suicidal thoughts, along with an admission of having lied about what she'd heard from others. The more that Braelin urgently searched for validation from others, the more desperate and off-putting her behavior became, creating a horrible cycle of impulsive acting out and self-deprecation.

Many social and emotional forces drove Braelin's behavior but one large factor, I worried, was her parents' repeated declarations that Braelin was not responsible for how others treated her. "It's not your fault," I would hear her mother tell Braelin, "that some kids choose to be mean."

Well, sure, no one deserves to be treated meanly, but that kind of statement releases Braelin from any responsibility for how her words and behavior impact those around her. She's not responsible for having been bullied, but she is in large measure responsible for the irritation evoked in her peers by her provocative behavior. Telling Braelin that what's happening is not her fault was a disservice to her. I understood that Braelin's parents were trying to preserve whatever self-esteem their daughter still had, but their strategy reinforced her victim status and discouraged the cultivation of personal self-reflection necessary for healthy relationships.

Within weeks of beginning of her eighth-grade year, Braelin was already feeling targeted and marginalized by her peer group at school. On a video call with Braelin's parents, I had the chance to speak to them about the liabilities of a parenting approach that tried to elevate a child's self-esteem by labeling others as the aggressors and disregarded the role that their own child might have played in the problems that have materialized.

> "Monica, I know you've made a point of telling Braelin that she's not responsible for how others treat her, and you're right – she's not. But I think it's also important for you to point her attention toward the role of her words and her behavior on what happens between her and her classmates. I think you could say, *'Listen, I hear you tell me what happens during many of these upsetting situations at school. Because I've always wanted to show you that I'm on your side, I never bring up anything that might make you feel bad, but I realize now that there's a missing part to these conversations – and it's the part that you play. I've always felt so bad for you that I didn't want you to think I was blaming you, but it doesn't help you if I don't also say* Hey, what's your role here? *and try to help you look at that as well.'"*

I encouraged Braelin's parents to start interacting with their daughter as the kid she *could* be, rather than the regressed version she presented in the wake of the problems at school. In other words, instead of jumping in to "rescue" her, or provide her with the external emotional regulation she appeared to need to develop for herself, I wanted them to believe that their daughter was indeed capable of a better response, but just not incentivized to do so because she got so much gratification (attention, support, responsiveness, kid glove care) from her regressed response. "I think Braelin's meltdowns are old habits – defaults, if you will. I see in her strong hints of a more mature way of relating, but I think you have to invite it to come forward."

I also encouraged Braelin's parents to (kindly and thoughtfully) use their genuine emotional responses to Braelin's behavior to help her understand the impact of her choices on the people around her. For example, that time Braelin called from her seventh grade prom saying the girls there were calling her a "disgusting rat" and then proceeded to yell at her mom when she said she couldn't come get her right away … could Monica say to her daughter something like the following?

> *I want you to know I always will have your back … But when I found out that you lied about what was happening at your prom, I felt played and resentful. I wish you'd have just been honest with me from the start.*

I also recommended to Braelin's parents that they help Braelin find an environment where she could be respected for her organizational skills and casual sociability. Soon afterward, Braelin got a job on Saturday mornings at her local farmer's market with one of the vendors. This experience allowed her to see who she could be at her best and appreciate the positive response she got when she pulled back on the attention-seeking acting out and related in a more relaxed, age-appropriate manner.

## Parents who dismiss their teenager's problems as "typical teen angst"

Our misleading cultural narrative about teenagers suggesting that unruly or immature behavior is a "teen phase" or a function of raging hormones or an undeveloped brain is one of the things that stands between sound parental decision-making and the overwhelming indulgence we see today in so many parenting approaches. Mistaking behaviors of choice as behavioral imperatives, too many parents dismiss poor behavior as just "stuff that teens do," allowing *bad* behavior to be seen simply as *teen* behavior.

A reasonable starting place when meeting parents who hold to these beliefs can be some point in the conversation where, in response to an incidental remark, such as, "Well, you know he does that because of all the hormones raging through his body now …," you say, "I know a lot of people believe that to be true, but I don't know that we can say it is all about hormones (or just a phase or will self-correct)." Here's an example of such a case:

Brazen insults and a disrespectful tone were fifteen-year-old Faith's weapons of choice in her battle to neutralize her parents' authority in her family.

"I think it's just a phase she's going through," Faith's mom was telling me in a parent consultation session. "You know, teens ...."

"It's not a phase, Norma" I say in response. My comment is purposefully stark, in order to break through all the dogma surrounding adolescence. "Insulting your parents, being rude, that's not a phase. That's a problem," I add. "Parents are led to believe it's a phase because that's how we talk about teenagers, that they all do it and will grow out of it. But they don't all do it, and none have to do it, and many never grow out of it. I think Faith needs you and her dad to think about this differently, not as typical teenager stuff but as a bad habit that needs to be extinguished. I can help you with that. And I can help Faith, too, with whatever it is that's going on for her that's fueling this behavior at home."

## Parents who have trouble establishing boundaries or following through by imposing consequences that matter

Many parents struggle to consistently set limits around their teenagers' behaviors while others have trouble with the follow through, or both. Here are some reasons why, each one as valid as the other:

- too tired
- tried it, doesn't work
- teen out maneuvers them anyway
- teen pushes back too hard, makes parent feel worse
- it becomes an ordeal
- teen consistently convinces them that they're misguided
- can't think of an appropriate consequence
- teen says "Here, take my phone, I don't care ..."
- don't want the hassle
- don't want the conflict that will ensure
- don't care anymore (okay, maybe this one's not so good)

Help for parents like these can be a conversation about what appropriate consequences are and which ones are ineffective or worse, adding fuel to the fire of resentment that entraps the parent and teen. In addition to the obstacles listed above, parents may ...

- *... not know which consequences will be effective with their teenager.*

203

- *... not realize that they can take time to think about how they want to respond to an incident, that they don't have to know on the spot what they're going to do.*
- *... believe they are already doing the consequences thing.*

Appropriate consequences should never be anything that shames or embarrasses the teenager or manipulates his or her emotions. Here are consequences that don't work:

- yelling, threatening, lecturing, scolding
- not telling the teen when the consequence will end
- holding grudges
- telling teens how disappointed you are in them

The purpose of a consequence is not to be punitive but only **to disincentivize the undesired response.** Basically, what the kid loses in terms of privileges or his free time (because maybe now he has extra work to do around the house) isn't worth what he gains from acting out. It also serves to balance power inequities in the family. Let's say a teenager has a younger brother who loves to annoy her to the point of bullying, for example, singing loudly while standing in front of her room early on Sunday mornings for the express purpose of waking her up. Rather than threatening to take his phone or some other device or privilege, he's told to make breakfast for her on that Sunday, or to do her chores for her on whatever the day he disturbs her privacy. It's not always about taking things away. If he doesn't comply, *then* he loses his phone.

Ideally, consequences...

- ... are something that matter enough to the teen to make him reconsider what he was about to say or do because it's no longer worth the price he'll have to pay.
- ... last for one day at most so that the next day everything starts over again.
- ... are imposed in the spirit of "that was an unfortunate choice" rather than of anger.
- ... are inconvenient or unpleasant but never punitive.

### Parents who are easily manipulated or put on the defensive regarding their parenting approach or judgment

Kids are astute readers of personality and know just how to take advantage of their parents' weaknesses in order to get what they want. These liabilities include anything from wanting to be that kid's "favorite" parent (especially in cases of divorce), to worrying about being a "good enough" parent, to wanting to be sure their kid knows that they care about them or feel bad for them or appreciate how lousy they feel.

### Coaching parents on how to respond to manipulative remarks

*Where teenagers exploit a parent's doubt or anxiety
regarding their parenting style*

> "I can't believe you actually called your sister to find out how to deal with me," criticizes fifteen-year-old Henry, whose single parent dad is flummoxed by Henry's most recent run in with the police.

> "Sure did," is how I would advise Henry's dad to respond to his son. Owning the decision to have called his sister is far better than trying to find some excuse that would appease his son. Henry wasn't looking to be appeased. He was looking to neutralize some of his father's authority.

*Where teenagers convince their parent they've been
offended by something the parent said.*

> "I cannot believe you don't trust me!" exclaims Hedy to her mother, who had just said that she wasn't ready to let Hedy sleep out at her friend Lila's house again, since the last time she did the two girls got smashed on vodka and spent the next day in bed throwing up.

> "Oh, honey, ...." is usually how the parent starts, feeling a need to back pedal so that the teenager doesn't *actually* think that her very own parent doesn't trust her. And right there, the teen knows she's "got" her.

> So when Hedy's mom replies with, "Of course I trust you, sweetheart ..." Hedy digs in even more deeply.

> "I can't believe this. It happened *one* time, mom, and it's like you won't let me go out ever."

> "Oh, no, hon, you can go out –"

> "So, I can go to Lila's then this weekend?"

> "No, you can't go over to Lila's but if you want she can come here –"

> "Forget it then ..." says Hedy, who ends the conversation abruptly.

How can we help parents who suddenly feel burdened with the responsibility to defend a sentiment toward their child that's not unreasonable? Let's say that exchange between Hedy and her mother took place during a session:

ME: "Your daughter is very good at getting you on the defensive." Hedy likely would be looking over at me, wondering where I'm going with this.

P: "You're not kidding."

ME: "Trust is a big word that can mean a lot of things, Colleen. You may trust Hedy to take care of her little sister by herself, to stay out of the liquor cabinet at home, to make good decisions when it comes to boys or who she drives with, but the truth is that, after last weekend, *you just don't trust her to stay out of trouble at Lila's house.*" Now I'd turn to the daughter. "Hedy, my friend, you went over to Lila's last weekend to bake cookies and the two of you ended up hugging toilets all night. Of *course* your mom doesn't trust you to go back over to Lila's yet – but who's really surprised at that (undermining the righteousness that is causing Colleen to doubt herself). Your mom trusts you to do all the important things, but not this one thing, so your question about trust isn't really a fair one. Instead, ask your mom what she needs to see in order to feel comfortable with you going over to Lila's house again, and start there."

## I can't believe you're going to punish me for being in a bad mood

"I'm not punishing you for being in a bad mood. I'm giving you a consequence *because I don't like how you talk* to me and your brothers when you're in a bad mood. Big difference."

## You're so mean

- I'm sorry you see me that way - I can't say I agree. And you leave it there, without giving the teen an opportunity to draw you into a protracted debate about whether or not you're actually really "mean."
- I think I do get mean sometimes and I hate it. I've just grown so tired of all the fighting and of having to work so hard to get your cooperation that it's affected how I am with you. I'm sorry.
- You say that every time I say no to something you want. It's kind of a shitty dilemma for a mom who just wants to be able to parent her kid who she adores.

## If you don't let me XYZ, then I'll do something you'll regret

If the teen threatens to cut or kill herself or run away, then it's important that she live with the consequences of her *statement*, which could mean that a parent sleeps over in her room on an air mattress rather than feel anxious about what the daughter is doing in her room, alone and angry. Parents have to be able to say no to their teenager, especially in response to something like the threat above, which sounds more like a behavioral issue than a mental health crisis. No lecture, no threats in return, just "I can't stay up all night wondering what you're feeling bad enough to do, or capable of doing. So I'm going to stay with you – not going to bother you or even talk to you if you don't want me to. And if you tell me you still feel that way in the morning, then we'll call your therapist/

crisis services/your doctor .... Sorry, love, but if you're going to say something that you know is going to scare us, then it should come as no surprise that we do something that assures us you're safe."

*Other comments like this ...*

- "Fine, I'll just keep everything to myself."
- "Well, I'm sorry I'm such a difficult child."
- "Sorry I cost you so much money."
- "Everything you say is negative and it just makes me feel worse."

Comments like the ones above are expressed for the sole purpose of putting parents on the defensive. In response, parents would do well to respond with a flat comment such as "I'm sorry you feel that way," or "I see it differently but that's okay," or "Not sure how you got that impression, but I hear you." *None of this is said sarcastically.* It's said in an even tone that suggests to the teen there's not much to fight here. Then later, on a different day, when the teen is not as angry, parents can return to what the teenager had said, giving her a chance to be taken seriously if, in fact, there was something serious about what the kid said. For example, "Tell me more about what you said the other day, Wren, about everything I say being so negative and making you feel worse. Is that something you really feel?"

TEEN: *No, I was just mad, forget it.*
MOM: *Okay.*
or,
TEEN: *Yeah, I do feel that you're always so negative, like I can never do any-thing right.*
DAD: *I'm sorry, I know I get angry a lot, but I never want it to affect how you feel about yourself. I think we've gotten into this weird cycle, where I almost ex-pect you'll do something that will upset me, so I take on an attitude before you even do anything. I'll try to stop doing that, and not be so negative ...*

I recognize that this kind of processing and responding is a tall order for many (most?) parents (or adults in general). Too few have ever seen it modeled for them in their families of origin or have gone out of their way to intentionally acquire an expanded emotional awareness and the skill set needed to create emotionally sensitive dialogue like the ones suggested above. But just because we don't see a lot of it doesn't mean we don't keep trying to raise a collective awareness of the beauty and potency of using language in a way that enhances connection and stimulates a desire in others to respond in kind. We can't ex-pect kids to pick this up on their own, or to even know such communication exists. It will have to start with their parents/caregivers, which means it will have to start, for the most part, with us.

## When kids are unkind

*My kid is so nice to everyone but us!"* This is a parents' refrain heard around the country. Teenagers display their more gracious side to everybody except to the ones who love them most. The reason? "Oh, they're my family. They can take it." Or "My parents know I don't mean it." Huh?

Painting broadly, American parents are more demonstrative than most when it comes to reassuring their kids that they are loved unconditionally. Unfortunately, in too many families, this translates into a free-for-all for kids, where they feel emboldened to brazenly push back on parental limits, values, and behests, or ignore them altogether.

Kids won't say as much, but they do find it hard to respect adults who play to their favor, who promise everything and expect nothing in return, who naively presume that demonstrating unbridled compassion and understanding without the balancing arm of personal accountability will draw out the best in them.

I think it's important that the mental health community stand strongly behind a shared push for parents to create family climates where members are not taken for granted as emotional dumping grounds but seen as deserving of the most considerate and generous treatment a person has to offer. For the sake of the respect and self-respect among family members that serves to hold families together in loving, healthy, and mutually caring ways, we need to do what we can to *de-normalize* this phenomenon where kids curse in their parent's face and the parents respond with something along the lines of, *Well, at least she feels safe with us at home and can express herself ….*

Some of the disrespectful comments are said with the intention to cause a parent emotional pain, neutralize a parent's power, or bully a parent into acquiescence. But others are mirrored reflections of the parents' style of relating to their child or teen. Respectful exchanges within a family require that *everyone* demonstrate respect, and while the disdain in a teen's comment may be evident to everyone in the room, that of the parent may not be, and it goes undetected. Kids who are addressed by adults in ways that make them feel patronized, invisible, underestimated, or dismissed will find ways to preserve their self-esteem that mimic the bully but are borne of a very different dynamic; their acts are more defensive in nature than they are aggressive. These kids, and the bullies, are very different kids, and in order to heal and change, they require from us very different interventions.

## Disrespect versus Defiance

A lot of teen bullying or disrespect ends up being rationalized by parents as simply teen "defiance" – a less personal offense than being disrespected and one often misunderstood as a requisite phase of adolescence. Whether or not you believe defiance to be a customary part of adolescence, it's still very different from disrespect.

Defiance is saying NO. It can be done respectfully or disrespectfully. Disrespect, however, is always inappropriate, and all bullying is disrespectful. There's an element of, *Whoa – I can't believe you just said that*. And its purpose is to DISABLE the parent.

I think of a teen's defiance as more of a communication about the self than it is an attempt to neutralize the power of the other person. Puberty, hormones, or changes in the brain – these are NOT the reasons why a kid decides to say "F%*@ you" to his mother or put his fist through the living room wall.

That said, we are way more familiar, however, with the ways in which kids disrespect their parents than we are with the ways in which parents disrespect their kids. Kids, and teenagers in particular, are able to disrespect their parents in big, showy, obvious ways. They make fun of or mock their parents in front of their siblings or friends, curse at them, act dismissively toward their suggestions or ideas, or respond to them with insulting remarks such as, "Dad, you're really pathetic, you know that?" Because of this, it is the teenager who is seen as the aggressor in many parent~teen conflicts, and the parent an unfortunate victim.

Most parents won't go that far or be that blatant when they're angry at their kids, but that doesn't mean they don't hurt them any less. In fact, I could argue that barbs from parents hurt kids much more than the other way around:

1)  Unlike with the teenager who does a better job of owning his aggression, the barbs thrown by parents are rarely acknowledged by the parent, creating disharmony between what the parent is expressing and what parent *says* she is expressing; this dissonance is disturbing and frustrating to the teenager, and the reason behind much of the rage we see in kids who cannot address the duplicity in communication in the family.
2)  I also believe there is a fundamental assault on a child's personal sense of self every time a parent says something hurtful; parents are simply not supposed to hurt their children.

## Helping parents to break the cycle of disrespect and bullying at home

Here are three ways you can help parents break the cycle of disrespect and bullying in their own families:

1)  Help them to recognize offensive or disrespectful remarks for what they are and to consider them unacceptable, rather than dismissing them as "things that all teens say to their parents."

2)  Coach them to employ effective consequences and to respond more constructively. For example, *That was an unfortunate comment, Nigel. For whatever pleasure you derived from calling me a 'serious asshole', you've lost your phone privileges for an hour.* Now, an hour away from one's phone might not seem like much, but it's not about how severe the consequence is. Besides, kids are offended by any threat to what is experienced as their proprietary right to their electronics, and any time at all that's taken from them is a big deal. All any consequence really has to do is *dis-incentivize* the undesired behavior (name-calling the parent, in this case). Its job is to prompt them, the next time they're about to let loose, to think, *Ah, I'll probably end up losing my phone, not worth it* and find another (more acceptable way) to express displeasure toward the parent.

3)  Teach parents to identify times when their own guilt or their teen's manipulations are compromising their judgment, and to try their best to follow through with their plan even if they don't feel great about it.

4)  Guide them in using the natural disincentivizing influence of self-consciousness, described below.

## *The natural disincentivizing influence of self-consciousness*

Self-consciousness draws on the fact that we are social beings and that, for most people, the need to be accepted by society is a powerful force in shaping behavior and conscience. For that reason, it is a very powerful vehicle through which we, as parents, therapists, teachers, and mentors can influence behavior change, especially in those whose resist our direct attempts.

A mother of a teenage daughter was once asking me what she could do about her daughter's disrespectful tone of voice and manner of speaking to her at home. She said it always got worse when her daughter's friends were around. The mother had tried talking to the girl about it and had taken away her cell phone and other privileges a few times, to no avail. Her daughter would simply flip her hair through the air, and act as if she hadn't been planning to use the phone for a while anyway.

I suggested to the mother that the next time her daughter had friends over and talked to her disrespectfully in front of them, instead of ignoring it (because of not wanting to embarrass the daughter in front of her friends) or making a joke of it (as if, yeah, they were all just kidding) or walking off with a slow burn (to avoid a conflict), she should simply stop whatever she was doing, and look directly and pointedly at her daughter. The mother wouldn't necessarily need to say anything, because halting her action and focusing on her daughter – the visual track of which would be followed by the friends in the room – would very suddenly and unexpectedly put the attention on the daughter, instead of on the mother, which the daughter had grown accustomed to expecting.

Part of the power of this intervention comes from the sense of drama that's evoked. All movement stops. There is no conversation. (There is no argument, either.) There is nowhere for the attention to go but on what's happening between parent and teen and, eventually, solely on the teen.

Kids don't like it when their attempts to control events leave *them* in the spotlight instead of the intended person, in this case the mother. This is the power of self-consciousness, I explained. The mother was now able to intervene with her daughter's inappropriate behavior without having to talk with her, which would be used by the girl as a springboard into rebuttal, negotiation, or frank defiance. There is nothing for the daughter to fight here. There is nothing for her to object to. She can only stand there and make some attempt at dismissing her mother's stance as ridiculous in some way which, in all likelihood, would come off as lame to her friends, or quickly change the topic and pretend that nothing happened.

No matter what the daughter says at that moment, the mother need only to stay the course in order to underscore her point. If the daughter were, say, to try and define her mother's response as an overreaction, her mother just stands there, maybe raises her eyebrows, as if to say, *Really?*

These actions on the mother's part, express everything that needs to be said in that moment:

- that what her daughter said was unacceptable,
- that the mother was no longer going to pretend it didn't affect her or that she didn't hear it,
- and that anytime her daughter took the liberty of saying something like that she should expect to have to account for it in the presence of whoever was around to hear it.

While on the topic of parents whose children and teenagers take advantage of them, consider for a moment the parent who wants to know if it's okay that she feels angry toward her son. "That's not a choice you make," I would tell her. "If you're feeling it, the anger is already there, and I can appreciate why after what you've told me." I've found that when a parent's compassion for their child or teen morphs into anger, it's usually because they're now feeling terribly imposed upon, and that the teen isn't really working with them in good faith.

One way to move things forward in this kind of situation is by helping parents *reduce the level of resentment* they feel toward their son or daughter. Resentment is often the reason why parents are so reactive and angry with them, and unable to hold a space where genuine conversations can happen without the barbs or heavy-handedness that dooms so many attempts to talk things out. They find it increasingly difficult to extend their good will or to see positive changes that the adolescent has been trying to make. When we help parents to reduce their level of resentment, we are clearing the way for relationship recovery. Here are two ways to do this:

1) helping parents *detach from the outcome of their teenager's decisions,* and
2) helping parents to *free themselves from feeling at the mercy of their teenager's behavior.*

An example of the first is when a mother who had been desperate for her daughter to pass algebra lets go of that and realizes that if her daughter allowed herself to fail algebra it would be unfortunate, but manageable.

An example of the second is when a father who, at his son's request, tries to help the boy improve his basketball game only to be berated, and finally decides he won't subject himself to the boy's hot-headedness any longer, to which of course the boy reacts with feigned disbelief.

The other problem for parents can be that after years of fighting, arguing, accommodating, and trying to appease, they are too tired and too resentful – just too tapped out – to have the psychological reserves necessary to maintain clarity in their perspective and in their reflection of events.

Unfortunately, that kind of prolonged stress also makes it hard for some parents to soften and see the pain behind their teenager's scowls, rolled eyes, and snarky retorts. Self-reflection isn't the first thing that comes to mind when you're angry at your teenager, and our beliefs about teenagers make it easy to assume that their angry or rejecting reactions to what you have said or done are a part of their separating from adults, or a function of adolescent rebellion, rather than a sign that they are hurting, too.

### Handling situations where your client's parents ask you for advice on consequences for their teenager

One challenging situation that almost any therapist working with teenagers comes across is that of supporting parents in their efforts to hold that teen more accountable for their behavior or choices than they have been able to in the past. This sometimes involves helping them to set firmer limits and/or boundaries and impose consequences when their teen doesn't oblige. Here's the question I get from therapists struggling to balance their alliances within the family:

"I don't know how to handle situations where parents ask me for advice about consequences for their kids. I worry that if I talk with them about taking away their kid's phone or restricting other privileges, their kid will be mad at me and it will affect our relationship."

And here's my response to this seeming dilemma: Painting broadly here, I believe that deep in their being, where they are their most authentic and honest with themselves, most kids can recognize parental over-accommodation or an absence of accountability within the family. It may be harder for teens who are depressed, very anxious, emotionally immature, or feeling extremely stressed to see the value in changing things up at home to bring them more into balance, but this is something you'll need to talk with them about, helping them to see the ways in which their growth and development is being compromised by not being asked to become more self-aware or patient or responsible. For most teens who are being frankly disrespectful or demonstrating a cavalier disregard for rules, curfews, and personal space, there's no need to explain why their jig is up, despite the barrage of excuses or flashes of anger they unleash. They know. In fact, many have been waiting a long time to be told to knock it off.

## Encourage parents to have a "heads-up" talk with their teenager prior to making changes

Whenever I speak with parents about making changes in how they're going to respond to their teenager's behavior, attitude, or choices, I encourage them to sit down with their son or daughter when no one is angry or upset with anyone else and tell them that they're going to try to address problems at home differently.

I suggest to the parents that they tell their teenager they probably won't like a lot of the changes, but that they're necessary for the health of the family, the health of family relationships, and the teenager's own emotional health. I let parents know that their teen is unlikely to agree with anything they're saying, but that the conversation is not about "getting them onboard."

Some mental health and educational professionals advise parents to invite their kids to join them in coming up with house rules and responsibilities so that they feel included. The idea is that, given the inclusion, these kids will be more likely to follow through with the program. This is one of those things that looks great on paper, but rarely carries over into real life application. Kids don't care whether they were in on the ground floor of a new plan that ultimately leaves them with a higher level of personal accountability and fewer opportunities to indulge their wishes; in the end, they just want to be able to do what they've grown accustomed to being able to do. Okay, we get it.

The heads-up talk is a courtesy to the teenager, and nothing more. But the courtesy part is important, and says to the teenager – *Look, we have some new ideas for how we want this family to operate, and we don't want to spring it on you because there are parts of it you probably won't care for. So we figured we'd tell you ahead of time. ...* Some kids might be relived to find their parents finally taking charge of an untenable situation or family climate, but they'd probably never let on that they did. And that's okay. I think we get that, too.

## A Dangerous Untethering

One of the most powerful and genuine ways to inspire kids to invest in their families and in their communities is to help them see how their contribution – whether in the form of labor, affection, intellect, artistry, or humor – is seen as vital to the group's functioning or existence. It's more than knowing you matter; it's understanding that you're needed. It guards against disconnection and indifference by offering a sense of purpose, and a sense of place. Unfortunately, what could be a good opportunity to learn this in vivo has, in most families, deteriorated into a mess of a situation in homes commonly known as "getting kids to do their chores."

This is why the dissociation of obligation from belonging (to a family, to a community) should be seen as a dangerous un-tethering. It's why children raised as if only their needs matter don't grow up into gracious young adults who leverage their good fortune in order to give back to their communities. It's why allowing adolescence to be romanticized is not good for teens or for their families, and why helping our adolescents become their best selves is so much more important than helping them become better students or better athletes.

# CHAPTER EIGHTEEN

# Enhancing Self-Awareness in Critical, Reactive, Defensive, and Controlling Parents

## Invisible fractures

Parents come in all shapes and sizes but it's the parent whose posture toward their teenager is defensive, critical, demoralizing, dismissive, or controlling that looms largest of all. They are quick to hijack conversations in order to make a point, lecture, or assert control and are slow to recognize the legitimacy of their teenager's distress, as well as their own role in it. Consider this exchange, benign to the casual observer but disastrous for the mother–daughter relationship:

> Jacki comes home from school on a Monday and begins to share with her mother some of the stories she's heard from friends about the weekend. Jacki's mother is delighted that her daughter wants to tell her about these things and gives Jacki her full attention.

> There's history here, though; Jacki has often felt that her mom questions her judgment, so she has always tried a bit too hard to "show" her that she makes good decisions about friends.

> One of the stories that Jacki shares with her mom references her friend Emily, who she's talked up to her mom as being a kid who never puts a foot wrong. Jacki does this in part to allay any fears her mom has when she goes out, "You don't have to worry, mom. I'm going with Emily …."

> Over the weekend, however, it seems that Emily got a little drunk and messed around with this guy she likes, and her parents found out and grounded her. Thinking it wasn't a big deal, Jacki mentioned it to her mom.

DOI: 10.4324/9781003257080-18

*"Oh,"* responds Jacki's mom, *"I thought you said your friend Emily would never get involved in anything like that ..."* her head cocked a bit and eyebrows raised. The mother's remark really has nothing to do with her daughter's friend, Emily. She has already exited the conversation her daughter was trying to have with her in favor of doing something else – which was to make a point, an unfortunate effort. The point was to get the daughter to realize that she's not always right, and that is the message which comes through loud and clear to the daughter, who feels offended and angry. It's one more of those invisible fractures between parent and teen that jeopardize their relationship in the long term, when it's too late to be able to trace the antagonism back to its source.

A cleaner and more genuine response to her daughter would have been something along the lines of, *"That sounds so different from the Emily you've been telling me about. What's changed?"*

Kids feel blindsided when remarks they make in one context are cross-referenced in another by an adult who is trying to prove a point. The teenager will never say anything about it because she's busy processing the experience, usually at a level below conscious awareness. But she *feels* it for sure.

Parent education and coaching desperately needs a break from the same old topics of "communication skills" and "listening skills," or at least a more nuanced and sophisticated illumination of the dynamics at play within families. It needs to include aspects that will help parents develop the emotional intelligence and matching skill set so they can engage authentically and respectfully with their children and teenagers. I have no idea where such things are or could be taught, but maybe we can fill the gap a bit, by being more specific and more pointed in our feedback to parents about the things that keep them and their teenagers from the closer relationships they wish for.

## How parents offend or get their teenagers on the defensive

### Sarcasm's wreckage

In many families, sarcasm is the default mode of communication. Members think it's funny or witty, but sarcasm always has an edge or a challenge to it. It's not warm, it's not kind. It never makes anyone feel better.

McKenna hides in her room for a little while to get a break from her six annoying nephews and nieces who've come to visit for the day. She doesn't like kids to begin with, and has a hard time with loud noises as well as with being around a lot of people for extended periods of time. When she comes back downstairs to rejoin the group, she runs into her mom, who chooses to say, "Oh, nice of you to join us again."

That McKenna made a point to share that story with me in one of her sessions told me it was important. Her mother would probably have been puzzled to discover that her daughter took the time to recount such a seemingly minor interaction to me; she'd already forgotten about it, I'm sure. But when I hear something like that I think about what has been lost – the opportunity for that parent to have expressed a measure of understanding and empathy to her daughter, "Lucky you, getting to hide out for a little bit!"

And when you think about it, which of the two remarks says to McKenna, *I understand that for you this is no picnic*, fostering a resolve for her to stretch a bit the next time her relatives come over, and which builds resistance?

## Not acknowledging changes in a teenager's behavior

Sometimes parents need coaching on how best to respond to their teenager's efforts to change their behavior. Some kids want to hear from their parents that they've noticed differences in how they're doing things, or talking with them, or responding to events. At the very least, they want a measure of faith from the parent in their sincerity. If what they hear from parents is,

- "Well, I haven't really noticed anything different yet – he's still the same kid who's always trying to get his way ..."
- "Yeah, well, we'll see how long that lasts ..."

and we're there to hear it, then that's where we can jump in and give the kid a boost:

> **Me**, to a parent: "Here's how I look at it: Dan has been ruling the roost with his temper for a long time but I think he realizes it's not doing him any favors in the long run. I think he's started to do some things differently, but for now they may be small things – some of which you'll notice, and some of which you won't. Dan needs to know that you see he is trying to change how he speaks with you, how he reacts to what you tell him he can't do. Look for small signs that he's doing something, anything, a little differently, and let him know that you appreciate it, without making a big deal about it. He's not a kid who wants a lot of applause. Just a smile and a, 'This was different, and I appreciate it' will do fine."

Then there are always parents who go overboard on the praise and embarrass their son or daughter with their exuberance when finding out their kid has opted to make a change for the better. High fives and comments like "That's so awesome!!!" aren't accolades that most teenagers will appreciate; it's too much, it's infantilizing, it makes everything too obvious that the teenager has decided to go along with what everyone has been asking them to do for a while (be less argumentative, do their homework, stop hitting their brother, refrain from cursing at mom). That alone can prompt a kid to back pedal, as in, *Yeah, not doing this ...*

Helping parents to understand the psyche of teenagers who feel they have subjugated themselves to the wishes of authority figures can be useful here:

> **Me**, to a parent: "Um, I think it would be a good idea to tone it down a bit .... The high five – just, no. No teenager is going to want to slap that hand of yours even if they appreciate the sentiment. It's just too weird.

## Reacting defensively

My fourteen-year-old client Clementine comes into her therapy session upset about the fight she and her mother had on the way over to my office.

> "She always wants to know why I don't like being at home so I told her why. I told her that somebody's always mad at someone so there's always all this fighting and yelling going on and I hate it. And she and my dad have no idea what to do with my brother, who is just so rude to them and I can't stand it and he doesn't stop and they can't make him stop. And you know what my mom says to me after all that?"
>
> "What does she say?"
>
> "She says, 'Oh, well, I'm sorry you hate all of us!'
>
> I said, 'Mom! I never said that I hated anyone. All I said was that with all the fighting and yelling and seeing Brian be so mean to you I don't like being at home." Clemmie sighs, looking away for a moment. Then she turns back to me and, continuing, says, "And so then she goes, 'Well, I guess we're just failures as parents then ...' I mean, really, mom? Come on."

That mother could do better and would reap such rewards in terms of her relationship with her daughter were she to have held off on reacting so defensively to Clemmie's comments and instead considered ...

- …how difficult it probably was for her daughter to have raised these points with her,
- … and given how difficult it probably was to bring these points up, it's a testimony to how affected her daughter was by the issues raised, and, finally,
- … could her daughter have been right?

CRITICAL, REACTIVE, DEFENSIVE, AND CONTROLLING PARENTS

And that's where I would go with this family. Had this taken place in a family session, I'd have said,

ME: "Whoa, Sheila. Where are you going with this? What's wrong?"

S: "What do you mean what's wrong? She's telling me I'm a bad parent!"

ME: "I didn't hear Clemmie say you're a bad parent. I heard her say that there's a lot of arguing at home and it's hard to feel at peace there, and I heard her say that she doesn't like seeing her brother take advantage of you and her dad. I didn't hear her say you were a bad parent."

S: "Well it's the same thing, isn't it? If she's not happy at home, then there must be something I'm doing wrong."

ME: "Hang on, this isn't about right or wrong. Your daughter is just saying that the arguing is too much for her. It's uncomfortable –

S: (interrupting) "Well c'mon, it's her dad and I who are the ones arguing so who else could she be talking about?"

ME: "Of course she's talking about you and her dad. And her brother. But Clemmie's point isn't to say you're bad parents. It was to answer your original question about why she doesn't always like being at home. It was a good question, and she gave a good and honest answer. Would you hear what she's saying more easily if you understood that she wasn't being critical?"

## Asking their teen a question when it's obvious they are surreptitiously trying to get info about something else.

TEEN: *Mom, I'm going to go over to Jenna's. She's having a small party.*

MOM: Oh, that's nice, so who else will be at the party tonight?

TEEN: *(Mom, do you think I'm an idiot? the teen is thinking. It's so obvious that you want to know whether Michael is going to be there.* This annoys the daughter, who doesn't say anything about the deception she feels and just answers angrily before going up to her room.)* "I don't know yet. I'll let you know when I find out." Her mother brushes it off as Jenna "being a teenager."

That mom would have been so much better off saying,

MOM: I'm happy for you to go to Jenna's party, but to be honest I am wondering if Michael is going to be there ….

TEEN: Why? What does it matter?

MOM: Because I don't like how he treated you at the last party you went to.

TEEN: Mom, I'll be fine.

MOM: I think so too. But I asked because if you guys are going to be drinking then I worry that you'll lose sight of things as you see them now, and be vulnerable to making decisions you'll regret later.

TEEN:   Mom, you worry too much.

MOM:   Maybe. But I want to put some safeguards in place …. Can we talk about this a little more later on?

## Not respecting their teenager's privacy, space, time or person

And then there's this one: Parents who knock on their teen's door and, without pausing, walk right into the room. I don't care whose name is on the title of that house. It's about respect, not who owns the property.

Walking in before you've gotten some sign to enter communicates to teenagers an utter lack of respect for their personal space, privacy, and person. It especially infuriates kids because they have to "go along" with the pretense that the parents did in fact "knock first," so it's hard to challenge.

And then you have Melanie's mom, who says, "I do it *because* I trust her, I don't think she'd be doing anything that I couldn't know about …" Omg. That's even worse.

## Working with parents who try to control their teenagers and lose the opportunity to influence them

"If I had ever said that to my mother, my dad would have killed me right there on the spot!"[1] This is the voice of a million parents, lamenting what they see as a loss of respect for adults among the younger generation. Many say it's because kids aren't afraid of their parents anymore, that they've grown so emboldened by permissive parenting that they don't even try to clean it up around their folks.

Fear being a lousy agent of parental influence, I'm happy to bid it adieu. Parents don't need their kids to be afraid of them in order to get them to do what they want, but they do need their kids to respect them – and not their authority or status, but *their person*, that is, who they are and how they've chosen to show up as a parent. They'll never get respect by commanding it from their children; respect like that is bestowed, not extracted, which of course makes it devilishly elusive for the controlling or authoritarian parent, not unlike Tantalus, in his pool of ever-receding water and retracting fruit.

Many controlling parents don't try commanding respect as much as they simply don't earn it. Their kids have learned to tolerate, endure, or desensitize themselves to communication styles ranging from insensitive to belittling to dismissive to downright harsh. In the process, their parents have forfeited the opportunity to be influential in their children's lives for the long run in favor of levying some form of control – a costly and ineffective medium for relationship-building. Besides, control always has an expiration date: kids grow bigger, kids grow up.

This feeling of expiring control over her son, Jack, was what brought Donna in to see me for consultation on her parenting. She had come by herself, and I never felt a need to meet with Jack or with the two of them together. Theirs was a dynamic driven largely by Donna's parenting style, and I believed that were she able to adopt a different approach to being with, talking to, and challenging her son, the tensions between them would diminish enough for him to begin to respond in kind, allowing them to create a new template for relating.

Twelve-year-old Jack was one of those polite boys whose teachers and coaches and friends would have been astonished to find out that he spent most of his time at home arguing, and often rudely, with his mother. Jack's father lived nearby and saw Jack and his younger sister regularly. Much to the mother's dismay, the father reported having no problems in getting Jack to comply with various requests.

When kids like Jack are brought to therapy, their therapists are often alarmed by the brazenness of some of their remarks. Less attention is paid to what's been said to kids by their parents or parent, whose verbal assaults in the form of sarcastic quips and self-serving assumptions are masked by their unfortunate over-familiarity and subsequent normalization. Luckily for this family, however, Donna was paying attention to this herself.

My introduction to how Donna related to Jack was her account of an incident that had recently taken place at home. Following a long day of digging out in the wake of a giant snowstorm, Jack went inside and refused to shovel the one last sidewalk his mother was asking him to clear. The more Donna insisted, the angrier and more defiant Jack became. In fact, Jack became so enraged that he lurched at his mother, to which she responded by chasing him around the kitchen table. Donna caught up with him, and when she did, she put him on the ground, pinning him with her knee in his chest and her hand around his collar. Then she said, "Now go shovel the fucking sidewalk."

"I'm not proud of it but that's why I'm here," Donna said when she finished her story. "I know that what I'm doing isn't working, but I don't know what else to do. I just wanted him to do the sidewalk. If he had done it, everything would have been fine. So tell me, what should I have done?"

This was a gift of a story, both because it exposed so much about their relationship and because of the candor with which Donna had chosen to share this story with me. Clearly, the failure of physical force to wrest compliance out of her son marked the end of Donna's ability to leverage control as a parenting strategy. The problem was that she had nothing with which to replace it. Her words and feelings held little currency with her son, largely because the relationship Donna had been building with Jack over the years was missing the critical dimensions of trust, credibility, and reciprocity. I began to see part of my job as helping Donna infuse her words and wishes and personal presence with the power her physical body had carried for years. It needed to be a different kind of power, though, the force of which came not from "might" but from mutual respect.

## Approaching problems with curiosity rather than anger

The first thing I did was to invite Donna to revisit Jack's refusal to do that last sidewalk with a sense of curiosity rather than outrage. "I mean, here's a kid who did a few hour's worth of shoveling for you when you originally asked him to," I said, "so his saying no to the sidewalk is probably not about him wanting to be difficult. I'd have been curious to find out what changed from earlier in the day, and might have asked, 'I don't understand, Jack. You were so helpful all day, and this is so different. What's going on?'"

Donna's response to this was immediate and revealed the value she put on power and control in her relationship with Jack: "But isn't the most important thing that he shovel the sidewalk? Otherwise, he wins."

## Deciding what's important in the moment

There are any number of things a parent could identify as important at a time like this – maintaining a sense of control, extracting an apology, or making sure the job gets done, which, for Donna, meant winning the battle. How many parents, though, think of *taking care of the relationship* as the most important objective? In such a situation as this, it could take as simple a form as finding out whether something was troubling the boy.

To Donna's question about the importance of getting the sidewalk shoveled, I replied, "No. I don't think that was the most important thing. I think a more important thing was seeing the big chasm opening up right there in front of you between you and your son, and figuring out how the heck you got there, and how the heck you get out."

"But I feel like if I don't end up making him do the sidewalk, he's won. Like I'm kowtowing to him."

"The sidewalk's not important anymore," I said. "What's important is understanding Jack's decision to say no after having said yes for most of the day. Go *there*. Ask him about that but be sure to ask with genuine interest in your voice."

"I can't. I'm too angry by then."

"I thought that might have been the case. I'm starting to think there are years of resentment sandwiched between the two of you, making things heat up pretty quickly. It makes it hard to respond thoughtfully, and easy to just react – to go from zero to sixty in a flash."

"It makes me sad to think that but it's probably true," said Donna.

"What's sad to me is that something that could have been a conversation wound up being an argument. You know, maybe Jack was cold or tired. Maybe he felt he'd done enough. It'd be great if he would tell you first what he was thinking at times like that, but most kids don't volunteer that on their own. They need somebody to ask them. Would it have been easier for you to ask him if you knew there could be some reason other than him being defiant?"

"I don't know, Janet," Donna said. "That's not how the real world works, though. I think he just needs to suck it up sometimes."

Taken aback for a few moments, I replied by saying, "It can be how *your* family works though, Donna. Your home doesn't have to be training camp for the real world. It can be a place where your son learns what respect and being understood look like, while still being held accountable for the choices he makes. That'll help him in the real world a lot more than anything he's going to get out of the school of hard knocks."

Donna's way of speaking to her son points us to an even larger issue than what goes on in her family. Parenting is exhausting and challenging work, but few are the opportunities for parents to reflect on how their particular approach is helping or hurting their relationship with their kids or their kids' well-being. Most people are busy trying to just make it through the day.

But I think we owe kids our best attempts at elevating the level of emotional awareness among parents and the corresponding skill set as well. Too often, parent coaching is hijacked by a pressure to appease the anxiety of parents who wonder why their teens won't talk to them or why they treat them so disrespectfully. Our current narrative about adolescence tells us that it's just what teenagers do and doesn't tell us to ask ourselves what our own role might be in the untold strained relationships between parents and teenagers.

## Working with parents who are very reactive toward their teenagers

### "I want to be a normal family."

Seventeen-year-old Hana was a therapy client of mine I'd been seeing for about four months. She was depressed, and fought frequently with her parents, with whom she shared little of her life or thoughts. Concerned about making her feel worse, Hana's parents gradually expected less and less from her around the house until she did virtually nothing at all to help. In addition, they accepted Hana's rude remarks and dismissive comments she directed toward them as something they'd have to put up with until she began to feel better.

One day Hana asked her mother to join us in her therapy session. Almost right away, the mom started pressing her daughter to explain why she was so unhappy. "You have a great life, dad and I love you to pieces, you have a little sister who thinks the world of you, you're smart and go to a great school, you have lots of friends … I don't get it. What could possibly be the matter?"

To my surprise, Hana answered right away. "I want to be normal family."

Beautiful, I thought. An invitation to talk about their family as they each experienced it. But Hana's mother had an altogether different reaction.

"Normal!? What do you mean we're not normal?!" Paula screamed. "What's your definition of a normal family?!"

Not,

- *Wow, I had no idea you didn't think of us as a normal family.*
- *If we were a normal family, what would be different?*
- *What do so-called normal families have that we don't?*

but "What's your definition of a normal family?!"

A dicey conversation like this needs somebody to place just one more domino at the end of the last sentence uttered in order to keep it moving. But that's not what Paula did. Paula flipped the table on its side so that all the pieces flew around the room. Game over.

I jumped in here, in an effort to do some damage control and stop the derailment. "Paula, let's find out what your daughter means. I'm very curious about her comment."

"That's exactly what I was trying to do!"

"I know, but your questions don't invite Hana to explain why she thinks your family isn't normal. Tell her you're surprised by what she said, but that you want to know more."

"Hana, can you tell me more about why you think we're not normal?" says Paula, her anger showing right through her gritted teeth.

"Paula, whoa, hang on …. What offends you so much about Hana thinking you're not a normal family?"

"Well, wouldn't it bother you if your kid said that?"

"I never thought of my family as normal from the get-go, so, no. I don't even know what that really means. Hana, help us out here. What did you mean by normal?"

"I don't know, we're just so weird around each other," Hana responds. "No one says what they really mean and everyone's angry all the time."

"Paula?" I ask.

"Well, that's true," Paula says. "But it doesn't mean —"

"Stop," I interrupt, gently, leaning toward Paula. "That's a good beginning to a good conversation. Let's just stay with that for now, that you can see truth in that one statement …."

## How Parenting Defensively Can Create Bigger Problems

Many problems come about in the wake of a parent's attempt to prevent problems. Take, for instance, Morgan's mom. She wants to set strict rules for her fourteen-year-old daughter based on her worry that Morgan might act out irresponsibly with boys and alcohol the way her older sister did when she was in high school. "I don't want to have to repeat that all over again," the mother said to both Morgan and me in a therapy session, referring to years of conflict and multiple but unsuccessful attempts to get the older sister to help.

I look over at Morgan and then back to her mom. "Has Morgan ever given you reason to think she would travel down that same path?" I ask. "She seems to me to be very different from her sister and, for the most part, making good choices with regard to friends and going out."

"Well, I'm just trying to prevent the same thing from happening," Morgan's mother said, defensively. "I'm not taking any chances."

"That just makes me want to break all the rules!" screams Morgan, frustrated with her mother's inability to see her for who she is instead of for who she might (but is unlikely to) become. Morgan has told me she feels invisible to her mother, that when her mother looks at her she sees only her older sister. So of course she thinks of pushing back by intimating that if her mother is going to impose that "bad girl" identity on her, she might as well act like one.

It's a perfect example of how parents' misguided attempts to prevent problems with their teenagers leave teens feeling disrespected and cause altogether different problems to arise.

The takeaway for Morgan is not that her mom is trying to keep her safe. It's that her mom has expressed a vote of no confidence in her judgment and failed to make a distinction between Morgan and her older sister. Conflating the two girls, the mom was treating them as "a teenager" – a monolithic, featureless humanoid partial to impulsive and dangerous decision-making. It reminds me of what another teenage client of mine had said after her parents asked in a family session why she was so unhappy. Sky, their daughter, turned to them and said, in a voice of resignation, "It's because you don't see *me*. You just see a 'teenager'" – as if being a teenager were a bad thing, untrustworthy, irrational, void of common sense.

## The Message to Get Out to Parents: Your Teenagers Want Your Attention, Not Your Advice

### Intervening with a jokester, patronizing parent

Olivia calls her dad a shithead every chance she gets, but what she really wants to say is: *Every time you talk to me you're trying to make some point and it gets old. Plus, you think you're being funny but it hurts my feelings and that's why I don't talk to you, not because I'm a "mopey teenager".*

Olivia is not the only teen who feels this way. Kids want connection, not counsel; it's easy for parents to underestimate the value of presence – something that doesn't do, but rather, is. Let's unpack this conflict and see how a father and daughter who are genuinely trying to connect can miss this badly.

Olivia was a client of mine, brought by her parents for therapy because of declining grades, withdrawal from the family, and a bad attitude around the house. Olivia's native temperament was challenging, no doubt; she was easily agitated, unforgiving, and impatient. But in a classic case of parent~child mismatch, Olivia's parents' parenting style was to press and provoke, probe and pry, which only exacerbated the tension in the relationship between them and their daughter.

The dad was a jokester, but his jokes were bad, and always came at someone's expense – usually Olivia's or her brother's. The jokes were demeaning or dismissive, and always sarcastic. This father knew of no other way to make his points, and his children resented it greatly. In one family session, he said of his daughter, "I really don't know why she's so mad at me all the time." He practically winked at her. "I'm a good guy," he added, smiling broadly, "best father she's ever gonna have!" Olivia's response to her dad's attempt at humor spoke volumes: she simply turned away, and stared down at the floor, silent.

Olivia tells me, in private, that anytime her dad talks to her it's to deliver a lecture about something she should have done, or reprimand her about something she did do, or advise her on something he thinks she should do in the future. The two have never learned how to just talk with each other, without an agenda or the need to impress a point upon the other.

Olivia's dad tells me, also in private, that he wants only to pass down to his kids some of the wisdom he's gleaned from his life experiences. "I want my daughter to be able to take advantage of the things I've learned over the years," he says, "and save her from making the same mistakes I did." Of course he does; that's what loving parents try to do. They try to save their kids from the heartache or turmoil they see coming down the pike at them. But some things are best learned in vivo and, honestly, even if you could save your kids a little heartache along the way, good luck getting them to listen to you.

The problem isn't that the information or wisdom itself is bad. The problem is when it ends up being the only or primary thing parents share with their child, or when it's not what their kids need from them in that moment, or when it's delivered as a lecture, or shrill reminder, or long-winded soliloquy. In these situations, parents are likely to lose their audience of one before they've even rounded the first corner. That's because any time you use an encounter with your teenager as an opportunity to Make a Point, you squander their fleeting attention.

Kids don't need parents for their wisdom. They need them for their undivided attention, their unfailing support, their affection. Case in point, Olivia's dad shared with me that he felt "irrelevant" to his kids when he couldn't advise them about something. "Yet, whenever I open my mouth," he said, "I can see them already rolling their eyes – they can't wait for me to finish talking." *This is good information*, I tell him. *Please don't get defensive with them. Understand it as their way of saying, "I need something else from you." You're anything but irrelevant, Adam, but understand they want* you *– your person and your listening presence – more than they want your advice.*

The greatest currency in any relationship between two people is respect, something that can be hard to identify or isolate because it's often an act of restraint, of not doing something: a person waits for the other to finish speaking before commenting; a person waits for the person to say "Come in" after knocking on their door; a person waits for a sign that the other actually wants their advice before spilling it out. People don't often "see" respect, but they feel it, and moreover, they especially feel its absence.

In families challenged by conflicts like the one between Olivia and her father, respect shows up when the parent chooses to give his children what they need over what he feels like giving them. It's a beautiful gesture, and kids will see it for the generous act that it is. They do recognize times when their parents start to look for ways to connect differently, to connect better – something that is more persuasive, more compelling, and more arresting than any "point" will ever be.

## Helping parents exercise new communication skills in order to have more thoughtful, emotionally sensitive conversations with their kids

Many parents have no template for talking with their teenager other than lecturing, questioning, informing, and reminding. They often struggle to have the types of conversations they have with others in their lives – free flowing, effortless chats or discussions in which each party is as engaged as the other. Somewhere along the line from childhood to adolescence, casual dialogue becomes self-conscious and guarded, re-purposed for making points or for the business side of parenting, i.e., *What time should I pick you up from practice today?* Or maybe it was never there to begin with. There are families that go a lifetime without ever having had more than a handful of conversations that aren't marked by low-level chronic hostility, power battles, one-up-manship, and defensive posturing, which are then carried forward into the next generation.

- Parents ask, "How was school today?" when they want to say, *I miss you and feel so in the dark and don't know how else to start a conversation with you.*
- Parents say, "Well, I'm stressed too but I still get done what I need to get done!" when their teen needs them to say instead, *I'm sorry to see you so stressed. Are you stressed about things that you feel I pressure you about, or is it just everything you have on your plate?*

## Everly

I'm meeting with Everly's mom, Amelia. Everly is a newly minted seventeen-year-old who I've been seeing seen in individual therapy for about six months. She has debilitating social anxiety, which has resulted in isolation and depression. Everly is also exceedingly withholding, and at times, such as in the initial family session, can come off as a selective mute. With her parents in the room during the initial appointment, she barely spoke.

I'm meeting with Everly's parents because Everly had been saying that she was doing pretty well overall, and that during the past several weeks she'd been feeling much less anxious and less depressed. Everly recently came out to her parents as a lesbian, so she no longer struggled privately with that secret. She thought she didn't really need therapy anymore.

Everly's parents were of a different opinion. So they came in together after Everly green-lighted the idea. One story stood out: Everly's mother was telling me about having taken Everly shopping for her prom, to which she was going with her girlfriend of two months. Her parents had done a wonderful job of being supportive, despite the poor delivery of coming out, in which one evening Everly abruptly said, "Oh I'm going out on a date tonight and it's with Morgan and she's a girl," before sprinting out the front door.

Okay, so there was that. Then, after having spent days together with Everly helping her get ready for her prom, Everly's mom was deflated and disappointed to get almost nothing from her daughter when she arrived home after the prom. "So how was it?" Everly's mom inquired, eager, hopeful. "It was fine," Everly replied, walking back out the door with her date.

This struck me as exceedingly unkind on Everly's part. She could tell that her mom was eager to hear about the evening, and she pointedly denied her the pleasure of finding out. It's one thing, I feel, to be reserved in your relaying of important and perhaps private events, and especially when you're with someone in front of whom you might feel self-conscious talking about such. But it's another to leave someone in the lurch ..... Everly could have said, "It was good, I'll tell you later, mom," and that would have been fine. But *It was fine*, followed by a deliberately quick exit, was stingy.

I said to Amelia that she had a beautiful opportunity to speak with her daughter about the impact of her choices on her and her dad, such as how she chose to respond to her mother after the prom. Amelia worried that Everly would feel criticized, but I said,

> "There are ways to say these things gently, without criticism, and with an expression of your wish for engagement." I added, "You can say something like this, **'Everly, I loved helping you get ready for prom ... I enjoyed the whole thing from shopping for a dress to looking for shoes to laughing about you wearing your Converses. And then that part was over, and you went to your prom and you can probably imagine that I was there at home thinking about you and wondering how it was going, and looking forward to hearing about it ... but then you came home, and said, 'Oh it was fine and just walked out the door.'"**

> I went on. "Tell her that it made you sad to be so left out of things. Tell Everly that you know she appreciated your help and that you aren't looking for a thank you or anything like that but that she didn't seem to recognize you were sitting there feeling totally left in the dark."

> "I can do that," Amelia said. "I can tell her I need her to –"

> "No," I interrupted. "Amelia, it's not about you needing her to do something. The purpose isn't to leave Everly feeling as if there's something you want her to do differently. That's implicit, but you're not asking directly for that. It's the difference between saying **I need you to do...** and saying **I'm sad because you don't seem to be thinking about what I would like**

> *or need sometimes...* One imposes a directive and the other is simply an expression of how you feel in your relationship with her."

This is an example of the more nuanced parenting skills that we can help cultivate among those parents who have both the interest and the emotional capacity to embrace them. They may be fewer in number than we'd like, but each time we're able to help one, it helps a whole family.

With others, you'll get "I already tried saying that" where you see a wide gap between what you're suggesting and what the parents think they've said that's similar. It's the parent who's willing to understand the impact of tone and body language and word choice on their messaging who will also be open to new ideas. Others might have been willing at some point but are just so time-starved and overwhelmed that they can't even begin to think of adding another thing to their plate.

In those cases there may be other interventions that are helpful, even if they won't directly affect the parent~teen relationship. I think about such things as self-care for the parent, or a parent support group, or a weekend away from the family to get a break. Are there other people in that family's life who could also help? An uncle, grandparent, godparent? They don't have to replace the role the custodial parent would have taken in trying to help the teenager, but there may be other ways of lightening the load, and therefore some of the tensions in the relationship (e.g., rides, meals, sitting the younger kids, spending time with the teen, teaching the teen to drive if no one has been available, helping the teen apply for a job, etc.).

An African proverb counsels that it takes a village to raise a child, conveying the message that it takes an entire community of people to provide a safe, healthy, and secure environment for children in which to grow and thrive.[2] Implicit in this is an alleviation of the expectation that any one family, with its set of two or one or sometimes no committed parent, should necessarily be able to supply all the emotional or material resources that the children in it need.

We have almost 3 million kids under the age of eighteen who don't live with either parent in the home, and another 1.7 million children who have a parent in prison, making this adage ever more germane to our concerns about raising healthy, happy, well-adjusted kids.[3] Overwhelming parental responsibilities coupled with the discomfort so many adults feel asking for help leaves a lot of parents struggling to raise their kids rather than enjoying it. Sadly, not wanting to step on toes or offend, a lot of family and friends on the sidelines who see what's going on and would love to help refrain from doing so. After all, we are socialized in this country to not comment on other people's parenting. Sure, it's polite, but it's not what we need.

I said earlier that doing therapy with kids and adolescents was not for the faint of heart. Neither is raising them.

CRITICAL, REACTIVE, DEFENSIVE, AND CONTROLLING PARENTS

# Notes

1 A version of this material was first published as, From tough love to empathic love: Teaching parents to earn their children's respect, *Psychotherapy Networker,* September/October 2017.
2 https://en.wikipedia.org/wiki/It_takes_a_village
3 https://thewriteofyourlife.org/it-takes-a-village-to-raise-a-child/

231

# CHAPTER NINETEEN

# Failing with Grace
## The Power and Limits of Helping Encounters

Sometimes, there's nothing we can do to make anything better for our clients. There will always be personal, familial, institutional or other systemic resistances or roadblocks, or simply hurdles that were too big, keeping us from moving anything forward or improving the mood or living conditions of these clients we've grown to care about. Sometimes the situation is just bigger than the both of us.

And sometimes it's us. We miss the mark. We weren't a good match for our client because of our personality, therapy approach, relational style, background, biases, countertransference, lack of expertise, or just the logistics of meeting which made it untenable to work together. We tried, and it wasn't enough. Being able to accept that without the need to blame anyone or anything, without bitterness or disillusionment – I call this failing with grace.

There's this, too: Therapy isn't for everyone, and doesn't have to be. There are so many ways to recover, and get better, and evolve in this world. Nature, wilderness therapy, equine-assisted therapy, music, and the arts each, in their own way, offer contexts within which people can heal. They might be better places for adolescents whose faith in adults has been lost after years of neglect or abuse or manipulation, or who have simply become immune to the healing influence of another human being.

Facing the anxiety that you might not be able to help your client(s) in the way you had hoped to means understanding the limits of helping encounters and of oneself. Lynn Ponton, in her book *The Romance of Risk: Why Teenagers Do the Things They Do*, [1] wrote about the importance of knowing when it's time to take a step back, look at other perspectives, or weigh in on the balance of how much your client is really capable of benefiting from your help with how draining the process of helping that client has become.

DOI: 10.4324/9781003257080-19

Help can be defined in a myriad of ways, however, and doesn't have to necessarily mean the direct and concrete resolution of problems. At times, focusing solely on the humanity of a person, or an important relationship, or a meaningful community, and instilling hope where there had been only the dark, can be exquisitely healing.

This is what Kenneth Hardy and Tracey Laszloffy spoke of in their book, *Teens Who Hurt: Clinical Interventions to Break the Cycle of Adolescent Violence.*[2] They point to the disruption in community among disenfranchised and violent youth as being a major reason why so many have lost their sense of security, connectedness, acceptance, and identity, and, worst of all, hope. Reconnecting these kids with their communities of immediate and extended family, neighborhoods, schools, and houses of worship, as well as with their larger cultural communities, is a positive step toward helping them recoup a sense of belonging and identity, find meaningful relatedness, and feel supported and accepted.

So too says distinguished family therapist Harry Aponte, in his book, *Bread & Spirit: Therapy with the New Poor: Diversity of Race, Culture, and Values.*[3] Helping people to find meaning in their identities, traditions, or legacies can be a way of compensating for the loss they experience in their way of living, their livelihood, or their ability to sustain themselves. Dealing with the humanity of the family's struggle becomes ever so more important than the details.

Reconnecting kids with their communities and helping them find meaning in their identities and traditions goes a long way no matter the socioeconomics or the nature of their most prominent problems. No population and no community is safe from emotional anguish that can cripple, eviscerate, and sometimes kill. The community in which I live and work is made up largely of middle- and upper-class families. Some mental health professionals look askance at those of us who spend our days helping kids of relative privilege. My guess is that they believe the psychological distress of less privileged children and teenagers is greater, or maybe it's just that there are fewer resources for them within their families and communities; the latter of these is undoubtedly true. I'm not interested in comparing the misfortunes, traumas, or emotional suffering of our respective clients, but I will say that privilege doesn't protect kids or families against that which ravages the heart or mind: just a couple of years ago and within a period of two years, there were *six* suicides in my local school district. The source of problems may be different, but despair is despair.

In summary, here are some meaningful ways to be present with troubled young clients from all walks of life when traditional talk therapy isn't in the cards:

- By being an aural witness to their story, pain, fatigue, or incapacitation. Just the fact that somebody else knows.

- By leaving kids who have gone through shattering experiences with a reference to what they can find for themselves later – for example, relationships characterized by honesty or trust or authenticity or accountability or a degree of respect previously unknown; relationships in which they really matter to someone and in which they can find dignity and solace. By holding on to what they have experienced with you, these kids might just bide their time until later when they are no longer at the mercy of others and can make their own choices about the people they want to keep close to them in their lives. Their exposure to this deeper sense of humanity or empathy may be brief, and may be on only a few occasions, but at least your client knows that such things exist. It can be your way of saying, *Don't let the way you've been treated become your blueprint for future relationships. Always remember that there's this, too.*

- By validating the emotional logic behind their actions. "To the casual observer," you tell them, "your decision to do XYZ is going to look crazy. But if anyone were to look behind the behavior and take the time to understand what it means, they might at least be able to appreciate and respect your choice, if not agree with it."

- Barring abuse or situations of severe neglect – by helping kids avoid automatically buying into the marginalization typically imposed upon adults and caregivers suffering from substance abuse, mental illness, and/or incarceration, where their abilities and desires to parent are categorically dismissed. You would be saying, *Don't let anyone dismiss your father as an important person in your life. He may not be able to show up in the way most fathers do, but he shows up as much as he can, and you continue to matter to him very much.* You can then help your clients decide how much contact is healthy for them, case by case.

- There's just one other point I want to make here, and it's this: If you are thinking of helping some of your clients by resuscitating their sense of hope, *you need first to make sure they want that feeling*. Maybe hopelessness is exactly what a kid wishes to project. In that case, it would be so much more helpful to talk with him or her about why feeling and/or showing up as hopeless holds such appeal rather than trying to steamroll over it. It's rarely productive (nor respectful) to try to pry clients away from a sentiment or stance that you find objectionable but they do not. Instead, maybe you can figuratively sidle over to them and see what they like about it, why they want to stay there, and what it does for them or gratifies in them.

As Kenneth Hardy[4] says, "We hold the hope for our clients until they're ready to take it."

And that, I just love.

## Notes

1 Lynn Ponton, *The romance of risk: Why Teenagers Do the Things They Do*, Basic Books (HarperCollins), 1997.
2 The Guilford Press; 1st edition, 2006.
3 W. W. Norton & Company; 1st edition, 1994.
4 Hardy, Kenneth V. "Working with violent and aggressive youth." (Workshop), Psychotherapy Networker Symposium, Washington, DC, 2002.

# Index

Note: Page numbers followed by "n" denote endnotes.

attention deficit hyperactivity disorder (ADHD) 72, 200
attention of parents 226–227
authenticity 36, 38, 39, 52, 101, 122, 156, 171, 192
authority 183; figures, therapists as 154; parental 5, 203, 205, 218
autonomy of clients 39, 54, 192

banter 89–94
behaviors, adolescent 38; aggressive 139–141, 142; antidotes to 128; and brain development 8–13, 202; defiance 208–209, 221; disincentivizing undesired behavior 204, 210–212; disrespectful 9, 12, 56, 194, 203, 208–212, 213; narrative about 8–9, 13, 202; normalizing behaviors that embarrass clients 86; parents not acknowledging changes in 217–218; rationale behind 132; resistance to adult input/support 123–126; rudeness 121–122, 143, 171, 224; teenage angst 6–7, 12, 202–203; see also accountability
being in charge, client's need for 140–141
blind spots 126–127, 194
body language 29, 230
boundaries 54, 104, 193, 197, 203–204, 212
brain development, and behavior 8–13, 202
bridging, conversation 147–148, 149
bullying 9, 43, 116, 130–131, 204, 208–212

choice(s) 54; parents struggling to hold teens accountable 193–194; protect their teens from consequences of 196; teenager's behaviors as 38–39, 55, 121–122, 200–202; see also accountability
communication: mosaic patterns 29–30; nonverbal 29; with parents 6–7; sarcasm 216–217, 221; skills, of parents 228–230; skills, of therapists 29–30
communion, self-disclosure as an expression of 42–43

compassion 3, 24, 34, 36, 56, 145, 179, 193
competency of therapists, parents challenging 183–184
confidentiality 183; clients weaponizing 155–157; in family therapy 182, 183, 186
conflict(s) 11; avoidance 39, 56, 144; connection with clients through 171; handling 51; resolution 147–148
congruence, and credibility 52–53
consequences of teenagers' behavior 10, 197; effective, parents employing 210; parents asking for advice on 212–213; parents having trouble following through with 203–204; purpose of 204; see also accountability
content 120, 126–127; see also process
control 154; clients exerting 161–162; controlling parents 220–223; teenagers' sense/need of 6, 32, 43, 44, 112–113, 125, 211
conversations, strategies for bringing forward: avoiding asking a lot of questions about feelings 80–82; banter 89–94; demonstrating curiosity about client's world views 88; handling dead end conversations 86–87; helping clients getting past misunderstanding/bias about therapists 84–85; naming ambivalence 85–86; normalizing behaviors that embarrass clients 86; not withholding emotional expressiveness from clients 82–84; removing pressure on clients to speak 77–80
conversations, things that stop: appealing to logic/rational thinking 67–70; ignoring the forces of natural law 70–71; motivation of clients 65–67; reluctance to follow negative affect of an individual or family 74–75; suspending common rules of decency and courtesy 71–74
counter-intuitive strategies 95–96; avoiding fixing the problems of clients 96–99; contradictions in client's